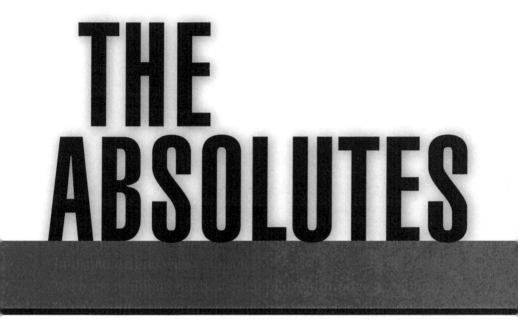

THE ABSOLUTES

James Robison

TYNDALE HOUSE PUBLISHERS, INC., WHEATON, ILLINOIS

Library of Congress Cataloging-in-Publication Data

Robison, James, date.
   The absolutes / James Robison.
     p. cm.
   Includes bibliographical references.
   ISBN 0-8423-6897-3 — ISBN 0-8423-6898-1 (pbk.)
   1. United States—Moral conditions. 2. Social values—United States. I. Title.
   HN90.M6 R59 2002
   306'.0973—dc21   2002010173

Printed in the United States of America

07 06 05 04 03 02
8   7   6   4   3   2   1

CONTENTS

ACKNOWLEDGMENTS

Words seem inadequate to express my heartfelt gratitude for the special people who invested in the writing of this book. I must begin by acknowledging my precious family, every one of whom is a source of encouragement, inspiration and joy:

My wife, Betty, who has demonstrated throughout the forty years of our marriage the importance of relying on absolute principles and values to guide our daily lives and govern our relationships. I marvel at the strength of her character. Her steadfast patience was a continual source of encouragement to me as this project demanded so much of my attention.

Our three children—Rhonda, Randy and Robin—are living proof of the powerful effect of the truths shared in this book. Their love for their spouses and children, and their gratitude for what they observed while growing up in our home has confirmed to me the beautiful impact of the absolutes.

Thanks to Rhonda's husband, Terry Redmon, who continually shoulders great responsibility for our organization and brings out the best in everyone. To Randy's wife, Debbie Robison, who is, as Randy says, "another person like Mom." To Robin's husband, Ken Turner, who loves God, his family, and life, and is a constant inspiration to me.

Thanks also to the spiritual heroes in my life, for the priceless inspiration I've drawn from them: Billy Graham, who began encouraging me in my early twenties and who suggested I use the powerful medium of television to convey my heart's message when I didn't think I could do it. His life has inspired me. Franklin Graham, a true friend, colaborer and fellow outdoorsman. Jack Hayford, Peter Lord, T. D. Hall, Dudley Hall, Tommy Barnett, Dennis Baw, John Hagee, Jack Taylor, Charles Stanley, Willie George, Ed Young Sr., Robert Morris, Jack Graham, O. S. Hawkins, and the many other pastors who have blessed me beyond words.

Special thanks to Mark Rutland and Ravi Zacharias, who graciously agreed to read the manuscript and offered their suggestions and encouragement.

How could I ever have completed this work without my intuitive editor, Dave Lindstedt? His honesty, commitment, and determination to get it "just right" kept us on course during the editing process. I am indebted to him—and the other Tyndale House editors who contributed their talents—for going the extra mile. I am also grateful to my son, Randy, who helped me develop the manuscript in the early stages.

Special thanks to George Grant, who researched volumes of material for powerful quotes and historical perspective.

To Tammy Faxel, acquisitions director at Tyndale House, for believing in my purpose in writing this book and helping to keep everything on track.

I could write several pages concerning my gifted assistant, Carol Stertzer, a shining example of what a life lived according to the absolutes can look like. Carol is willing to "tell it like it is," meet every challenge, and never settle for less when the best is possible. I appreciate her greatly.

To Jim Rogers, my right-hand man and executive vice president who has stood by me for more than twenty years and provided dedicated leadership for Life Outreach. His wisdom and oversight have been great stabilizing factors.

To Peter and Ann Pretorius, our missionary partners in Africa. God used this beautiful couple to show the importance of Good Samaritan acts in life and ministry.

I couldn't possibly fail to mention my deep love and gratitude for our friends Michael and Susan Ellison, and Pete and Jody Claytor, who have modeled unconditional love.

To my foster brother, Clayton Spriggs, who was a continual inspiration to me from the time I was a boy until his death in 1999.

To Presidents Ronald Reagan and George Bush, who heard my heart and seemed to appreciate my prayers and friendship. And to President George W. Bush, for setting aside special times to pray with me, and for his willingness to incorporate biblical principles into his leadership. I will always treasure the moments I've had with these men of great impact.

Thanks to my staff and all the supporters of our mission efforts around the world. Together I hope we can help to inspire everyone to fulfill their God-given purpose as we seek to apply the absolutes in our daily lives.

INTRODUCTION

A nation which does not remember what it was yesterday, does not know what it is today, nor what it is trying to do. We are trying to do a futile thing if we do not know where we came from or what we have been about. Ours is a rich legacy. Rich but lost. **WOODROW WILSON (1856–1924)**

No abounding of material prosperity shall avail us if our spiritual senses atrophy. The foes of our own household will surely prevail against us unless there be in our people an inner life which finds its outer expression in a morality like unto that preached by the seers and prophets of God when the grandeur that was Greece and the glory that was Rome still lay in the future.
THEODORE ROOSEVELT (1858–1919)

Without such common belief no society can prosper; nay, rather, no society can exist; for without ideas held in common there is no common action, and without common action there may still be men, but there is no social body.
ALEXIS DE TOCQUEVILLE (1805–1859)

Our Moment
of Truth

Standing at the threshold of a new decade, a new century,
and a new millennium, we have an extraordinary opportunity
to live up to our high ideals. If we don't, we face
a dangerously uncertain future.

I began writing this book long before the devastating terrorist attacks that hit New York City and Washington, D.C. Even prior to the events of that tragic day—which many refer to simply as 9/11—there was no question in my mind that as a nation and as individuals we needed to dial 9-1-1 to request emergency help from a power source far beyond ourselves.

Over the past several years in particular, I've seen how our national prosperity and security have given rise to a prevailing mood of complacency. I've seen how the blessings of our freedom and our affluence have enabled many in our society to be misled toward the prideful condition that precedes an inevitable fall. It's easy in a free society to begin to neglect the very foundations of freedom. If we forget the many sacrifices—great and small—necessary to maintain liberty, encourage progress, ensure safety, uphold justice, protect the innocent, strengthen families, and preserve hope for the future, the things that matter most are too easily lost in the hustle and bustle of everyday life. Lately, it has become evident that in our comfort, satisfaction, and security, we have begun to take for granted the very things that made us comfortable, satisfied, and secure in the first place.

Long before that fateful September morning, another deadly attack had been launched against our freedom: Many Americans, including many of our national leaders, had begun to forsake the moral absolutes necessary to preserve our nation's security and stability. Although subtle, the decaying effects of this dangerous trend had already set in, leading to increased vulnerability for our nation. As a result of this decay

– Many leaders lacked the character necessary to make wise decisions.
– Radical partisanship prevailed at the expense of the people and our better interests.
– Comfort and economic prosperity had become more important than principled living.
– Human compassion for those who were suffering desperately needed to be rekindled.
– Our national defense and security deteriorated, becoming bogged down in mindless debate.
– Our intelligence and protection agencies failed to safeguard our security because of bureaucratic tendencies to protect their "turf," thereby short-circuiting clear communication and cooperation.
– Spiritual and eternal values were blatantly sacrificed on the altar of selfish material pursuits.
– Protecting innocence and the innocent became an object of scorn.

Perhaps more now than at any other time in our history, we need God's direction and protection, or else we in the United States of America and others in the free world will one day find ourselves living in a continual state of emergency. Unless we respond positively to the absolutes, our freedom will ultimately drown in a sea of relativism, indifference, and selfishness. No longer will we enjoy the comfort, security, peace, and opportunity that our matchless liberty has afforded us thus far. And now that attacks on our freedom and our way of life have become open and violent, we face the very real prospect that the type of terrorist attacks plaguing Israel will become commonplace in America and other Western nations.

The Roots of Our Freedom

The absolutes are the foundation stones of our society—and these same principles have been foundational to all stable societies throughout history. When those societies began to depart from the absolutes, they also began to decay. That's a strong statement, but you don't have to take my word for it. Look at the testimony of history and judge for yourself. To acknowledge the absolutes and abide by them is to invite prosperity, success, and the blessings of freedom. To ignore them—or worse, to defy them—flies in the face of reality and courts disaster.

The founders of the American republic knew they were taking great risks in their efforts to establish an enduring basis for freedom. A century before the Constitution was written, Cotton Mather, the colonial pioneer whom George Washington described as "the father of the founding fathers," said, "Religion hath brought forth prosperity, and the daughter may well destroy the mother—there is a danger, lest the enchantments of this world make us forget our errand into the wilderness."[1] The founders were willing to take the risk of freedom, but they were always wary, ever vigilant, and persistently attentive to first principles—supreme authority, a reliable source for truth, and time-tested values to guide the affairs of free men—lest Mather's prophecy inevitably come true.

Nevertheless, it seems clear by almost any standard of measure that by the final decade of the twentieth century most Americans had indeed been beguiled by the enchantments of this world and had forgotten their greater purpose. Distracted by the demands of our moment in history, we lost sight of the very standards that made our country the great nation that it is.

As it relates to first principles, many Americans have come to agree with the proposition that the only absolute is that there *are* no absolutes—a self-canceling philosophy known as relativism. Although relativism collapses of its own weight when subjected to even the most casual scrutiny, the negative impact of such foolish thinking has taken its toll. As the brilliant contemporary philosopher Ravi Zacharias has said on numerous occasions while lecturing at Harvard, Oxford, and other venues throughout the world, "The pure relativist cuts off the branch on which he is sitting while telling you the branch cannot be severed. The landing is mind-shattering."[2] How true! Nevertheless, relativism has gained currency in our society, greatly weakening our foundations, and corrective measures must soon be taken.

The Wake-up Call

On September 11, 2001, we were jolted from our complacency. In the weeks and months immediately following the terrorist attacks, we Americans began to reassess our priorities as a nation. People took stock of the blessings of freedom—and were reminded of their source. For a moment it seemed we might begin to recover our national and moral sensibilities as we recognized anew the importance of family, community, and free-

dom. Patriotism burgeoned across the land. Debates over
political correctness, multiculturalism, and ethical relativism
faded into the shadows as Americans once again embraced the
distinctive values and moral standards that made our nation
great. The heroic instincts of the human spirit were again
lauded. The vocabulary of faith, courage, sacrifice, honor, and
fortitude reentered our daily discussions. Prayer once again
became our first and ultimate recourse.

Although our suddenly aroused zeal for what really matters
has already begun to fade, many Americans at least recognized
September 11 as a serious wake-up call. I believe we now have a
unique window of opportunity to restore the principles of freedom to their proper place, to once again put first things first,
and to recalibrate our moral compass to true north. It is an
opportunity to reenergize the great experiment in liberty that
has long been the hallmark of American civilization. As President Bush acknowledged in his inspired address to the world in
the aftermath of the terrorist attacks, "Our nation has felt great
sorrow. Yet this can be a time of great achievement. A great evil
can be turned to greater good. The terrorists did not intend to
create a new American spirit of unity and resolve, but they are
powerless to stop it."[3]

There are no quick fixes to the grave threats we face as a
nation and as a people. Plenty of daunting challenges lie ahead.
Yet poll after poll suggests that we Americans really are ready to
start reevaluating our values, reaffirming our morals, and rees-
tablishing our principles.[4] Perhaps we are once again ready to
consider how to make the absolutes an essential aspect of our
lives.

I'm not proposing that we "go back" to the founding of our
nation, but history has shown that much of what the Founding
Fathers did was right—and we ought to continue to build on

that solid foundation. Look at it this way: If you purchased a two-hundred-year-old home that was still standing strong while surrounding homes had been demolished or had fallen into disrepair, and then you found out that the other homes had been built on a different type of foundation, you'd look at the foundation of the house that was still standing to find out what the builder did right. Why is that particular house still standing? Why has it not been shaken? That's what I mean when I say we must return to our founding principles: Let's look at the foundation of this nation that is still standing strong after 226 years and let's keep building on what the founders did right.

Despite my great enthusiasm for this project, I have to admit that writing a book about the absolutes is not without its hazards. After all, I am hardly perfect, and I have all too often missed the mark in upholding absolute standards. I thank God, however, that even when we fall short, the absolutes continue to stand, constant and true, undiminished by our failures. I like what the prolific Christian writer G. K. Chesterton wrote when the *London Times* asked him and some other writers to submit essays on the topic "what's wrong with the world?" Chesterton's essay amounted to four words: "Dear Sirs," he wrote, "I am." What an honest and powerful response! I, too, admit that along the way I have made many mistakes and often exercised poor judgment, yet through those trying times I have learned important lessons and my character has been strengthened. I am certainly not the standard by which to measure. But I have fixed my heart in hot pursuit of the rock-solid principles that made America great, and having acknowledged my own failures, I stand ready to offer hope and encouragement to all who in weakness or rebellion have resisted the absolutes.

It is my fervent hope and prayer that my words here will inspire and encourage a healthy debate and a meaningful dialogue about the absolutes and the principles of freedom. May we be willing as individuals and as a nation to pursue the vision expressed by John F. Kennedy in his 1961 inaugural address to "pay any price, bear any burden, meet any hardship, support any friend, oppose any foe to assure the survival and the success of liberty."[5]

The assault on our freedom and our beliefs will continue—and likely will intensify. But if we are standing on the firm foundation established by absolute truth, the attacks will only serve to strengthen our resolve. The enemy's attempts to knock us down will inspire us to stand taller than ever before. Efforts to diminish the light will enhance its radiant glow.

With firm conviction, I believe the wisdom necessary for freedom's survival must come from God above. This source, often referred to by our Founding Fathers as "divine providence," can secure our hope for the future. If we will diligently seek to live up to our high ideals, and if we are willing to uphold the absolutes and recognize their source, then our future is bright and the light of freedom shall endure for yet another generation. To that end, I prayerfully offer this book as both a catalyst for change and a practical guide for this moment of truth.

WHY THE ABSOLUTES ARE SO IMPORTANT

PART ONE

1

CHAPTER ONE

Time after time mankind is driven against the rocks of the horrid reality of a fallen creation. And time after time mankind must learn the hard lessons of history—the lessons that for some dangerous and awful reason we can't seem to keep in our collective memory. **HILAIRE BELLOC (1870–1953)**

Unless a man become the enemy of evil, he will not even become its slave but rather its champion. God Himself will not help us to ignore evil, but only to defy and defeat it. **G. K. CHESTERTON (1874–1936)**

Oftentimes, to win us our harm, the instruments of darkness tell us truths, win us with honest trifles, to betray us in deepest consequence. **WILLIAM SHAKESPEARE (1564–1616)**

1

Evil Is a Horrible and Present Reality

*The reality of evil exposes the
bankruptcy of relativism.*

No sane person who watched the unfolding horror at the World Trade Center or saw the destruction at the Pentagon could deny the reality of evil in the world. In those terrifying moments, our perspective changed. The nation was jolted out of its complacency by the sheer wickedness of the attacks. Almost immediately our vocabulary—including that of otherwise politically correct journalists, politicians, and law enforcement officials—became downright theological. The tension and uncertainty of possible further attacks dramatically adjusted our priorities.

The events of September 11 reminded us once again that evil exists in the world. In the glare of such purposeful brutality and devastation, the shabby ambiguities of relativism no longer seemed adequate. Out of the rubble of Ground Zero, the truth of the absolutes began to reemerge with extraordinary poignancy and power: Our beliefs and our actions matter. Life and death matter. Justice and injustice matter. Right and wrong matter. The absolutes matter.

Throughout human history, the existence of evil is a reality that people have had to take into account—in dealing with one another, in commerce, in passing laws, and in building civil societies. Because the world is infected by sin and populated by sinners, evil wreaks havoc on our best-laid plans and our sincerest intentions. The existence of evil is self-evident. Its effects are the most basic observations of both anthropology and sociology. No one ever has to teach a child how to do wrong. It doesn't take a bad environment to teach someone how to be cruel, selfish, or perverse. No one needs a role model to learn about greed, pride, or dishonesty. Sin is inbred in us.

Our natural inclination to sin is no petty or trivial matter. Evil is destructive. It runs roughshod over everything and everyone—including the person who perpetrates the evil. Left unrestrained, evil morbidly embraces death. "There is a way that seems right to a man, but in the end it leads to death."[1]

The consequences of unrestrained evil are all too familiar to us. We have seen their tragic end far too many times over the course of the last century. The memories are carved on our hearts with a dull familiar blade—a blade variously wielded by Adolf Hitler, Josef Stalin, Mao Zedong, Ho Chi Minh, Idi Amin, Pol Pot, and Saddam Hussein. Indeed, the gruesome results of evil clutter the pages of human history. Every great society has had to take evil into account—and decisive, principled action has been the only proven remedy. In response to evil, the bankruptcy of relativism and appeasement are clearly evident. What is needed is a return to the absolutes.

The absolutes are the principles that undergird our most basic assumptions about life. They are the underlying foundations of common sense, the standards by which we determine the difference between right and wrong, truth and falsehood, essential and trivial. They are the truths that support our truisms. They form the bedrock of our civility. The absolutes are the fixed points on the horizon by which we navigate the river of life.

Nineteenth-century historian and philosopher Robert Goguet argues that the genius of the Constitution was that it took the necessity of the absolutes fully into account:

> The more [the founders] meditated on the biblical stan-
> dards for civil morality, the more they perceived their
> wisdom and inspiration. Those standards alone have the
> inestimable advantage never to have undergone any of the
> revolutions common to all human laws, which have
> always demanded frequent amendments; sometimes
> changes; sometimes additions; sometimes the retrenching
> of superfluities. There has been nothing changed, nothing
> added, nothing retrenched from biblical morality for
> above three thousand years.[2]

The founders, fresh from the experience of the Revolutionary War, were well aware of the consequences of moral disarray. They knew that in order to build cultural consensus—let alone a nation—they needed an identifiable, objective standard of good. Although many of them were not practicing Christians, the priority they gave to biblical morality was a matter of sober-minded practicality.

John Jay, the first chief justice of the Supreme Court, affirmed the necessity of having a standard of virtue to ensure the proper maintenance of civil stability and order:

> No human society has ever been able to maintain both
> order and freedom, both cohesiveness and liberty, apart

from the moral precepts of the Christian Religion applied and accepted by all the classes. Should our Republic e'er forget this fundamental precept of governance, men are certain to shed their responsibilities for licentiousness and this great experiment will then surely be doomed.[3]

The founders recognized the futility of creating and implementing a system of laws without a foundation of absolute principles. Constitutional provisions such as the separation of powers, mixed government, checks and balances, jury trials, and civil rights were all predicated on the notion that people are bent toward chaos if left to their own devices. Laws were designed with the understanding that in a fallen world both sin and sinners must be restrained if justice is to prevail. For a system of law and order to succeed, the difference between right and wrong must not only be defined, it must also be accounted for in the very fabric of our relationships.

Abandoning the Absolutes

During the waning days of the twentieth century, as a society we began to contradict many previously held assumptions about life by turning the absolutes upside down. According to our topsy-turvy logic, "bad" came to mean "good," and "good" was a label that every status-conscious teen desperately wished to avoid. Some people began to take pride in things that once would have shocked, shamed, and silenced us. As the apostle Paul said, "Their future is eternal destruction. Their god is their appetite, they brag about shameful things, and all they think about is this life here on earth."[4] Breaking traditions, violating conventions, and upsetting taboos became fashionable. Rebels were seen as heroes, whereas true heroes were either forgotten altogether or became the object of cynicism.

The relativists recast certainty as intolerance. Virtue was considered a potential liability, if not an actual vice. Orthodoxy was labeled as radical fundamentalism—giving fundamentalism a negative connotation—while heresy was praised for its honesty, courage, and ingenuity. Society began to question whether there was any such thing as a standard by which we could judge truth from falsehood or right from wrong. Judgment and discretion were abandoned for fear of being found guilty of judgmentalism and discrimination. Thus, adherence to absolutes no longer seemed reasonable, normal, and practical, but small-minded, mean-spirited, and insensitive. Even the gentlest reminder of their relevance served as an unwelcome distraction to our "politically correct" society.

In dismissing objective standards upon which right and wrong were judged, our culture came to value all ideas as equally valid and good. As philosopher Richard Weaver observed, "That it does not matter what a man believes is a statement heard on every side today. This statement carries a fearful implication: It does not matter what a man believes so long as he does not take his beliefs seriously."[5] To a great extent Americans have not taken their beliefs—or any one else's, for that matter—seriously for quite some time. As a result, we have become embroiled in a running battle over the meaning of values and truth. In the face of an increasingly subjective or "relative" mind-set, it has become harder and harder to forge consensus, build community, nurture families, uphold freedom, and develop trust.

Ravi Zacharias shared the following observation in his important post-September 11 book titled *Light in the Shadow of Jihad:*

> The relativist who argues for the absence of absolutes smuggles absolutes into his arguments all the time,

8

while shouting loudly that all morality is private belief. Alan Dershowitz, professor at Harvard Law School, spares no vitriol in his pronouncements that there are no absolutes and that that's the way it is. "I do not know what is right," he contends. It all sounds very honest and real, until he points his finger at his audience and says, "And you know what? Neither do you." So it is not just that he does not know what is right. It is also that he knows the impossibility of knowing what is right so well that he is absolutely certain that nobody else can know what is right either. There is his absolute.[6]

Zacharias later added that Professor Dershowitz, "who denies our ability to define good, says with equal vehemence that he does recognize evil when he sees it. Fascinating!"[7]

Are All Ideas Equally Valid?

In practice, relativism is an attempt to create "out of the mosaic of our religious and cultural differences, a common vision for the common good."[8] But that is just so much wishful thinking. After all, if "everything's relative," who decides what is and what is not a part of the common vision? Who defines *honesty,* or *loyalty,* or *justice*—or any other ideal, for that matter? Under relativism, the public opinion poll becomes the voice of virtue—subject to continual update and a certain margin of error.

Perhaps the most destructive trait of modern relativism, so common in our culture today, is the brash and cavalier attitude it has toward the existence of an objective standard of goodness and morality. In the name of civil liberty and cultural diversity, the conscience of the individual is elevated to the role of moral compass. What's good and true for me might not be good and true for anyone else. Of course, if all ideas are deemed equally valid, there can be no action or idea that is objectively "worse" (i.e., more harmful) than another. Reaching that logical conclusion, however, forces people to fudge the reality of good and evil, because the existence of an objective standard would negate the assumptions of relativism.

To disregard objective standards in the name of liberty only serves to undermine that very same liberty. First, by denying the existence of evil, relativism by definition precludes the ability of a society to restrain evil. How can we legitimately criminalize something that might just be the result of a difference in values? You can see how relativism quickly becomes a self-defeating philosophy. It should be clear that unrestrained evil is the enemy of all free societies.

Further, relativism cheapens our freedom by seeking to bestow liberty as an unearned, undeserved, and unwarranted entitlement, ignoring the fact that with great privilege comes great responsibility. Throughout the history of our country, freedom has been bought with a price—through moral diligence, virtuous sacrifice, and ethical uprightness in opposition to objective evil. Relativism shuns the idea of sacrifice because it implies that no idea is more valuable than another. Unless the sacrifices and responsibilities of freedom are recognized, however, those freedoms will be neglected and then lost, because people only truly value those things for which they have worked or sacrificed.

As Thomas Paine so aptly said, "The harder the conflict, the more glorious the triumph. What we obtain too cheap, we esteem too lightly; 'tis dearness only that gives everything its value. Heaven knows how to put a proper price upon its goods; and it would be strange indeed, if so celestial an article as Freedom should not be highly rated."[9]

By confusing liberty with license, relativism threatens our freedom rather than upholds it. Also, by its very nature, relativism weakens the common vision and destabilizes the common good by its emphasis on the primacy of the individual. Aleksandr Solzhenitsyn, the brilliant Russian novelist, historian, and Nobel laureate, was alarmed by this drift in Western cultures and offered a stern critique:

> Fifty years ago it would have seemed quite impossible in America that an individual be granted boundless freedom with no purpose but simply for the satisfaction of his whims. The defense of individual rights has reached such extremes as to make society as a whole defenseless. It is time to defend, not so much human rights, as human obligations.[10]

According to political analyst James Q. Wilson, those who embrace relativism end up disguising their wrongheaded thinking in a cloak of reasonable-sounding euphemisms:

11

> Many people have persuaded themselves that no law has any foundation in a widely shared sense of justice; each is the arbitrary enactment of the politically powerful. This is called *legal realism,* but it strikes me as utterly unrealistic. Many people have persuaded themselves that children will be harmed if they are told right from wrong; instead they should be encouraged to discuss the merits of moral alternatives. This is called *values clarification,* but I think it is a recipe for confusion rather than clarity. Many people have persuaded themselves that it is wrong to judge the customs of another society since there are no standards apart from custom on which such judgments can rest;

presumably they would oppose infanticide only if it involved their own child. This is sometimes called *tolerance;* I think a better name would be barbarism.[11]

Although relativism purposely blurs the distinctions between good and evil—so much so that one might wonder if there is any distinction at all—every now and then a tragic event will snap us to attention, bringing back into stark focus the great chasm between right and wrong, righteousness and wickedness, good and evil.

Waging War against Evil

If freedom is to survive, we must re-engage with the truth of the absolutes to govern our lives and our society, and we must steadfastly resist the forces of evil. The testimony of history is that evil will always be a present and horrible reality. And as long as evil exists, there is potential for destruction. Although we may never completely eradicate evil, we can keep it from destroying everything that is good and right in the world.

I believe that God has given us an example—in our own bodies—of how righteousness and goodness can prevail over the forces of evil. Inside your body right now, germ warfare is being waged. Your natural defense system protects you from the attacking forces of bacteria, viruses, and other nasty invaders, even though some of them may still be present in your body. As long as your immune system remains strong and no destructive intruders gain a foothold or overpower your defenses, you will experience good health. But as soon as a rebellious cell takes over—be it cancer, a virus, or the destructive elements of arthritis that degenerate the body's natural joint lubrication—disease, discomfort, and sometimes death are the result. Sometimes, like with HIV, it isn't the virus itself that causes disease, but the virus suppresses our defenses, making us vulnerable to other aggressive organisms. In society, such things as violence, sensuality, and depravity in our entertainment media can make us numb to the destructive effects of violence, sensuality, and depravity in real life. Environmental factors, such as allowing a neighborhood to become run-down, can create an atmosphere where crime will breed and flourish.

Everywhere in life, there are deadly forces looking for opportunities to overcome all that is good. Like arthritis or cancer, these forces can be hidden, subtle, progressive, and degenerative, gradually wearing down our defenses and causing friction, or they can strike suddenly and catastrophically like an epidemic.

The destructive forces of greed ate away the integrity of Enron, which led to a spectacular collapse that affected shareholders, employees, and the accounting firm of Arthur Andersen.

Unhealthy forces of self-interest have led at times to support dictators and thugs with our foreign policy and foreign aid, leading to a loss of freedom and a profound suspicion of the United States in certain parts of the world, while leaving millions starving.

Deadly forces of inequality and prejudice led to the institution of slavery in our country's history, the effects of which still linger 150 years after the Emancipation Proclamation. We need a strong prescription of love, forgiveness, and reconciliation—coupled with compassionate concern and assistance for those who are still in need—to finally heal the disease of injustice.

As we seek to treat these "illnesses" in our society, we need to make sure that the remedy is not worse than the disease. For example, we can take an antibiotic to combat a bacterial infection in our bodies, but in the process we also destroy the good bacteria that keep our digestive systems in tune. If we don't restore the proper balance, we can be susceptible to other problems. Likewise, when we apply legislative remedies to social problems, we run the risk of killing off natural safeguards and private initiatives that might actually be more beneficial.

Often the best way to counteract the forces of evil is by strengthening that which is good. So we might try to bolster our immune system by taking vitamins and other supplements, exercising, and watching what we eat. The same principle can be seen in the field of agriculture. If the farmer concentrates more on killing the weeds than on growing the crops, the result is likely to be damage to both. But if the farmer grows good, healthy, vibrant crops, they tend to choke out the weeds—or at least the weeds that do grow are on the fringes of the field or between the rows where they're more easily contained. Perhaps you've had a similar experience with your lawn. A well-watered, healthy lawn is more resistant to weeds, and those that do grow are readily eliminated.

In our society, if we would strengthen everything that is good, raising our standards to conform to the absolutes, focusing on providing water, nourishment, and sunlight to the value system that produces life—if we would pour our time and energy and other resources into positive action that benefits people of every description—we would produce a bumper crop of goodness in our society and the influence of evil would be pushed to the margins where it could easily be controlled. Our laws must be just and enforced. Our military and defense must be as strong as possible and diligent to protect our shores and interests against evil's fierce assault.

We may always have red-light districts and areas of crime in our communities, just as there will probably always be terrorists and others bent on destruction in the world, because the forces of evil are tenacious and persistent. But we don't have to give in. Would we like to eradicate every weed and deadly germ? Yes, but we can't. However, we can isolate those negative factors while we continue to impact the lives of those caught up in destructive behavior and vices with the transforming power of love and truth.

We must be diligent because the moment we begin to give ground to the forces of evil, the moment we stop looking out for one another—especially the poor, the weak, and the disadvantaged—evil will creep in like a fox in the henhouse or a wolf among the sheep, and destruction will be the inevitable result.

Breaking Evil's Deadly Grip

We live in a spiritual world, and we are undeniably spiritual beings. Evil powers in the realm of darkness can affect and even control the actions of people. The crucifixion of Jesus, the only perfect person ever to walk the earth, was the work of spiritual forces of hatred and darkness. The nature of such spiritual control was revealed in Jesus' prayer on the cross: "Father, forgive them; *for they know not what they do*" (emphasis added).[12]

15

This implies, very clearly, that individuals are not only out of control on occasion, but they are far too often under the control of evil forces. The Bible refers to these powers as evil spirits, tormenting spirits, unclean spirits, seducing spirits, deceiving spirits, spirits of bondage and murder and destruction. It is important to realize that not all destructive spirits are as obvious and despicable as those responsible for the tragedy of September 11 and other atrocities. Seducing spirits are often subtle, sophisticated, and in some ways attractive. They can control professors, politicians, artists, and even religious leaders, including Jesus' own disciples. Although all evil spirits are ultimately destructive and deadly, they most often use subtle deception as the means to bring about the bondage of their subjects. The entertainer, teacher, or leader who undermines the relevance of absolute principles is no less demonically manipulated than the terrorist.

Although the negative impact is less obvious and may take much longer to be revealed, the damage is just as real and just as destructive.

Merely recognizing the problem of evil is not enough. We must seek to free our hearts and minds from the deadly grip of evil forces beyond our control through the power of prayer. We must evaluate all areas of our lives—both personally and as a nation—and turn those areas over to God. We must examine our own hearts individually and nationally by asking questions like the following:

– Do we sacrifice the well-being of others while trying to ensure our own personal well-being?
– Do we guard our economic interests while giving too little consideration to the interests of others?
– Do we adhere to business practices that exploit rather than assist others?
– Do we disregard the true value of human life, including the unborn? (The consequences of this practice are more severe than words can ever communicate.)
– Do we fail to protect the rights of those with whom we disagree?
– Do we place more value on material gain than character development and spiritual maturity?
– Do addictive practices and appetites control us?

Consider the prayer of the psalmist David: "Search me, O God, and know my heart; test me and know my thoughts. Point out anything in me that offends you, and lead me along the path of everlasting life."[13]

In this lifetime we will never be free from the struggle against evil and the negative effects of those who practice it, but we can battle and overcome much of the evil we encounter, especially in our hearts, through the power of prayer. In the prayer recorded in John 17, Jesus prayed not only for the immediate protection of His disciples, but also for all who would later believe in Him as a result of their testimony. This includes us. We can be protected from the adverse effects of the evil one, but we must continue living and abiding in the spirit of Christ's prayer. We ask not only to be delivered from evil, but also to be protected from evil's deadly effects. In Christ, there is hope and help because He came to overcome the evil one and set free the captives. Our freedom as a nation will be secured only as individuals experience release from the grip of evil and begin to walk in personal liberty.

The Bible teaches that believers in Christ and those who receive the fullness of the Holy Spirit will have spiritual discernment. This gift enables individuals to identify the spirit that often controls a person's actions. Consider the importance of accurately reading the hidden intentions of a potentially dangerous person. It is well known that some dogs can recognize the spirit of fear or evil intentions in human beings and immediately go on guard or point. If a dog can recognize evil traits in people, surely God-given discernment—an indispensable asset during these perilous days—can safeguard us against harm.

President George W. Bush has rightly referred to those behind the attacks on our country as "evildoers," and he no doubt has the unanimous agreement of sane thinkers and peace-loving people throughout the world. But we must not forget that supernatural powers are influencing those who are caught up in evil, and supernatural power of a different kind will be required to break, not only the threat of terrorist attacks, but also the grip that evil has on the hearts of so many people.

17

Our Government Is Not the Answer

I've had the privilege of spending time with George W. Bush before and during his governorship in Texas, as well as for brief periods since he was elected president. Through close observation and open, honest dialogue, I have come to believe wholeheartedly in his commitment to Jesus Christ, his character, his courage, and his calling. But even though I personally admire and appreciate the president and have confidence in his leadership, and even though his decisions and the counsel of his advisers will, in many ways, determine the path and progress of our personal and national liberty, freedom's hope does not rest upon his shoulders. His ability to make the right decisions will largely be determined by the faithfulness and prayers of those who understand the importance of the absolutes.

I had occasion to visit with President Bush on his ranch in Crawford, Texas, one month prior to the September 11 terrorist attacks. That day, more than a dozen people were killed in Israel by a terrorist attack, and the president and I briefly discussed the rising tension in the Middle East, but little did we know that only a few weeks later terrorism would come to our own shores.

At the conclusion of my visit, I asked President Bush how I could best assist and encourage him. He replied by repeating something he had said on numerous previous occasions: "James, there is not one thing you or anyone else can do that is of greater importance than prayer, and I mean that." Before I left the ranch, he and I prayed together, asking God for wisdom, direction, and a spirit of peace to guard our hearts.

I count it a deep privilege to be able to pray with and encourage our president, especially during these strategic times. I've long had a sense in my heart about George W. Bush's divine destiny and responsibility, and I pray continually that God will impress him with the significance of the role he has been chosen to play in human history. He has a unique opportunity to reshape world thinking and redirect the greatest nation in the world. I believe that is God's purpose for President Bush, and that now is the time. We must all pray for our president, and especially that he will never compromise his God-given convictions. Although his public approval ratings have soared to all-time highs, and he has even gained the approval of many former critics who have acknowledged the wisdom of his approach to the terrorist situation, his lasting effectiveness will be determined by his ability to inspire the nation to return to the rock-solid principles of the absolutes.

Although it is not the government's responsibility to share spiritual truths, it is the responsibility of our leaders to maintain our vigilance and our strength as a deterrent to terrorists and rogue nations:

– Our law enforcement and intelligence gathering agencies must set aside past tensions and work together for the good of the nation. Our commander in chief must receive good information and wise counsel.
– We must maintain the best equipped and strongest military in the world, and we must develop a defense system and missile shield far more effective than our present one.
– Our borders must be made more secure, and we must diligently enforce our immigration laws.

As important as these measures will be in the years to come, we must not place our hope of lasting security in the might of our military or our defense shield. Our response as individuals and as a nation to the principles shared in this book, to the Word of God, and to God Himself will ultimately determine the future of our freedom. No political party, no president, no leader will save us.

They can certainly contribute to a positive move in our nation toward the absolutes, or they can impede our progress; but our future will be determined by our proper response to the absolute, unshakable principles of God. We *must* love people. We *must* love the Lord, and we must be serious about demonstrating our faith through acts of righteousness and compassion.

The forces of evil have launched a direct attack on the truth of the absolutes, and all of human history bears witness to the deadly consequences of this assault. The Bible declares that evil "prowls around like a roaring lion, looking for some victim to devour."[14] It desires to destroy everything that life is intended to be, and it seeks to devalue human life and diminish our freedom.

Evil is an ever-present reality, and it is only as we recognize absolute truth and the supreme authority of God that we will be able to determine evil's intent and properly deal with its perpetrators. Prayer is without a doubt the most vital factor in overcoming the evil that lurks around us. "Pray, too, that we will be saved from wicked and evil people, for not everyone believes in the Lord. But the Lord is faithful; he will make you strong and guard you from the evil one."[15]

CHAPTER TWO

It is absurd to consider any theory without first examining the theology and philosophy which lies behind it. Theological and philosophical concerns underlie every idea, every policy, every work of art, and every practical behavior. Those who recognize as much are to be accounted as wise. Those who do not are but fools.

CHARLES HADDON SPURGEON (1834–1892)

Worldview is the most important thing that we can know about a man. Ideas have consequences. And those consequences affect everything in the practical realm as well as in the theoretical realm. Discernment of worldview is therefore the most necessary of all the tasks of wisdom.

RICHARD M. WEAVER (1910–1963)

Ideas Have Consequences

Every belief system will ultimately bear fruit—and the fruit will be consistent with the root from which it comes.

Nobody is completely open-minded or genuinely objective. It's simply not possible. We all carry in our heads "a mental model of the world, a subjective representation of external reality," according to Alvin Toffler, author of the groundbreaking classic *Future Shock*.[1] This mental model, he says, is like a giant filing cabinet that contains a slot for every item of information we take in. It organizes our knowledge and gives us a grid from which to think. Our minds are not blank slates.

"When we think," says economic philosopher E. F. Schumacher, "we can only do so because our mind is already filled with all sorts of ideas with which to think."[2] These more or less fixed ideas make up our mental model of the world, our frame of reference, our presuppositions—in other words, they make up our worldview.

The term *worldview*, translated from the German word *Weltanschauung*, means "life perspective" or "way of seeing." It refers to the way we look at the world. Everyone has a worldview. It is the means by which we interpret the situations and circumstances around us. It is what enables us to process the information that comes to us through our senses. It determines our basic outlook on life and faith.

We might be tempted to think of a discussion about worldview as something only for philosophers or ivory-tower intellectuals. It's not the sort of thing we would associate with the practical, nitty-gritty details of life. But in truth there is nothing more relevant to our day-to-day lives than the subject of worldview. Ultimately, understanding the importance of worldviews is more practical than understanding how the stock market works, how laws are passed through Congress, or how e-mail messages travel through cyberspace. It is one of the most down-to-earth and important subjects we can tackle.

In his helpful book *How to Read Slowly*, James Sire writes:

> A worldview is a map of reality; and like any map, it may fit what is actually there, or it may be grossly misleading. The map is not the world itself, of course, only an image of it, more or less accurate in some places, distorted in others. Still, all of us carry around such a map in our mental makeup and we act upon it. All our thinking presupposes it. Most of our experience fits into it.[3]

All people—without exception—have a worldview, whether they realize it or not. Their worldview not only affects what they think about, it determines what they do. Writers write from the perspective of their worldview. Painters paint from the palette of their worldview. Politicians pass laws in accordance with their worldview. Teachers teach from the framework of their worldview. Their worldview shapes their perceptions, preferences, prejudices, and priorities. It is not possible to separate what we do from how we think. We simply cannot escape from our worldview.

Pablo Picasso believed that the modern world was a place of randomness, fragmentation, and impersonal force. Because he painted and sculpted in a manner consistent with his worldview, his works—most notably the large abstract canvasses he painted later in life—evoke randomness, fragmentation, and impersonality. In a sense, his worldview necessitated cubism.

Johann Sebastian Bach viewed the world as a place of beauty, goodness, and truth. He wrote, played, and performed in a manner consistent with his theology, which was reflected in the beauty of his music—especially in the concertos he composed during his tenure as choirmaster in the city of Leipzig.

Karl Marx believed that the world was a place of inequality and injustice. His worldview, espousing class struggle and the inevitability of social change, was reflected in his writing—most notably in *Das Kapital* and his Communist Manifesto, which helped to spawn the socialist revolutions of the late nineteenth and early twentieth centuries.

So we see that ideas have consequences. Orderly ideas have orderly consequences, revolutionary ideas have revolutionary consequences, and inconsistent ideas have inconsistent consequences. Ideas can also have unintended or secondary consequences. If we follow a certain line of thinking by adhering to a particular behavior for any length of time, we will experience a kind of worldview domino effect, with one consequence leading to another, and so on.

For example, if we allow our minds to dwell on forbidden fantasies, before long our thought life will be marked by unfaithfulness. Over time, we might begin to grow restless and discontented, which in turn could lead to adultery—which might

result in separation or even divorce. The ripple effect of consequences expands until it affects our spouse, our children, our
neighbors, and our friends. Because our actions have consequences, the ideas behind them have consequences as well. You
may have heard the saying, "Sow a thought, reap an action. Sow
an action, reap a habit. Sow a habit, reap a character. Sow a
character, reap a destiny." This is worldview thinking at its most
practical level.

The Modern Worldview

Sadly, in our culture, people are generally not concerned about
their worldview. They act as if they can separate their ideas from
their actions—in effect establishing a worldview in which
worldviews are irrelevant! If this ironic paradigm, rooted in
relativism, is allowed to stand, it strips all worldviews of their
functional value.

More than twenty years ago, in his landmark bestseller *A
Christian Manifesto,* Francis Schaeffer described the fragmentation that has accompanied the shift toward relativism in our
society. Schaeffer suggested that the basic problem with our
culture was that parents and leaders had only "seen things in
bits and pieces instead of totals."[4] The result was an inability to
deal with the full scope of society's dilemmas.

"They have very gradually become disturbed over permis-
siveness, pornography, the public schools, the breakdown of
the family, and finally abortion," Schaeffer said. "But they have
not seen this as a totality—each thing being a part, a symptom,
of a much larger problem. . . . They failed to see that all of this has
come about due to a shift in worldview—that is, through a fundamental change in the overall way people think and view the
world and life as a whole."[5]

In other words, according to Schaeffer, part of the reason it

25

has been so difficult to address the cultural challenges of our day is that we have largely ignored the fact that these changes in our society have occurred primarily because of changes in our *thinking*. Not only have we failed at times to acknowledge the consequences of our ideas, we've often failed to recognize the ideas themselves. We have not clearly seen how our worldview affects our decisions and our values. If we are to have any hope of maintaining a civil society, it is essential that we recognize not only that ideas matter, but that having the *correct* ideas makes all the difference. If we fail to see this basic reality, we will be morally and culturally hobbled.

In the book of Romans, the apostle Paul expounds on the ill effects of a life lived without regard to the consequences of ideas:

> God shows his anger from heaven against all sinful, wicked people who push the truth away from themselves. For the truth about God is known to them instinctively. God has put this knowledge in their hearts. . . .
>
> Yes, they knew God, but they wouldn't worship him as God or even give him thanks. And they began to think up foolish ideas of what God was like. The result was that their minds became dark and confused. Claiming to be wise, they became utter fools instead. . . . Instead of believing what they knew was the truth about God, they deliberately chose to believe lies. So they worshiped the things God made but not the Creator himself. . . .
>
> That is why God abandoned them to their shameful desires. Even the women turned against the natural way to have sex and instead indulged in sex with each other. And the men, instead of having normal sexual relationships with women, burned with lust for each other. Men did

shameful things with other men and, as a result, suffered within themselves the penalty they so richly deserved.

When they refused to acknowledge God, he abandoned them to their evil minds and let them do things that should never be done. Their lives became full of every kind of wickedness, sin, greed, hate, envy, murder, fighting, deception, malicious behavior, and gossip. They are backstabbers, haters of God, insolent, proud, and boastful. They are forever inventing new ways of sinning and are disobedient to their parents. They refuse to understand, break their promises, and are heartless and unforgiving.[6]

In the wake of September 11, some people sought to attribute the terrorist attacks to the judgment of God. But according to Paul, God's wrath has already been revealed against the ungodliness and unrighteousness of people. In fact, God's judgment against those who embrace a God-less worldview is to allow them to experience the consequences of their lifestyle choices. God gives them what they ask for! The resulting bad ideas, unhealthy practices, and addictive tendencies reveal that God's judgment has already been released. It is revealed in the degenerative lifestyles of those who reject absolute truth. When we refuse to honor God and instead begin to present vain, foolish speculations and assertions, our hearts are darkened and those beliefs lead us down a deadly spiral, as individuals and as a nation. Professing ourselves to be wise, we become a nation of fools.

For example, some people in our society will defend the rights of plants and animals with greater zeal than they do the rights of people. They worship the creation more than the Creator, just as Paul predicted in the first century. Others defend their right to engage in unnatural sexual practices, and anyone who disagrees with them is immediately labeled an extremist, a hatemonger, homophobic, or intolerant. Who would have thought we'd see the day when a woman's freedom of choice would not be constrained by her unborn child's right to life? Who would have thought that an individual's freedom to choose to have a sexual relationship with a person of the same sex would not only be defended as normal, but would become the basis of proposed changes in our laws governing marriage and family? A nation of fools—one with a God-less worldview—cannot long preserve a productive and healthy society.

Still, we should not wish God's punitive judgment against those who engage in self-destructive behavior. Under no circumstances should we ever encourage unkindness, discrimination, or attacks on those with whom we disagree. Instead, we must extend the love of God to them, demonstrate compassion, and show them the way to find healing for their deep-seated spiritual unrest. Corrupt ideas and their harmful consequences will not be redeemed through condemnation and shame. The underlying illness can only be healed by love, truth, and a reaffirmation of the absolutes.

The American Idea

The founders of our nation made certain to ground their hope for building a great society of freedom and liberty on the established principles of the Judeo-Christian worldview, which they knew had resulted throughout history in the world's most remarkable flowering of the arts, freedom, prosperity, and progress. For all the shortcomings of the West, no other society has known the kind of independence, affluence, and advancement as those founded during the Christian era. For contrast and perspective, we need only look at those societies developed under the influence of communism or Islam. Those ideologies have resulted in far less freedom for people, the arts, politics, and

28

economics and have had profound implications for crime and punishment, foreign policy and domestic stability, and war and peace.

Unlike other nations, which have forged their identity and cohesion from a common ethnicity, geography, or cultural tradition, the United States of America was founded on certain ideas—ideas about freedom, opportunity, and the pursuit of dreams; ideas about religious tolerance, human dignity, and social responsibility; ideas about community, charity, and civility. The American founders wanted to perpetuate—and perhaps even enhance—the legacy of freedom for the sake of their children and all succeeding generations.

Modern relativists who wish to remove Christian ideas and ideals from public life are not simply trying to ensure objectivity and tolerance in our culture, they are seeking to exchange the influence of one worldview for another. We need to be clear about this. The idea of a "separation between church and state" was designed to keep the government from interfering with the free practice of religion; it was never intended to eliminate the influence of religion from the public square. The founders viewed that prospect as a "devil's bargain," in Patrick Henry's words, and rejected it out of hand. They decided early on that they preferred the consequences of a Judeo-Christian worldview to any other— even though they themselves did not all hold to the Christian faith. It was an informed choice—rooted in a remarkable intellectual and spiritual command of history, theology, and philosophy. They understood that to remove the biblical identity of our nation would be to subvert its creed. It would stifle the very essence of what Alexis de Tocqueville called "American exceptionalism." It would deny the American idea.

Thus, the tendency of some in our day to downplay the relevance of the Judeo-Christian worldview, except as a means of spiritual solace, has paved the way for a dramatic shift in the character of our culture. When the task of faith is limited merely to offering individuals inner peace and tranquility, then virtually all moral influence is removed from the world. There is little or nothing to restrain the ambitions of evil people and movements. There are no checks, no balances, no standards, and no limitations. The wise counsel of the ages goes unheard and unheeded. And the foundations of civil society are threatened.

The worldview of the American founders was comprehensive. It included sociology as well as salvation, a new social order as well as a new birth; it included reform and redemption, culture and conversion, a reformation as well as regeneration. Read the literature of the great theorists of the American experiment in liberty and you will see that balance—they applied the Judeo-Christian worldview to the whole of life, knowing the importance of worldview because ideas have consequences. The founders clearly understood that true spiritual salvation would have such a transforming effect on people that they would be compelled to care for those in need. Christian faith, rightly understood, does not refer only to "life up there in the hereafter," it also engages fully with life in the here and now. Evangelism is not divorced from charity—in fact, true charity springs to life as a result of salvation. Having received freely from God, we will be anxious to give freely to others.

A spiritual rebirth leads to newness of life—not just in word, but also in deed. The redemption that brings about conversion leads also to the reformation of culture and practice. Reformation is the outgrowth of supernatural transformation. In their practice of Christian faith, the founders were not mere "hearers of the word"—they were "doers," as well.[7]

Any other approach to building a civil society is bound to be shortsighted and woefully impotent—as history amply attests. A worldview based on anything less than the absolutes fails to live up to the comprehensive high call of the American idea. It is therefore essential that we release the restraints of a partial and passive Christianity in order to mount a full-scale assault on the evil and privation that now threaten the safety of our country and the stability of the world.

When we fully apprehend the truth of the absolutes, we are able to answer the gravest and deepest questions that arise out of the human experience. The philosopher Immanuel Kant asked, "What can we know? What must we do? What can we hope for?" Likewise, the French impressionist painter Paul Gauguin asked, "Where do we come from? Where are we? Where are we going?"[8]

Such are the universal cries of the human heart. If we grasp the importance of basing our worldview based on the absolutes, we can begin to answer those questions. If we do not, then we are doomed to live in a society filled with the aftereffects of wrongheaded thinking, and we will leave a moral and intellectual void begging to be filled by some ideological or religious fanatic who will not hesitate to impose his worldview on us. Damaging and deficient worldviews are not overcome using bullets or missiles. They are defeated by the love and forgiveness that result from embracing a worldview based on the absolutes.

The Transforming Power of Better Ideas

The best way to overcome the negative consequences of bad ideas is with better ideas. It may not happen overnight, but eventually truth and wisdom will prevail. Take the fall of Communism in the Soviet Union and Eastern Europe, for example. Karl Marx had an idea about how society should be governed. Influential people who shared Marx's worldview were drawn to

31

his ideas and eventually formed systems of government based on his principles. As a theory, communism had some appeal for the disenfranchised, but in practice it turned out to be a really bad idea with even worse consequences. Far from bringing about a proletarian state of equality, it devalued humanity, destroyed freedom, and denied the reality of God.

The negative consequences of Marx's vision took decades to run their course; but eventually they did, because a better idea—freedom—was continually knocking at the door.

In our nation, we enjoy incredible freedom, but it's a freedom that must be guarded carefully. In the marketplace of ideas, truth and error continually collide; freedom takes her stand against the forces of bondage; and good faces off against evil. We cannot afford to ignore the consequences of our ideas, thinking that freedom will somehow be self-perpetuating. History tells us otherwise—loud and clear. Unless our liberty is hemmed in by truth and constrained by common sense, it will eventually lead to license: the attempt to have freedom without responsibility. License inevitably erodes the foundations of freedom, resulting in some form of bondage—addiction, corruption, slavery, or death—and loss of our essential humanity.

Come, Let Us Reason Together

It's time we considered as a nation the consequences of our ideas, good *and* bad. If the results of our ideas turn out to be destructive to life and liberty, we need to change the underlying ideas—we need to change our minds and our hearts. I'm not suggesting that one person or group should impose their ideas on others, but let's make a place at the table for all ideas to be considered, and may the best and the brightest prevail on their own merits.

The ideas on which our nation was founded have served us

well for more than two centuries. We ought to acknowledge the roots of our freedom and diligently protect our ideals from the inevitable erosion of time and the corrosive effect of lesser ideas that would undermine our firm foundation. If we hope to maintain our civil and free society, we must recognize the truth that ideas have consequences, that ideas make all the difference, and that they shape the course of human events. If we fail to see the connection between our ideas and our outcomes, we will suffer the consequences.

Perhaps the most fundamental debate in American society today is about which ideas will prevail. Will we continue to govern ourselves and establish public policy based on the absolute principles on which this country was founded? Or will we shift our values and our policies based on the prevailing winds of popular opinion? The answers to those questions will determine the future course of our nation.

Let's bring *all* ideas to the table, from every quarter, and let's weigh them in the balance of reason. Let's look at the consequences of our ideas and decide which ones we want to govern our society. I'm not trying to *impose* my convictions on others, any more than I want them to impose their convictions on me. But neither am I afraid to place my Christian ideas and convictions alongside ideas from other faiths and perspectives—because I know that truth will prevail. If I'm wrong, I'm willing to be corrected. If I'm misguided, I'm willing to be set straight. I'm not afraid of the truth. Sometimes the truth hurts, but I've also seen how the light of truth brings incredible freedom.

C. S. Lewis said, "I believe in Christianity as I believe that the Sun has risen, not only because I see it, but because by it I see everything else."[9] He understood that ideas have consequences. Such an understanding would surely serve us well in these difficult days in which we now live. Such an understanding is consistent with the hopes and dreams of future generations that our great legacy of liberty may yet be passed on. Let's debate the great issues of our day. Let's stop hiding behind empty rhetoric and political positions. Let's take an honest look at the consequences of our ideas in a spirit of fairness and truth. The foundations, on which all who live in the free world are building their lives, are about to be tested as never before. Let's resolve to take our stand on absolute principles that have stood the test of time.

3

CHAPTER THREE

Faith is the force of life. LEO TOLSTOY (1828–1910)

Faith declares what the senses do not see, but not the contrary of what they see. It is above them, not contrary to them.
BLAISE PASCAL (1623–1662)

If I find in myself a desire which no experience in this world can satisfy, the most profitable explanation is that I was made for another world. C. S. LEWIS (1898–1963)

O Lord, Thou made us for Thyself, and our hearts are restless until they rest in Thee. ST. AUGUSTINE (354–430)

We Are
Spiritual Beings

*To ignore our spiritual nature is to deprive ourselves of what
makes us most essentially human. To deny the existence
of God is to set our minds at war against our hearts.
God exists, and He created us with the capacity to know Him.*

After the terrorist attacks on the Pentagon and the World Trade Center, people across America experienced a resurgence of interest in spiritual matters. Church attendance skyrocketed, and prayer services spread from churches and synagogues to town squares, stadiums, and homes. Bookstores couldn't keep Bibles and other religious books on the shelves, and many people logged on to Web sites like spirituality.com, which saw the number of hits to its site triple in the hours and days following the attacks.[1] On the steps of the U.S. Capitol, our nation's leaders united in singing "God Bless America," the anthem that also replaced "Take Me Out to the Ballgame" during the seventh-inning stretch at major-league ballparks. Our national crisis drew us together and turned our attention beyond ourselves. When confronted with the unmistakable reality of evil, people instinctively drew upon spiritual resources.

Such a remarkable impulse is not unique to these difficult days in which we live. In fact, it is a universal tendency, common to all people everywhere, in every age, because we are spiritual beings. In any crisis, our first and most natural reaction is to cry out to God. We don't have to learn how to do this. We simply know, deep down inside, that there is a God. His character is etched on our hearts. When there is nowhere else to turn, we know beyond a doubt that we can turn to God. Although in the course of daily life our awareness of the spiritual dimension may be suppressed or ignored, it can never be altogether forgotten—regardless of how hard we might try.

Consider this famous quote, which is widely attributed to Blaise Pascal, the great seventeenth-century French mathematician and philosopher: "There is a God-shaped vacuum in the heart of every man which cannot be filled by any created thing, but only by God the Creator made known through Jesus Christ."[2] Whether or not we are consciously aware of this "vacuum," each of us has an innate sense of our own spiritual nature—that vital essence that sets us distinctly apart from the animals. Part of being human is having an inner curiosity, a longing for meaning and understanding—a longing for God. Our tendency to want to worship, as well as our capacity as humans to *feel*—compassion, conviction, regret, remorse, desire, love, joy, to name just a few—are visible outworkings of a deeper reality: We are essentially spiritual beings. There's something in us that draws us to look beyond ourselves.

The Bible teaches that we are not only spiritual, we're eternal. When a person passes from this life, far more than a final breath leaves the body. A living essence departs. Jesus taught that the departed spirit lives forever—either in God's presence or in hell. We're on a journey toward eternity, and the decisions we make in this life will determine our destiny. A lot of people resist the idea of a personal God who holds us accountable, but it takes more faith *not* to believe in God than to acknowledge His existence.

Getting in Touch with the Heart of God

As a young boy, I always believed there was a God somewhere "out there." At one point I became marginally involved in a religious group, but this had very little impact on my life at the time. God might really exist, but He didn't have much to do with a shy, lonely boy named James Robison. (Or so I imagined.)

I had heard people talk about Jesus and "the Father," but somehow they had never seemed real to me. Yet as I look back, I can now see that my true Father was reaching out to me even then.

Many people today chafe or rebel at the suggestion that we should derive our moral base from something outside ourselves, such as the Bible, but those people are no less moral creatures than I am; they have simply chosen to base their morality on something other than God's revealed truth. I believe in God and what He says about how we should live our lives, but let me say right up front that if you don't believe in God, I respect your right to differ with me. That's part of the freedom we have in America, and I'm grateful for it. However, even as I respect your right to disagree, I hope that you will read what I have to say with an open mind, and I pray that before you set this book down you will have come to see God the way I see Him—as a real Father who loves you with an everlasting love and has a good purpose for your life.

You might say, "James, how can you believe in a God you can't see or prove exists?" The answer is, I do see Him. I see Him in what He has created; I see Him in what He has designed. And perhaps most of all, I see Him in other people who have surrendered themselves to Him and who allow His love to overflow in their lives.

If you've ever met a person who overflows with the love of God, you know it—it's unmistakable. Just as a tree is known by its fruit, so too a life that is rooted in the love of God will be known by its fruit of love, joy, peace, patience, and a host of other good things. A truly God-centered life, lived out with integrity, is the best theological argument you'll ever encounter. And that's how I want *my* life to be. I want to live with integrity, and when I open my mouth to speak, I want the genuine love of God to pour out. There's nothing in this world that can withstand the love of God.

I'm not talking about religion. I'm talking about a relationship with God that is so real, so energizing, and so vital that when you get around people who have that energy, you know that something has happened in their lives, something that is the visible revelation of everything you've ever tried to find. Those people know how to live. They know how to love. They know how to forgive. They know how to deal with pain and adversity and loss. They know how to handle the difficulties of life, because there's a source of power within them that is greater than any force in this world, seen or unseen.

Jesus said that He came to bring us abundance of life. Too often, though, in our materialistic Western mind-set, we try to interpret what He said to mean abundance *in* life rather than abundance *of* life. I've met a lot of people who have abundance in life but don't have abundance of life. Some of the wealthiest areas in our country have more misery per square foot than in the slums. But when God gives us abundance *of* life, it not only fills us up, it also spills over into the lives of others. The real blessings of God are things that money can't buy.

Once you get in touch with the heart of God, you'll begin to extend hands of care. You'll look beyond yourself and your own self-interest, and you'll begin to take notice of other people. If God has already blessed you with abundance *in* life, you will want to share it freely with others. And even if you are materially poor, the abundance in your heart will flow out as a blessing to everyone you meet. As you surrender your heart and your will to God, His love will continue to grow in your life, resulting in boundless joy and indescribable peace.

The Power of Faith

Max Weber, the renowned political economist and founding father of modern sociology, argued in his classic work *The Protestant Ethic and the Spirit of Capitalism* that the remarkable prosperity of the West was directly attributable to the cultural, personal, and ethical prevalence of the Christian faith. In contrast to pagan cultures or societies dominated by other religious systems, where freedoms and opportunities were severely limited and where poverty and suffering abounded, Weber found that commitment to the intellectual precepts of the Bible brought people and nations both liberty and prosperity. He used the categories of social science to propose that faith in God makes a very real and tangible difference in the lives of people and society.

First, he said, the Christian faith "reorients fallen men to reality."[3] Because of sin, we are to some degree naturally blind, foolish, and self-destructive.[4] We tend to go our own way, following our passions and appetites. By engaging ourselves spiritually, we become reacquainted with what is right, what is real, what is true, what is good, and what is beautiful.[5]

Second, according to Weber, the Christian faith "counteracts the destructive effects of sin."[6] The concept of sin does not have much currency in our society these days—which may

40

account for our failure to come to terms with the deep needs of our social institutions and our civic communities. Sin is, in fact, the chief cause of our social, cultural, and personal woes. Think of all the horrors unleashed on the world by people who have pursued their sinful passions unchecked—all the rape, murder, pedophilia, slavery, racism, thievery, and abuse of women and children. By contrast, the Bible says, "Those who become Christians become new persons. They are not the same anymore, for the old life is gone. A new life has begun!"[7] Faith reforms sinners with new and constructive values. They are provoked to moral and upright lives of diligence, purity, sober-mindedness, thrift, trustworthiness, and responsibility.

Third, according to Weber, the Christian faith "establishes a future orientation in men."[8] The Christian faith teaches us to live thoughtfully, to plan, to exercise restraint, and to defer gratification in order to achieve higher ends.[9] Through self-control, wisdom, and careful stewardship, we are encouraged to build for the future.[10] Acknowledging our spiritual nature enables us to look beyond our circumstances. Faith allows for hope.

Fourth, according to Weber, the Christian faith "provokes men to exercise responsibility."[11] Outside the bounds of faith and piety, we are much more likely to yield to our destructive base natures of selfishness, wastefulness, and laziness.[12] However, when we embrace the life of the Holy Spirit, we begin to grow more and more toward selfless maturity.[13] In faith we are much more likely to be responsible to redeem our time.[14] We are inclined to take responsibility to make the most of every opportunity.[15] We are more likely to be responsible to fulfill our calling in life, to use our money wisely, to care for our families, to serve the needs of others, and to be an example of redemption.[16] As we learn to live according to biblical principles, we will admit our weaknesses, confess our sins, and seek diligently to repent and be restored to fellowship with God and others. Far from wanting to impose our beliefs on others, we hope to inspire the desire for positive change in others by offering a consistent example of attractive, godly living and being ready to give testimony to the power of God at work in our lives. It is the very fruit of faith that we all need if we are to preserve and enhance our civil society of freedom, progress, and prosperity.

Fifth, according to Weber, the Christian faith "empowers men with confidence."[17] "It is faith," says George Gilder, "[that] brought immigrants thousands of miles with pennies in their pockets to launch the American empire of commerce; and it performs miracles daily in our present impasse."[18] God blesses obedience.[19] So even though every believer suffers through life's normal struggles, we have the assurance that God's sovereign hand will set it all aright in the end.[20] We can confidently move forward into the future. We can work hard, raise our families, tend to our communities, and plan for the future with confidence and certainty.

God Wants Us to Seek Him

A man once asked a respected leader how he might find God. The leader did not reply directly, but he asked the man to walk with him down to a nearby river and wade in. When the two men were standing chest deep in the water, the leader suddenly forced the man's head beneath the surface and held him there. The man fought desperately, tearing at the leader's arms, until finally, gasping for air, he thrust his head above the water. The leader then explained: "You will find God when you want him like you wanted air!" The book of Hebrews in the New Testament says, "Anyone who comes to [God] must believe that he exists and that he rewards those who earnestly seek him."[21]

It is not my purpose in this chapter to argue for the existence of God. The Bible says that we know the truth about God instinctively, because God has put this knowledge in our hearts.[22] Our longing for a better world finds its source in God—as does our desire for relationship, significance, and purpose. My aim is simply to point you to the only One who can satisfy the deepest desires of your heart. You were designed for a meaningful relationship with your Creator, the one true God. Don't miss out on this most important relationship.

When God's People Get in the Way

Perhaps one of the greatest obstacles to cultural transformation is that many people have substituted religious affiliation for a genuine relationship with God. Some people doubt the reality of God because of the inconsistency they see in the lives of those who profess to know Him. Sadly, the imperfections and outright hypocrisy within parts of the Christian community cause the world to step back with a skeptical, critical attitude.

43

The Bible teaches that Jesus Christ is the head of the body (i.e., the church) and that those who believe in Him make up the rest of His body, the visible expression of who He is.[23] If we are disabled or disfigured because of an improper connection to the head or to one another, then the image of God we are supposed to reflect is distorted and sometimes even lost. But anyone who understands our tendencies to fail knows that our human frailties, inconsistencies, and outright sins do not invalidate the truth about God. In fact, they only serve to underscore our desperate need for Him. It is only as we surrender ourselves to God that others can clearly see His image in us. God says through the prophet Jeremiah, "You will seek me and find me when you seek me with all your heart."[24] If you truly want to know what God is like, don't look at the worst example you can find of someone who claims to believe in Him—go to the source. Read the Bible for yourself, talk to God directly, and draw your own conclusions. Ask God to reveal Himself to you and help you to understand His Word as you read, and He will.

God Speaks

God speaks to us through the Bible, certainly, but He also speaks directly to us, if we will listen. When we set aside our personal agendas and our self-serving motives, it's amazing how clear the voice of God becomes.

I was driving down the road with my wife one day when I heard God speaking in my mind and my heart. It was not an audible voice, but it was nonetheless real. I heard Him say, "I really like the way you come to me. You don't just come with a list of requests and concerns. Instead, you crawl up into my arms, lay your head on my shoulder, and rest. *I like that.*"

Immediately I found myself remembering my eleven grandchildren. When they all come to the house at the same time, they're everywhere, crawling all over me. It's like a circus. "Papaw, let's do this." "Papaw, let's go do that." "Papaw, will you take us fishing?" "Papaw, let's go outside."

But I'll never forget the time one of my grandsons, who was three or four at the time, climbed up in my lap and settled in. While all his siblings and cousins were tugging at my arm and saying, "Papaw, I want to do this" and "Papaw, do that," this little guy just laid his head on my chest and let me hold him. It felt so good. After a while, he looked up at me with his big brown eyes and said, "Papaw, what d'you want to do?"

That's a picture of how God wants us to come to Him. He wants us to rest quietly in His arms, then look up and say, "God, what do *You* want to do?" "What's on *Your* heart, Father?" And then we must wait until we hear His answer.

God and Society

We live in a day when the character of God is up for debate. The Islamic world says there is one God and He is Allah. Christians contend that the God of the Bible—the God of Abraham, Isaac, and Jacob—is the one true God. Anyone can argue with another person's convictions and say, "That's just your opinion versus mine," but if those convictions are backed by historical evidence that supports the truth of one's principles, and if the historical evidence shows the consequences of violating those principles, that's a different story.

In recent months we've had an opportunity to look more closely at the tenets of Islam. We've seen what happened to freedom when the Taliban imposed its religious regime on Afghanistan. If we compare that situation to the freedom we have in the United States, it should make us wonder why our nation is so uniquely different from any other in history.

It isn't because we're a "Christian nation"; let's be clear about that. The founders of our country resisted the imposition of religion. Instead, they established a secular, constitutional republic based on the principle of religious pluralism. It would be a mistake, however, to ignore or deny that the framers of the Constitution believed that the basic principles found in the Bible were a sound basis for government. Whether or not they quoted the Bible to affirm these principles or simply acknowledged that they were true, they nevertheless based the tenets of our liberty on biblical truth. Our spiritual heritage as a nation runs throughout our social and political history. The founders and early leaders of the American republic had no qualms about acknowledging the God-centered order of creation. Their politics were thoroughly rooted in the realization that God is sovereign. Here are a few examples:

- George Washington added the pledge "So help me God" to his inaugural oath, and he later said, "It is impossible to rightly govern the world without God and the Bible."
- John Adams made no secret of the fact that he studied the Bible often and with diligence. "Our constitution," he said, "was made only for a moral and religious people. So great is my veneration of the Bible that the earlier my children begin to read it, the more confident will be my hope that they will prove useful citizens of their country and respectful members of society."
- Thomas Jefferson, the primary author of the Declaration of Independence, wrote, "The Bible is the cornerstone of liberty; therefore students' perusal of the sacred volume will make us better citizens, better fathers, and better husbands."
- William Penn, founder and governor of the Pennsylvania colony, said, "If we will not be governed by God, then we will be ruled by tyrants."
- Andrew Jackson referred to the Bible as "the Rock on which our republic rests."
- Ulysses S. Grant, the nation's eighteenth president, urged his fellow citizens to "hold fast to the Bible as the sheet-anchor of your liberties; write its precepts in your hearts and practice them in your lives. To the influence of this book we are indebted for all the progress made in true civilization and to this we must look as our guide in the future."
- Even Benjamin Franklin, who was by no means a confessing Christian, said, "A nation of well-informed men who have been taught to know the price of the rights which God has given them, cannot be enslaved."[25]

Although these men were not necessarily known for their piety or their orthodoxy as Christians, neither did they suggest a rigid separation between faith and government, or between individual and civic morality. Instead, they left us a legacy in American political life of unashamed and unapologetic dependence upon the benevolent rule of a sovereign God as revealed in the Bible. Thus we have as our national motto, "In God we trust."

I'm not suggesting that America should become a Christian nation any more than it should become an Islamic nation or a Hindu nation or a Buddhist nation. We've seen only too clearly the inherent danger of religion-based political regimes in other parts of the world. What we should desire, however, is a nation that is influenced in a positive way by Christians who live according to godly principles, whose lives are governed by absolute truths, and who manifest the love of God in word and in deed.

During the latter half of the first century, the whole world stood in awe of the New Testament church because the love of God was like a fire burning in the believers' hearts. They were the most politically powerless group one could imagine—they didn't live in Christian countries; they rarely had access to the halls of earthly power; they were often persecuted—yet they were filled with the Spirit of God, and through them God altered the course of history and changed the world.

I believe that was just the beginning—and just an example of the way things can be. I really don't believe that God intended for us always to be looking *back* at the church in the book of Acts as the ultimate example, nor do I believe that the way our nation was in 1776 is the way it always should be. Certainly we need to learn from history—and I believe those times were an example—but I believe we can move forward into an even brighter future as we adhere to absolute principles. At the same time, however, we must recognize that when we depart from the principles that fostered our freedom and our success as a nation, we risk reaping the consequences of our error.

Absolute Principles in Practice

Over the years, I have been privileged to get to know several national leaders who have demonstrated a commitment to principled leadership. Certainly our current president is one. I also had an opportunity in the late 1970s to visit with Ronald Reagan as he prepared for his presidential campaign. I was part of a group of religious leaders with whom he met to discuss the future of our country. We talked fairly extensively about the global threat of Communism (which at the time was a paramount issue) and the massive arms buildup, which we agreed must be stopped. It was the consensus of the group that unless there were some major changes in U.S. policy, our freedom might cease to exist. I expressed to Mr. Reagan my conviction that policy decisions must be based on absolute principles, and he concurred. Later, when I had a moment to speak with him in private, I asked him a very pointed question. I said, "I want to ask you something very personal, and the only way I know to ask it is to phrase it in this manner: Is Jesus Christ real to you? Is He real in your life?"

Mr. Reagan paused and then said in his inimitable style, "Well, the only way I know how to answer is to share that my father was an alcoholic. I never really knew him. The strongest influence in my life was my mother. I want you to know that Jesus Christ is as real to me as my mother."

Later, during the eight years of his presidency, we came to see the fruit of his faith in Jesus, which I believe gave him the moral courage to take some very tough stands. In the end, the Berlin Wall came down, the Soviet military buildup was halted, and Communism collapsed in Eastern Europe, largely because of the principled leadership of President Reagan and his administration. Was he a perfect president and a flawless leader? No, but he understood the importance of governing according to absolute principles. During several phone conversations and other conversations when I visited President Reagan at the White House, he emphasized that principles, not preferences, would guide his decisions.

An Invitation to Meet God

God lives in my heart. He wants to live in your heart, too. I invite you to let Him. Christianity is not an *exclusive* religion, as some would portray it, because the love of God is available to *everybody.*

Do you know what genuine love feels like? Maybe you've never experienced it. When I was a boy, I didn't receive a lot of love from the people closest to me. They were too caught up in their own concerns and addictions. I know how it feels *not* to feel loved. I know how much that hurts. But I also know how it feels to have the love of God flow through me, and it's the love of God that I hold out to you as worthy of your acceptance, regardless of your circumstances. The love of God can reach you and rescue you wherever you are.

If the people of the United States of America were to give themselves over to the love of God, there would be no need for the imposition of more laws, and there would be little need for most of the laws we have now. If Americans were to give themselves over to the love of God, we would begin to see our nation transformed from the inside out.

The goal of Christian involvement in our society is not to usher in a God-centered order or prove an ideology, but to acknowledge the God-centered order that already exists.[26] It is to

49

honor God as the sovereign ruler He already is. God's purpose is not that we should try to live up to a long list of rules and regulations or that we should try to impose a religious standard on society. Instead, He wants us to be in a genuine *relationship* with Him as our loving heavenly Father—a Father who is real, approachable, all-knowing, full of love, holy, compassionate, unshakable, trustworthy, and vitally interested in every person's well-being—and then, as a result of that relationship, to exhibit His character here on earth by living lives that reflect His image. A truly God-centered society, far from being an oppressive religious regime, would be one of unimaginable freedom, far beyond even the level of freedom we now experience and enjoy in America. The Bible says, "It is for freedom that Christ has set us free. Stand firm, then, and do not let yourselves be burdened again by a yoke of slavery."[27] It is my heartfelt desire that everyone come to know such an incredible God and such indescribable freedom.

4

CHAPTER FOUR

Just as a mob may be easily swayed by passing fashions, fancies, and demagogue, so a majority may fall into grievous error and trample truth and justice. Therefore, sometimes it is the patriot's duty to oppose the will of the majority for the sake of what is good and right and true.
ROGER SHERMAN (1721–1793)

We do not need to get good laws to restrain bad people. We need to get good people to restrain bad laws. The problem is that the majority would rather not accept such responsibilities; therefore, it generally falls to the minority to protect the majority from its own predilection to foolish acquiescence to tyranny. G. K. CHESTERTON (1874–1936)

Public opinion is a flitting thing, but truth outlasts the sun; if we cannot own them both, possess the oldest one.
EMILY DICKINSON (1830–1886)

The Majority Is Not Always Right

History—both secular and biblical—demonstrates
that the majority is not always right.

The majority around us often ignores—and in some cases reviles—the absolutes. Does that mean the absolutes are an inferior basis upon which to build one's life? Hardly. People are often wrong, even when their views are shared by a majority of their peers. Objective truth, by definition, is neither subject to nor swayed by the extent of its opposition.

The Bible teaches that we should understand that the majority will often oppose the truth. Jesus said, "The highway to hell is broad, and its gate is wide for the many who choose the easy way. But the gateway to life is small, and the road is narrow, and only a few ever find it."[1] Lessons from history, from the Bible, and from the founding of our nation further illustrate that majority thinking is rarely an accurate barometer of what is right and true.

Examples from History

History is replete with examples of great heroes who stood against the tide of public opinion. Their courageous and principled stands provide us with a powerful reminder that the majority is all too often wrong and must be resisted if truth, justice, and freedom are to prevail.

Today, Abraham Lincoln is almost universally acknowledged as one of the greatest U.S. presidents. But Lincoln came to the White House in a swirl of controversy. More than 60 percent of the electorate had voted against him. He was so despised, and feared by some, that more than half the nation's states threatened to leave the Union if he took office—and seven states actually seceded before he was even inaugurated. A few weeks later, the Civil War broke out, dividing the nation for years.

Even in the North, Lincoln was controversial, often despised, and very rarely considered popular during his presidency. On the day in 1863 when he delivered the immortal Gettysburg Address, he was not even accorded the privilege of being the main speaker. Many of Lincoln's contemporaries disdained and mistrusted him. Clearly, the majority is not always right.

Winston Churchill, one of the more remarkable leaders of the twentieth century, rarely had the support of the majority during his political career in Great Britain. First elected to Parliament in 1900, Churchill was acclaimed at the time as one of the rising stars of British politics, but his outspoken commitment to his principles—popular or not—forced him to the periphery of the government.

After serving in a variety of governmental posts, Churchill was past retirement age when a desperate nation, on the verge of collapse in the face of the Nazi advance in Europe, turned to him for help in 1940. Over the course of the next five years, he was able to do the impossible—withstand Hitler's assault, help save the world for democracy and freedom, and lay the groundwork for postwar peace. Churchill's courage, grit, and gift of oratory inspired his nation to victory. So how did the majority of Britons reward him in 1945? By voting his party out of office.

Great Britain turned to Churchill once again in 1951. Socialism in Europe had wreaked havoc on the British economy, and Stalin's Cold War had begun to threaten the very existence of Western freedom. The majority waited until their beloved empire was on the brink of disaster before acknowledging the error of their ways. Clearly, the majority is not always right.

Not every hero is a government leader, of course. In 1955, Rosa Parks confronted the practice of racial discrimination in the South by refusing to move to the back of the bus. Instead, she boldly resisted the majority and its racist mind-set. From her courage, the modern civil rights movement took strength. Martin Luther King Jr. likewise carried the banner of civil rights and equality for all in the face of overwhelming odds and deep-seated, violent resistance. His life and actions exemplified what it means to stand firm in the face of the prejudice of the majority.

The gruesome French and Russian revolutions enjoyed majority support. Hitler's Nazi regime enjoyed the support of the majority of Germany's citizens. The majority in America, at one time or another, sought to uphold slavery and oppose civil rights. Clearly, the majority is not always right. Throughout history the greatest statesmen and reformers have often had to resist the tide of public opinion in order to fight for what was right. They had to be willing to stand alone—against the majority—in order to protect the innocent, uphold justice, and preserve the peace.

Examples from the Bible
Throughout the Old Testament, the nation of Israel rebelled against the truth, stoning the prophets and refusing to turn back

to the commandments of God. The Israelites often chose to trust the wisdom of the world for security rather than submit to God's authority. In embracing the will of the majority, they relinquished God's protection over their nation.

When Moses sent twelve spies to investigate the strength of the enemy in the Promised Land, the majority report came back negative. Ten spies reported insurmountable odds; only two believed the enemy could be overcome. Joshua and Caleb trusted God for protection despite the opinion of the majority, and God blessed them as a result.[2]

When Elijah stood on Mount Carmel to call down fire upon God's altar, he stood alone against wicked Queen Jezebel, the 450 prophets of Baal, and the 400 prophets of Asherah. Elijah was outnumbered more than 850 to one, but he never lost faith. Because of his stand, the power of God was revealed, and truth prevailed.[3]

Jesus Christ was bitterly opposed by the religious leaders of His day. He taught a gospel of forgiveness, humility, the necessity of a heart change, and help for the poor. His teachings, which upset the entire religious establishment, led to His arrest and eventual execution. After His trial, when the mob screamed for Barabbas to be released rather than Jesus—choosing a common criminal over the unblemished Lamb of God—the majority proved once again just how terribly wrong it can be.[4]

Examples from the Founding of the United States

Perhaps the most potent example of the dangers of majority rule is seen in the philosophy behind the creation of our own government. The founders of the great American experiment in liberty understood the importance of balancing the concerns of the majority with those of the minority. They made careful provision for it in the very structure of American democracy. In their wisdom, the founders created a remarkable system that preserved the importance of majority rule without yielding to its inherent weaknesses. The mechanism they employed, a system of checks and balances, included the electoral college.

History has proven the brilliance of the plan. During more than two centuries of social, cultural, political, and technological revolution, the American constitutional system has remained fundamentally unchanged. The Constitution's genius is, as President Calvin Coolidge once asserted, that it is "grounded upon a firm foundation of enduring principles, applicable to any society for any time."[5]

Checks and Balances

The founders were led by Roger Sherman, a cobbler who taught himself law and then went on to help draft four of the major American founding documents—the Declaration of Independence, the Articles of Confederation, the Constitution, and the Bill of Rights. Sherman quickly won the respect of his fellow delegates at the First Continental Congress (1774) for his wisdom, industry, and sound judgment in regard to both the strengths and the dangers of the majority. John Adams called him "one of the soundest and strongest pillars of the Revolution."[6] A Puritan of simple habits who performed his delegated tasks with thoroughness and accuracy, Sherman gained more legislative experience than any of his contemporaries in Congress—serving on more committees, drafting more legislation, and creating more policies than all the others combined.[7]

Sherman's greatest contribution—and the best known—was the "Connecticut Compromise" he put forward at the Constitutional Convention. Sherman proposed that Congress have two branches, one with proportional representation and one with equal representation. With this proposal, he satisfied both the small and the large states, providing a solution to one of the most stubborn problems of the convention—how to protect the minority from the majority without undoing the aspirations of democracy in the process.

Drawing on a great wealth of wisdom and practical experience, the founders codified in their national charter a host of carefully crafted provisions designed to preserve the freedoms and liberties of the people. They designed the government with a series of interlocking checks and balances. The executive, legislative, and judicial branches were given limited spheres of authority, and states, regions, localities, and even individuals were afforded certain hedges against the imposition of tyranny. Powers were carefully separated. Authority was judiciously delegated. Rights were vigilantly secured.

Rather than yield to the inherent weaknesses of existing forms of government—pure democracy, absolute monarchy, or elitist oligarchy—the founders created the Constitution as the bulwark of a new kind of mixed government known as Federalism. This provided the nation with a government of laws, not rulers. It established a legacy of limited government, "laced up straightly within enumerated powers," according to Thomas Jefferson.[8]

The principle of federalism allows distinctive and individual communities to join together for a greater good without losing their essential distinctiveness and individuality. Instead of the states becoming a part of some larger amorphous union, under Federalism they are able to unite in a mutually beneficial fashion so that the sum of their parts is greater than that of the whole.

A federal relationship is a kind of compact or covenant that allows states to bind themselves together substantially without entirely relinquishing their various identities. The federal nature

57

of the American constitutional covenant enables the nation to function as a republic—thus specifically avoiding the dangers of a pure democracy. A republic exercises governmental authority through mediating representatives under the rule of law. A pure democracy, on the other hand, exercises governmental authority through the imposition of the will of the majority without regard for the concerns of any minority, thus allowing the law to be subject to the whims of the people. The founders designed the federal system of the United States so that the nation could be, as John Adams described it, a "government of law, not of men."[9]

The founders thus expressly and explicitly rejected the idea of a pure democracy, because as James Madison declared, "Democracies have ever been spectacles of turbulence and contention; have ever been found incompatible with personal security, or the rights of property; and have in general been as short in their lives as they have been violent in their deaths."[10] The rule of the majority does not always respect the rule of law and is as turbulent as the complexities of political correctness. Indeed, history has proven all too often that democracy is particularly susceptible to the urges and impulses of "mobocracy."

Americans are one people under the rule of common law, but they are differentiated into a number of distinctive communities, sovereign states protected from the possible intrusions of the national government or from a majority of the other communities. As educator Paul Jehle explains:

> The nature of federalism is seen in the balanced structure of the states and the people throughout the Constitution. Both the national government and state governments are sovereign in their respective spheres. Our national identity as Americans and our federal identity as state citizens are both represented in Congress—in the Senate and House.[11]

The Electoral College

The heart and soul of the founders' balanced vision of government was the creation of the electoral college for the non-direct election of the chief executive—the president. It was one of the least controversial provisions of the new compact during the divisive debate for ratification. According to Alexander Hamilton, writing in the *Federalist Papers:*

> The mode of appointment of the Chief Magistrate of the United States is almost the only part of the system, of any consequence, which has escaped without severe censure, or which has received the slightest mark of approbation from its opponents. The most plausible of these, who has appeared in print, has even deigned to admit that the election of the President is pretty well guarded. I venture somewhat further, and hesitate not to affirm, that if the manner of it be not perfect, it is at least excellent. It unites in an eminent degree all the advantages, the union of which was to be wished for.

Afterward, the structure of the electoral college was never a matter of serious debate—even when the nation was forced to weather fiercely contested elections in 1824, 1876, and 1888, and the trauma of the Civil War.

The electoral college was designed to be a federal hedge against the domination of individual states by an absolute national majority. Indeed, without the electoral college, the delicate federal balance between national unity and regional distinctiveness would be lost, and the various states would lose much of their power over the executive branch.

The founders rejected direct popular election of the president because it failed to protect the states from the intrusion of massed, centralized forces. They believed that if a centralized government directly governed the people, there was likely to be more opportunity for corruption. Further, they reasoned that a pure democracy would be more easily corrupted than a federal constitutional republic, because it would essentially eliminate state borders and state prerogatives.

Direct popular election of the president would also fail to prevent a candidate from pandering to one region, or running up votes in certain states. Political scientist James Whitson explained the concept by using a sports analogy:

> In a baseball season you don't play 100-odd games, add up your total runs from all those games, and the teams with the most play in the World Series. Teams would just run up the score on weaker teams to balance the closer games against tougher opponents. In a direct election, Democrats would run up the vote totals in safe states like Massachusetts and Republicans would run up their votes in states like Nebraska. The electoral college forces candidates to concede states their opponents are winning handily and contest the tight races.[12]

Another problem with direct popular election of the president is that it would fail to protect minority interests from the tyranny of the majority. For example, because African-Americans make up about 13 percent of the population, in a direct election they would only represent 13 percent of the vote. Likewise, the nation's farmers, once a very influential constituency, now make up less than 4 percent of the population and a scant minority of the overall vote. In a direct election, why would candidates worry about these small groups? They wouldn't. But under the electoral college system, African-Americans and farmers represent sizable

60

constituencies in several states, and thus their voting strength in these states gives them more power and influence. Because minority groups are often concentrated in certain states and not spread evenly throughout the country, their influence is protected to a greater degree in a federal system.

Finally, the founders rejected direct popular election of the president because it would encourage candidates to ignore smaller states in favor of big metropolitan areas. In a direct election, New York City would have about twice the electoral clout of the combined states of Alaska, Delaware, Montana, North Dakota, Vermont, and Wyoming. Why would candidates even campaign in those six states when they could double their impact by spending more time and less money in a single city? The issues and needs of large urban areas would inevitably outweigh the interests of small rural communities.

The federal solution was to elect the president by a balanced representation of the states and the people. Electors, independent from either the states or the national government, were selected in accordance with standards established by individual state legislatures, and the electors then elected the president. The electoral college system represents a careful implementation of the essential constitutional principle of federalism. Without it, the genius of the entire Constitution would be jeopardized.

Critics of this system of checks and balances had a field day during the election of 2000. During this dead-even contest, the wisdom and foresight of Roger Sherman and the other founders were evident. Vice President Al Gore, the Democratic candidate, apparently won a slim plurality of the popular vote, but Texas Governor George W. Bush, the Republican candidate, secured a slight majority in the electoral college—thus winning the presidency.

Outraged calls for the abolition of the constitutional system of election were subsequently aired in both the corridors of power in Washington and in the national media. Concerned that "the will of the people" had somehow been "ignored by an archaic system" that "failed to weigh every vote fairly and equally," the critics demanded that the college be "scrapped for a more direct election process."[13] The system, however, worked exactly the way the founders had hoped.

Very simply, the electoral college provides protection against the tyranny of the 51 percent. The vaunted "will of the people" is not best expressed in the voices of just over half of the people if just under half of the people have their voices ignored. The brilliance of the constitutional system is precisely that every vote counts—not just those that belong to the majority.

What is the value of our constitutional form of government if not as a safeguard against the possibility of a foolish majority rule? The brilliance of the American system is that it recognized this fact and institutionalized it. Indeed, James Madison argued in the *Federalist Papers* that much of the genius of a nation of liberty is its "protection of the freedoms and prerogatives of the few against the freedoms and prerogatives of the many."[14] The founders' intentions make it clear that majority rule needs to be tempered for our freedom to be preserved.

A Need for Wisdom

If we can't trust the majority to be right, how can a government of the people, by the people, and for the people function properly? Clearly, we need wisdom as citizens and most certainly as leaders and elected officials. Instead of merely pursuing what is popular with the majority, we need to seek understanding and allow wisdom to govern our lives and our nation. According to the American patriot leader Samuel Adams, it is wisdom that will ultimately sustain us:

Many nations have come and gone with their vast stores of expertise. Only those peoples intent on the task of marshalling knowledge with understanding and wisdom can expect to perpetuate their hopes and dreams and visions of liberty from one generation to the next. Therefore take heed, that each new day dawns with the hope of knowledge, the light of understanding, and the practical energies of wisdom.[15]

For decades our educational system has emphasized the gaining of knowledge as its primary aim and objective. In our information age, we have assumed that if our children have a good grasp of facts and information, if they have all the knowledge they need, they will be able to make their way in the world. Unfortunately, in a "values-free" environment, minds that have been dulled by the smothering conformity of popular culture cannot plumb the depths of understanding necessary to make wise and prudent decisions. At the same time, wisdom has been marginalized in our society because it is deemed to be dangerous. (After all, it involves value judgments.) Because wisdom is not ethically neutral, it flies in the face of the postmodern worldview. But godly wisdom, as seen in the absolutes, is the only thing that can ensure the endurance of our nation's great legacy of freedom.

63

What Is Wisdom?
When we speak of wisdom, we do not mean the accumulation of knowledge or facts. Knowledge is a building block for wisdom, but it is not wisdom. Someone who has a firm grasp of facts in math, science, or literature, for example, does not necessarily have what it takes to relate those facts to real life. Understanding is necessary in order to put knowledge to good use. Understand-

ing involves making logical connections between facts. It is what makes knowledge useful. It is what makes knowledge practical and functional. Understanding *applies* knowledge, puts it in context, and makes it relevant.

The three-step progression of knowledge, understanding, and wisdom corresponds approximately with the three phases of the Trivium (grammar, logic, and rhetoric), which is the cornerstone of the classical model of education, the ancient system that gave rise to a remarkable renaissance of art, music, literature, science, and culture. The classical model is rooted in the desire for wisdom and understanding, not just the amassing of knowledge. It is a philosophy focused on putting rote knowledge (which is learned during the grammar stage) into the necessary framework of logic and rhetoric (the ability to reason and to articulate one's thoughts in rational and eloquent ways).[16]

Wisdom results when knowledge is matched with understanding—but this process is easier said than done. In Proverbs, the biblical book of wisdom, Solomon says that true wisdom is a gift from God: "The Lord grants wisdom! From his mouth come knowledge and understanding."[17] Only by turning to the Lord—that is, by embracing the absolutes—will we gain the wisdom needed to preserve and enhance our country's greatness.

Wisdom is what allows knowledge and understanding to go to work in the world. It takes knowledge out of the ivory tower and puts it to work. Solomon goes on to say, "Getting wisdom is the most important thing you can do!"[18] If we are to reclaim our culture from the relativist worldview that often seems to control the majority, we need to be willing to ask for and apply God-given wisdom to the issues, questions, and dilemmas that face us. Wisdom will unleash understanding upon a world rife with conflicting facts, contradictory evidence, and contrary notions. It will provide clarity to a worldview muddied by relativism.

Martin Luther said, "The strength and glory of a land does not depend upon its wealth, its defenses, its great houses, its powerful armaments; but on the number of its gracious, serious, kind, and wise citizens." Instead of striving for personal peace and prosperity, as so many do, we should pursue wisdom and let the wisdom of the absolutes shape our national discourse and priorities. Only then will our country attain and be able to maintain its true strength and greatness.

5

CHAPTER FIVE

Truth: that long, clean, clear, simple, undeniable, unchallengeable, straight, and shining line, on one side of which is black and on the other of which is white.
WILLIAM FAULKNER (1897–1962)

A man who knows that the earth is round but lives among men who believe it to be flat ought to hammer in his doctrine of the earth's roundness up to the point of arrest, imprisonment, or even death. Reality will confirm him, and he performs that greatest of all services in a free society: debate.   **HILAIRE BELLOC (1871–1953)**

The surest signs of a healthy society are open and free debates. We must be able to agree to disagree. In a democracy protecting the rights of our adversaries is as important as protecting the rights of our advocates.
THOMAS JEFFERSON (1743–1826)

5

Truth Withstands Debate

*We can agree to disagree, but we must reaffirm
our commitment to freedom of speech.
Only then will truth be given a voice and the
opportunity to transform society.*

When Alexis de Tocqueville, the French statesman and author, came to the United States early in the nineteenth century, he was struck by the open vibrancy of American cultural, political, and religious debate. Everywhere he traveled—in cities, towns, and villages, among the social elite and the common folk, in churches and state capitols—he witnessed the same phenomenon: citizens who happily and congenially agreed to disagree. From his cosmopolitan European perspective, this was one of the more outstanding features of the sprawling young republic. Not only had the American people found peaceful and legal ways to disagree, they had made freedom of speech part of the Constitution and part of life. Ordinary citizens seemed to relish their verbal tussles as a vital aspect of their private liberty. Indeed, America's freedom seemed to express itself best in continuous debate. Unaccustomed to such freedom of protest and diversity, Tocqueville wondered if such an innovation could possibly endure.

After Tocqueville returned to France, he published his observations in a massive two-volume work titled *The Republic of the United States of America*, later renamed *Democracy in America*. In it he wrote:

> I confess that in America, I saw more than America; I sought there the image of democracy itself, with its inclinations, its character, its prejudices, and its passions, in order to learn what we have to fear or to hope from its progress.[1]

In our nation's ability to tolerate dissent, withstand criticism, and endure disagreement—even to the point of embracing, supporting, and encouraging it—Tocqueville caught a glimpse of liberty's great power, promise, and purpose.

The First Amendment and Freedom of Speech

What Tocqueville observed was a reflection of one of the absolute principles on which our nation was founded: the right to freedom of expression. In fact, freedom of religion and freedom of speech were the first rights and liberties amended to the Constitution:

> Congress shall make no law respecting an establishment of religion, or prohibiting the free exercise thereof; or abridging the freedom of speech, or of the press; or the right of the people peaceably to assemble, and to petition the government for a redress of grievances.[2]

Notice that the First Amendment does not constrain the free exercise of religion, freedom of speech, freedom of the press, freedom of assembly, or freedom of protest. On the contrary, it specifically prohibits *the federal government* from interfering with or restricting such liberties. In fact, the founders were specifically aiming to protect the right of the people to hold and express opinions that opposed the government. They knew all too well the injustice of being refused the right to speak freely and worship freely, because the restriction of free speech—even free thought—was a matter of tradition throughout the history of the British monarchy. To criticize the king, to call him a fool or a tyrant, or even to wish him physical harm was considered an act of treason punishable by jail time, confiscation of property, life imprisonment, or death.[3]

The founders' first word on liberty was this: Give ordinary citizens from every walk of life the freedom to disagree. Let every voice be heard. Permit no argument to be silenced. Let no debate be censored. Ensure everyone the right to be heard—and the right to be wrong. In our ongoing pursuit of liberty and justice for all, we must reaffirm our commitment to the core American principle of freedom of speech. There must be a place at the discussion table for everyone, including the many well-reasoned, articulate people who hold to the absolutes. Unless we uphold the right of every viewpoint to be represented, our society will suffer irreparable harm.

Many of us in the United States may take the privilege of free speech for granted, but we have only to watch the evening news to be reminded of what life would be like without it. We've seen how the Taliban in Afghanistan outlawed music, television, and even the simple acts of clapping and cheering, and how the Chinese have imprisoned many who have expressed dissenting views. We've seen how citizens of other closed nations have suffered and how they long for the right to speak out.

Are We Still Free to Disagree?

The postmodern mind-set, with its emphasis on political correctness, has strayed from the founders' original vision.
Although the First Amendment still limits the power of the federal government, it seems that the media have in effect taken on
the role of "abridging the freedom of speech" by limiting the
scope of their coverage to "sound bite journalism" that selec-
tively presents news and information. People are still free to
speak, of course, but given the way that access to mainstream
media is governed by certain gatekeepers, can they get a hearing
in the public forum? And if they do speak up, can they avoid
being labeled according to the latest standards of political
correctness?

The popular slant in today's marketplace of ideas is to
smear opposing opinions, tagging them as narrow-minded and
unacceptable. Organizations that disagree with the majority are
labeled as "hate" groups. This marginalization of alternative   71
viewpoints is contrary to the founders' intentions and the
American tradition of political discourse.

Commentator Cal Thomas hit the nail on the head in a col-
umn he wrote following actress Rosie O'Donnell's appearance
on ABC's *PrimeTime Thursday* in March 2002 to discuss gay
adoptions:

> Journalism used to see its role as fairly and accurately
> presenting both sides of a story and letting the public
> decide which one makes sense. Now, too much journalism
> presents us with a conclusion and demands that we
> accept it or be called names like "homophobic" or
> "Neanderthal bigot."
>
> Would the mainstream media consider doing a story
> on women who regret having had abortions and think the

law is too lax? Would the media reveal that abortion clinics seldom tell women the truth and turn the sonogram machine away so they can't see the image of their unborn child? Would the media ever do a one-sided story on the benefits of lower taxes and less regulation on business? . . . Not likely.[4]

The issue is not so much whether the media bring a liberal bias or a conservative one, but that they would deny being biased at all, and that they would—without apology—present a carefully crafted version of the truth under the guise of objectivity. Let's be honest: We all have our personal perspectives, prejudices, and presuppositions that prevent us from achieving true objectivity, but certainly we can acknowledge our particular points of view while seeking to present a balanced story. It seems to me that a reporter who is genuinely in search of the truth would do everything possible to present a subject fairly and completely. Attempts to suppress or "manage" the truth ought to trigger a big red flag, alerting us that there's more to the story that should be told. But that's not always how it works, which is a tragic state of affairs in a country that prides itself on freedom of expression. When reporters suppress the truth or are afraid to uncover and report the truth because it might undermine a position that they themselves hold dear, the results are not much different than if the government was suppressing the truth—which of course the media would not tolerate.

The Media As Interpreters Instead of Reporters
Isn't it amazing how free the media are to *interpret* everything they see, rather than simply report the facts? They have even managed to interject themselves into the political process, training our legislators to speak in sound bites and slogans. And

rather than giving voice to dissenting views, the news outlets often silence or distort them.

Too many times someone in the media has interviewed me at length, but when the story is published or presented, my comments have been reduced to an innocuous statement that doesn't speak to the real issues, even though I covered those issues quite thoroughly during the interview. From my perspective, these reporters are trying to create an illusion of balance in their articles by dropping in a quote or two from a "conservative voice," regardless of whether or not the selected quotes are substantial or relevant.

The failure of the media to fairly and accurately present all sides of an issue is one of the greatest hindrances to open and honest debate in our society. Perhaps they fear that a good dose of the truth would change public opinion or even national policy.

A good example of how the media will bury an effective and persuasive presentation of the truth can be seen in the DeMoss Foundation's experience in trying to air a series of public service announcements promoting the right to life. Although the series included some of the most heart-touching, thought-provoking spots depicting the beauty of a child and innocent life, many major stations and networks refused to run them. Why? They were too effective in combating the mind-set that refuses to acknowledge the importance of protecting the innocent and unborn.

What would happen if we made a place at the table for every voice to be heard? What if instead of protecting partisan positions, we made the pursuit of truth our number one objective in public discourse? What if we refused to let counterarguments be silenced or whittled down to innocuous and ineffective sound bites? What if instead of censoring debate through selective

73

reporting, we encouraged the expression of dissenting viewpoints? I think we would discover that truth is like a lion: If you turn it loose, it will defend itself. Why would someone not want to pursue the truth? One possible reason was summed up quite forcefully by Jack Nicholson's character in the movie *A Few Good Men*: "You can't handle the truth!"

Jesus said that we would know the truth and the truth would set us free—but that works only if we want to be set free. There is no greater bondage than refusing to acknowledge the truth. Over the past several decades, our society's aversion to truth has become quite clear. It reflects the mind-set of a culture that runs counter to the absolutes.

Disingenuous Debate

It used to be that we appreciated eloquence and persuasiveness in public discourse. We respected the right of people to express themselves freely, even if we disagreed with or were offended by what they said. That isn't to say that all speech is equal or that public discourse has never been inflammatory. Certainly there is such a thing as dangerous speech or hate speech. Some people really are intolerant. But in America we have always allowed plenty of leeway for contrary views to be expressed. We have trusted the open forum of freely expressed ideas to expose error, foolishness, heresy, and hatred for what they really are: chaff in the wind.

In recent years, however, it seems the focus has shifted from evaluating the merits of a person's argument to labeling people in an effort to discredit what they say. Just watch what happens, for example, when someone makes the observation that homosexuality is unnatural (which should be obvious to anyone who has studied physiology). It won't take long before someone else will label that person a gay basher, homophobic, or intolerant.

Someone who criticizes the current welfare system or the administration of affirmative action is likely to be labeled a racist or a bigot. A person who speaks out against abortion will be derided as a hater of women, chauvinistic, or insensitive. But just because some people have strong moral views does not mean they want the government to police bedrooms, or that they want legislators to impose a rigid set of behavioral rules and regulations, or that they desire to have the church run the state. We must vigorously resist the trend in our society toward labeling and name-calling.

Another disturbing characteristic of our public discourse is the tendency of many to protect their partisan positions at the expense of the truth. It doesn't upset me when a member of Congress, for example, stands up and challenges the opposing party's positions. What troubles me is that too many of our leaders are more concerned with defending their spheres of influence than they are with focusing on solving problems and trying to find common ground to promote the common good. Sadly, this tendency is also prevalent among religious leaders. Instead of being "iron [that] sharpens iron," we have lost our cutting edge by our failure to focus on the common good during times of disagreement.[5] Only through the proper recognition and application of the truth can these disagreements be resolved. Unfortunately, our culture seems to have little concern for finding the truth.

Discovering Truth

The Founding Fathers believed that unhampered and unfettered truth was the only suitable ground upon which openness, honesty, and freedom could be established—whether in families and communities, or among societies and nations.

The truth is not merely a moral concept; it is a reflection of the way things actually are. It is the very fabric of reality. To veer

75

away from the truth is to swerve into the realm of fantasy. To deliberately and perpetually reject the truth is nothing short of insanity.[6] In a world where the forces of evil are continually pitted against the goodness of love, truth is an essential weapon in the arsenal of righteousness. Apart from truth, a civil society cannot long survive.

Unfortunately, we are not naturally inclined to affirm the truth even when we are perfectly well aware of it. In the book of Romans, Paul says that people deliberately choose to believe lies instead of believing what they know to be true. In fact, our first impulse is generally to pull away from the truth. The Bible says that wicked people "push the truth away from themselves."[7]

The problem with truth is that it is often uncomfortable. It calls us to account for our words, thoughts, attitudes, and actions. It compels us to look at ourselves honestly, and we don't always like what we see. When the truth hits too close to home, our first impulse is to recoil from it. We try to avoid it or ignore it, if not outright deny it. We might admire truth as a principle, but do we really want to hear it?

Truth confronts our preferences and prejudices. It tells us the way things have always been, the way they are now, and how they ought to be in days to come. Sometimes the truth really hurts; in fact, it can be downright offensive. Truth is often most offensive when it clashes with tradition. Just ask Jesus or any other courageous soul who has ventured to point out that someone's traditions are contrary to the truth.

None of us likes to hear that we are wrong, that we should adjust our way of thinking, or that we ought to make changes in the way we live. We are slow to confess that we are in need of repentance, forgiveness, or forbearance. And we are prone to persist in our pride even when we know the truth.

Friedrich Nietzsche, the famous existential philosopher,

once confessed, "We all fear truth."[8] Why would he say that? Because, in the words of writer Lionel Ceveada, "Truth may be stretched but it cannot be broken, and always gets above falsehood, as oil does above water."[9]

The battle for truth has been fought through the ages. As such, we need not manufacture new strategies for defending the truth. To be effective, truth simply needs to be presented faithfully and proclaimed fearlessly. As Thomas Paine said, "Such is the irresistible nature of truth that all it wishes, and all it needs, is the liberty of appearing." When applied to life, the truth proves to be powerfully liberating.

Throwing Down the Gauntlet

It is with the deepest possible conviction that I invite you to grapple with the truth of the absolutes. However, by boldly stating that our freedom depends on certain absolute principles, I do not mean to imply that there is no room for discussion or disagreement. In fact, I invite you to challenge these time-tested principles, because I am confident you will discover that truth can stand the debate test. Poke it. Probe it. Explore it. Turn it inside out. Put it under the microscope. Expose it to the harshest conditions. Truth will endure.

We never have to apologize for the truth. It is able to withstand every charge. It is able to bear up under every challenge. It is sufficient unto itself. In due course, it will prove its own value and veracity.

My staff and my family know that I desire to speak the truth at all times, but occasionally they will respond to one of my comments by saying, "That's just James." In other words, there are times when I'm just venting my opinion. I'm glad they know the difference, and I appreciate that they allow me to be myself even when I'm wrong.

The Bible tells us that we must be discerning when it comes to truth. Not everything we hear—or say—is going to be true. Still, the truth has an undeniable radiance and resonance. It stands up and it stands out.

Bill O'Reilly, the outspoken commentator on Fox News, is a great example of how truth and opinion can be interspersed. O'Reilly is undeniably a gifted communicator. He speaks such clear and piercing truth so often that he is having a positive effect on American thought. It is equally clear, however, that there are times when it's "just Bill on a roll" and his message is tainted with personal feelings (which everyone is entitled to, by the way). His willingness to speak out contributes to his audience appeal and works well in the context of his program, but as with anyone, we need to keep in mind that the views expressed may be opinion and not truth. For example, he could be better informed concerning positive progress in Africa, and he should be careful not to make light of efforts being made on this important continent.

For my part, I am ready to publicly declare and defend what I believe, and if I have missed the mark or fallen short in my own understanding, I'm prepared to be corrected. My views are considered by many to be conservative, but I have no problem engaging with other viewpoints or discussing the issues with someone whose views are more liberal than mine. I read all the editorials in the newspaper, regardless of the writer's ideology. I *want* to know what others think, and I want to find ways that we can agree about how to get things done. I'm tired of all the division in our country. I'm tired of people who are more interested in defending their own positions than in seeking the truth. This happens on all sides. Some people are so busy stating their own views that they don't have time to listen to anything else. That has to stop. We need to come to the table and find common ground—and not just *talk* about common ground.

I believe in the direct approach. When two people have a disagreement, they ought to get together face-to-face and work it out. Whenever I hear the Senate Majority Leader use the media to air his differences with the Bush Administration, I want to suggest to the president that he hop in a limo and go to Capitol Hill, walk up to Mr. Daschle's office, sit down with him and say, "Tom, I want to hear what you have to say. We have a meeting at the White House every week, but it doesn't seem to be sufficient. What is it you're trying to tell me that you don't think I'm hearing?" Do you see how quickly that would diffuse any dissension? I guarantee the general public will rally behind leaders who confront issues openly and listen intently because they want the truth and what's best for people.

It is my prayer that this book will help make a place at the discussion table for those who are willing to make a stand for the absolutes. Together may we practice the biblical command to reason together, to seek wise counsel, and to be ready to make full proof of our beliefs.[10] Our nation's hope for future freedom and greatness depends on an open and honest dialogue.

HOW THE ABSOLUTES WORK IN SOCIETY

PART TWO

6

CHAPTER SIX

Never will I sit motionless while directly or indirectly apology is made for the murder of the helpless. In securing any kind of peace, the first essential is to guarantee to every man the most elementary of rights: the right to his own life. Murder is not debatable. **THEODORE ROOSEVELT (1858–1919)**

Do unto others as if you were the others.
LEONARDO DA VINCI (1452–1519)

All the starry hosts of heaven and of earth declare with one voice the glory bestowed on these sublime creatures of the Living God, these creatures made just a little lower than Himself. We can do no better than to acknowledge our acceptance of Him by our acceptance of them.
DYMPNA OF GHEEL (c. 770–795)

People
Matter Most

Every life is worth affirming,
enabling, and protecting.

At 2:15 A.M. on March 18, 2002, a fire gutted the sanctuary of St. Michael Catholic Church in Wheaton, Illinois. Firefighters were able to keep the flames from spreading to other parts of the building, but the sanctuary was a total loss. Later that morning, when the parish priest was interviewed by a newspaper reporter, he said, "It was unbelievable, but we cry not for buildings. Thank God no one was injured."[1]

Whenever a crisis occurs, our first concern is for the people involved: Was anyone hurt? Is everyone all right? If a fire ravages an apartment complex but everyone gets out safely, we invariably breathe a sigh of relief. Even if the tenants have lost everything they own, we will say, "At least no one was killed. That is the most important thing." Indeed, it is the most important thing because people matter. I dare say that if no one had died in the attacks on the World Trade Center and the Pentagon—and if everyone had walked away from the crash of Flight 93—the prevailing response would have been, "At least no one was killed." We can rebuild buildings and replace airplanes, but we simply cannot replace people—and people matter most.

In the same news article about the church fire, a parishioner of St. Michael was quoted as saying, "My heart hurts. . . . I've been crying all morning,"[2] which prompts us to ask, Do we "cry for buildings" or don't we? The article went on to explain that the woman had been married in the church and had attended for twenty-five years. Her tears were not so much for the building as for the memories the building held—the essential human connections that make us unique, reflect our spiritual nature, and underscore our fundamental importance as people.

When disaster strikes, it's amazing how quickly the things we thought were important become relatively unimportant. Our latest work project, our favorite team's win-loss record, the status of our diet and exercise program, the current value of our stock portfolio, or how we look in the new outfit we're planning to wear this weekend all cease to matter very much to us. We often can't find time for the things we *say* are important, but when confronted with a family illness, a child's injury, or a neighbor's house fire, we will drop everything without a moment's hesitation to focus on what is really important. That's because we know that people matter.

Civil societies recognize the vital principle that people are precious, and those societies build their cultural institutions around that truth. When we understand that people are what matter most, we will do anything and everything to safeguard the dignity, integrity, and sanctity of life. We will affirm that every life is worth honoring, protecting, and saving. There are no expendable or disposable people. When a culture does not value human life, atrocities are inevitable. A few examples from the twentieth century alone are enough to prove the point: Nazi

Germany, Stalinist Russia, Cambodia under the Khmer Rouge, Uganda under Idi Amin. In any society, the rule of law ultimately depends on respect for the value of people.

Even in the Middle East, with the ongoing Israeli-Palestinian conflict, we must put into practice the absolute principle that people matter most. People are more important than places or property. I understand the importance of ownership, property rights, land and covenant promises, but I also understand that peace can't be bought with land. It will ultimately be secured by love for people—because people matter most.

In the wake of yet another suicide attack against Israel, someone asked, "When will it stop?" Years ago, a well-known Middle East leader, responded to a similar question by saying, "When they love their children more than they hate us."[3] I believe this was a wise and thoughtful assessment of the situation.

Wouldn't it be miraculous if the power of love would move the Israelis to say from their hearts to the Palestinians, "We want you to have land because of love, because we care for you and your well-being, and because we care for all families"? What if the leaders of other Arab countries, who openly express their concern over the plight of the Palestinians, said to Yasser Arafat, "Brother, we love you so much that we want to offer you some of our land"? Love does affect the peace process as much as the war against evil and terror. Ultimately, love must be the greatest part of the equation. It will also be love that demands secure borders and assures undying protection for the Israelis and their families. The Arab world must acknowledge Israel's right to exist—because people matter.

A Clash of Values

Throughout the history of our nation we have taken courageous action to protect human life when it has been threatened. We have supplied humanitarian aid to countries whose people were suffering. We have intervened in armed conflicts and helped to win two world wars to protect the cause of freedom and save lives. We have interceded diplomatically to oppose tyranny and contain violence across the globe. Tragically, our legacy of staunchly defending life and liberty around the world, as good and commendable as it has been, stands in stark contrast to the carnage we have allowed within our own borders.

In recent years, we've seen an alarming increase in the number of mothers who have killed their children. Susan Smith and Andrea Yates are two notorious examples. Across the nation, people said, "Oh, how appalling that they would kill those innocent children"—and they're right: It *is* appalling, and we should be shocked—yet we should also be appalled that every year in the United States more than one million of the most innocent and helpless lives in the world are terminated by abortion. In those cases, however, many respond, "It's a woman's choice! It's her body! Don't tell a woman what she can or can't do with her own body!" Well, I'm not saying a woman doesn't have a right to control her own body, but it is not only *her* body we're talking about here. Any pregnancy involves two precious and valuable lives, and we must consider both of them.

87

Every Life Is Precious

My heart goes out to every woman who has found herself pregnant without planning to be. And I want to say with the utmost compassion that there are better options for you and your baby than abortion. I thank God that my son's birth mother chose to place him for adoption when she was unable to keep him herself. Our lives wouldn't be the same without Randy and the four wonderful grandchildren he and his wife have brought into our family.

Recently, we interviewed a guest on *Life Today* who had become pregnant as the result of rape. At first, she was so horrified by what had happened to her that abortion seemed her only option. She felt as if having the baby would be an ongoing reminder of her horrific experience. Later, when she heard a song titled "A Baby's Prayer" by Kathy Troccoli, she felt the need to pray. And as she prayed, she realized that the "little mass of tissue" in her womb was really a person with purpose and potential. She decided to keep the baby and named her Alexis Kathleen in honor of Kathy Troccoli, whose song had touched her heart and caused her to reconsider her options.

As this young woman told her story on our show, I began to weep because I also am the product of rape. My mother was an unmarried, forty-year-old practical nurse who was assaulted by the alcoholic son of the man for whom she was caring. When she went to the doctor to have me aborted—because she had no husband, an inadequate income for caring for a child, and she had been raped—the doctor said, "Ma'am, I simply do not believe this is best." My mother later told me she went home, sat down on the screen porch and prayed. And God said, "Have this little baby, and it will bring joy to the world."

My mother chose to carry me to term, and I was born in the charity ward of the local hospital. Two weeks later, through an ad in the newspaper, my mother released me to a foster family, who raised me for the first five years of my life. My conception was the result of a crime, and my childhood and adolescence weren't easy, but God had a plan for this unexpected child born in difficult circumstances.

In standing against abortion, I am not in any way minimizing the trauma that accompanies an unexpected pregnancy—especially by rape or incest—nor am I in any way suggesting that a pregnancy under those circumstances would be easy. It would not. But I am saying, unequivocally, that every life is precious and there are better options than abortion for every case where a birth mother is unable to keep her baby. If, as a matter of principle, we affirm the value of every life, God will honor the intent of our hearts. If we will lovingly respond to the women involved in crisis pregnancies, we will find ways to alleviate their suffering and help them make the best of a difficult and painful situation. And through our actions we will affirm the absolute truth that people matter.

Anyone who insists "it's just a fetus" should have been at the funeral of our second grandchild, a little boy who was stillborn. The doctors did everything they could to save the little guy's life, but it was not to be. We watched as our daughter held his little body. He fit in her hand. His eyes were closed; his little fists were folded. We heard her say as she placed him back in the basket, "I didn't know you very long, but I loved you." Don't tell me it's just a fetus.

What can we do to change the status of innocent preborn children who have no voice of their own? The truth is, the only thing that will turn our nation away from the holocaust of abortion is a complete change of heart. Although poorly written laws and tragic court decisions need to be changed, we're not going to stop abortion by simply focusing all our attention on reversing *Roe v. Wade*. That would likely serve only to mobilize the proabortion forces to even greater militancy. Unless a woman has a fundamental change of heart, she'll find a way to terminate her pregnancy anyway. In addition to encouraging legislative action, we must take every opportunity to affirm the value of life. We must demonstrate love and compassion—not just emotionally but practically—to every woman who is pregnant, regardless of the circumstances, and we must provide alternatives to abortion so that every woman in need will know that she has other options for her unborn child. Many of these alternatives are already available, but as a nation we must choose them. Individuals must be inspired to make the best choices. It is critically important that we become as zealous in our desire and efforts to help children born into extremely difficult circumstances as we have been in our efforts to oppose abortion. While we boldly proclaim the right to life, we must also help provide hope in life.

If you have aborted a baby—whether you are the mother or the father—you need to know that there is a source of healing for the pain in your heart. That healing balm is the love of Jesus Christ, who died to set you free from sin and shame. He grieves with you over the loss of innocent life, and He can heal your broken heart.

Some of the most dynamic Christian women I know made the tragic mistake of aborting a baby, yet they will tell you firsthand that in spite of their decision, God's grace covered their sin and removed their shame "as far as the east is from the west."[4] Denial only compounds the pain. But you can choose to experience God's forgiveness and find healing and redemption from the mistakes you have made in the past. If, on the other hand, you are struggling with the pain of an unplanned pregnancy right now, I encourage you to choose life for your baby.

Guarding Life and Liberty

The great liberties we have enjoyed in America for more than two hundred years were secured against the arbitrary whims of men and movements by the rule of law. As Thomas Paine writes in *Common Sense,* the powerful pamphlet that helped to spark the Revolutionary War, "In America, the law is king."[5] Our system of government has never depended on the benevolence of judges, the altruism of the wealthy, or the goodwill of the powerful. Instead, every citizen, rich or poor, man or woman, native-born or immigrant, healthy or disabled, young or old, has been declared equal under the law. This is true, I believe, because the founders of our nation adhered to the absolute principle that people matter.

The opening refrain of the Declaration of Independence affirms the necessity of an absolute standard upon which the rule of law must be based:

> We hold these truths to be self-evident, that all men are created equal; that they are endowed by their Creator with certain unalienable rights; that among these are life, liberty, and the pursuit of happiness. That, to secure these rights, governments are instituted among men, deriving their just powers from the consent of the governed.

As we will discuss in a later chapter, this does not mean that everyone is equal in every respect—in ability, interest, or opportunity. But it does mean that we are committed as a nation to the equal value of every life, every citizen, every person. Whenever the principle of the dignity and sanctity of life is called into question, the rule of law is thrown into very real jeopardy. When the principle of absolute truth is removed from the constitutional vocabulary, our freedom is no longer absolutely secure. As Thomas Jefferson said, "The chief purpose of government is to protect life. Abandon that and you have abandoned all."[6]

Abraham Lincoln later pressed the same issue when he questioned the institution of slavery on the basis of the sanctity of all human life and the rule of law:

> I should like to know if taking this old Declaration of Independence, which declares that all men are equal upon

91

principle, and making exceptions to it, where it will stop? If one man says it does not mean a Negro, why not another say it does not mean some other man?[7]

Nullifying the right to life and liberty for some citizens jeopardizes the rights of every citizen. That is why the struggle to abolish the slave trade, to emancipate the slaves, and to guarantee their civil rights afterward was such a test of the American system. Not only were the dignity, integrity, sanctity, and rights of African-American lives threatened—at stake was the entire American constitutional vision, which was built on the foundation stone that all people matter.

Depersonalization

Over the course of the past several decades we have seen the American commitment to life and liberty come under assault by a host of depersonalizing trends. As the pace of life has continued to accelerate, we have less time to spend in meaningful interaction with other people. Perhaps the most insidious of these trends is the way in which our advances in technology have led to a splintering of society. Today, we rarely, if ever, meet at the general store, the water cooler, or the back fence to discuss our common interests. Instead, we hammer out e-mail messages, sound off on talk radio, and "meet" in Internet chat rooms, often anonymously, to express our views.

As more and more resources have been placed at our fingertips, we have steadily and inevitably become more and more wrapped up in ourselves. What do *I* want? How do *I* want it? What can *I* do to further my own self-interests? As our self-absorption has taken root, disrespect has become rampant; incivility is more and more common. Far too often we are rude and crude to one another, mocking and disrespectful of authority, and irreverent and contemptuous of time-honored conventions. Listening to five minutes of Howard Stern's radio program is enough to prove the point. Giving in to the error of humanism—the idea that humanity is the center of all existence—causes us not to care about other people except insofar as they entertain us or help us advance our "enlightened self-interest."

Other disturbing trends in our society are the proliferation of pornography, which exploits and degrades women and children, and the explosion of violence and revenge portrayed in movies and video games—two popular media that are absorbed by a disproportionate number of young males. According to many criminal investigators, the first and most important factor in stripping away a person's inhibitions against committing a crime—including rape and murder—is the ability to depersonalize the victim. In order to commit violence, a criminal predator needs to distance himself psychologically from his victim's humanity. His disrespect for the possessions or the life of his target depends on his ability to ignore or deny another person's integrity or sanctity. He justifies his actions by redefining his victim as a mere "thing." There's no question that violent movies and video games open the door to this dangerous type of thinking by gradually neutralizing our inherent shock over violence and bloodshed.

Killers are made, not born. In his frighteningly insightful work *On Killing: The Psychological Cost of Learning to Kill in War and Society,* Lt. Col. Dave Grossman writes, "In World War II, only 15–20 percent of combat infantry were willing to fire their rifles; in Korea, about 50 percent were; in Vietnam, the figure rose to over 90 percent." What made the difference? Training. Military strategists began to discover ways to condition soldiers to overcome their "powerful, innate human resistance" to killing. They began to put in place certain mechanisms that would enable soldiers to psychologically depersonalize the enemy.[8]

93

According to Grossman, the same dynamic is at work in society at large. Our natural inhibitions against criminal assault are strong. Without careful conditioning, most people are simply incapable of hurting, much less killing, another human being. Except in cases of extreme emotional trauma, we have a natural psychological resistance to murder. In order to pull the trigger, lunge with the knife, or swing the bludgeon, we must first systematically desensitize our innate sense of the sanctity of life or be convinced that our own life or the lives of our loved ones are in serious jeopardy.

Slavery became possible only when people were conditioned to believe that an entire race was somehow subhuman. The Nazis were able to commit the horrors of the Holocaust only after they conditioned the German people to see entire ethnic communities as somehow subhuman. Similarly, the great genocidal slaughters committed in Russia, China, Cambodia, Uganda, and Serbia were possible because partisans were conditioned to see an entire class of people as somehow subhuman.

Perhaps the most instructive episode of the growing desensitization of our culture was the recent political and media firestorm over partial-birth abortion. According to Robert Bork, senior fellow of the American Enterprise Institute and author of *Slouching Towards Gomorrah:*

> When it was proposed to outlaw this hideous procedure, which obviously causes extreme pain to the baby, the pro-abortion forces in Congress and elsewhere made false statements to fend off the legislation or to justify an anticipated presidential veto. Planned Parenthood stated that the general anesthesia given to the mother killed the fetus so that there was no such thing as a partial birth abortion. Physicians promptly rebutted the claim. . . . Two doctors

who perform partial birth abortions admitted that the majority of fetuses aborted in this fashion are alive until the end of the procedure.[9]

It is difficult for me to understand how anyone can fail to see that our culture is in serious danger of stripping away our natural inhibitions against killing in other arenas and spheres. Already, legal precedents for abortion have been recycled for the causes of euthanasia, assisted suicide, and mercy killing.[10]

The gruesome testimony of history is precisely why our societal trend toward depersonalization is so frightening. It is why our liberty suffers every time we indulge in dehumanizing rhetoric or behavior. Our legal and institutional drift toward death through abortion, infanticide, and euthanasia has further eroded our sensitivity to the value of life, already numbed by our exposure to violence in the media. We have begun the process of redefining whole categories of people as "things." In the media, in sex-education literature, in political discourse, and in the arrangements of daily life, we have begun to diminish the personhood of everyone by diminishing the personhood of a few.

Turning the Tide

Although "we hold these truths to be self-evident," we have not always practiced what we preach. Throughout our history, too many Americans have attempted to suppress the truth of equality and human worth in one way or another, which is why we still have inequalities of justice, opportunity, and protection. And that is why the struggle to maintain the dignity and sanctity of life has always been an uphill battle.

How do we stem the tide of depersonalization and once again actively promote and protect the sanctity and dignity of every human life? It won't be through legislation; it will only be through love. If we think we're going to stop abortion, pornography, and violence by winning at the polls or passing more laws, we're wrong. If we think we can legislate equality and "create a level playing field," we're misguided and mistaken. We may have abolished the practice of slavery by force of law, but we cannot force people to love one another and treat others with respect. What we need is a fundamental change of heart.

I once heard a black leader, who was speaking to a prominent U.S. senator, put it about as well as anyone could express it: "Senator," he said, "until we in the African-American community believe that you Republicans and all politicians love *our* children as much as you love *your* children and that you want for *our* children what you want for *your* children, neither you nor any other leader will receive the hearing and support you desire. We have to believe you really care."

We all need to hear this message. It doesn't matter whether we are Republican or Democrat, black or white, rich or poor— we need to remove these discussions from the realm of politics, class, and race and bring them to the realm of *people.* Forget political expedience. We need to stop appeasing the minority communities and start loving them. Only when others *know* that we genuinely care for them—not just for what we can get from them or for the political advantage we might gain by reaching out to them, but genuinely care enough to become personally involved with them—will we break down the walls of mistrust and resistance and truly be able to help. Genuine love dissolves differences.

As Alan Keyes so eloquently said:

America has once again arrived at a momentous crossroads. We are going to have to decide—as we have had to decide so many times in the past—whether we shall only *speak* of justice and *speak* of principle, or whether we shall *stand* and *fight* for them. We are going to have to decide whether we shall quote the words of the Declaration of Independence with real conviction, or whether we shall take that document and throw it on the ash heap of history as we adopt the message of those who insist that we stand silent in the face of injustice. When it comes to deciding whether we shall stand by the great principle that declares that all human beings are "created equal" and "endowed by their Creator" with the "right to life," it seems to me, there is no choice for silence.[11]

It's time to stop merely talking—trying to appear as if we care about other people—and begin involving ourselves in their lives. Like the good neighbor in the story Jesus told about the traveler who was attacked by robbers, it was the one who got involved at his own personal risk and expense who was worthy of commendation.[12]

As individuals, we cannot solve all of our community's problems, but we can solve some of them. We can touch one or two people in our sphere of influence and make a real difference. And although we cannot care directly for every person, we *can* care *about* them and support the efforts of others who can reach them directly. All I'm asking is that all of us do our part.

Reaching Out with Hands of Hope

I have spent many years trying to focus the attention of industrialized nations, especially the United States, on the people of Africa. They are Africa's most precious resource and are a tremendous asset to the world community. Africa is rich in natural resources, but its people have been plundered and ravaged from within and without. They need our love and our care. If we will reach out to them, as Americans and as Christians, we will have a profoundly positive effect on the African people—and they will respond.

Closer to home, when we consider the situation with our neighbors to the south, we must realize that the Mexican people who live in the United States truly love their families in Mexico. They work hard to help provide for them. Although we must safeguard our borders and bring illegal immigration under control, we must also look for ways to use our immigration laws to encourage the opportunity for labor and give our neighbors hope. It's not hard to understand their deep desire for a better way of life.

Because God filled my heart with love and I am the direct beneficiary of my mother's "sanctity of life" decision, I have made a personal commitment to meet the needs of starving, sick, and suffering children around the world. Over the years, God has graciously multiplied the efforts of Life Outreach International to feed and care for millions of children, and I've had the privilege of holding many of these children in my arms. Because my mother and her doctor agreed that "this child matters," my life was spared, and God has used me to touch the lives of others.

That's just one life. Imagine what could happen if you and everyone you know took up the cause of meeting the needs of suffering and underprivileged people at home and abroad. Imagine what could happen if we experienced a change in our hearts and minds about the daily sacrifice of countless lives at the hands of abortionists.

Life is precious, and we must do all we can to protect and enhance it. We will never accomplish anything through public debate and political discussion if we neglect taking positive action. Instead, minds must change concerning the value of all human life, and then we must put sound principles about our values into practice. When we willingly sacrifice our own rights and privileges for the good of other people, we will discover the true meaning of abundant life.

The apostle Paul, who wrote much of the New Testament, reemphasized the central principle of Jesus' teaching when he wrote, "For the whole law can be summed up in this one command: 'Love your neighbor as yourself.' "[13] He might well have added: "because people matter."

7

CHAPTER SEVEN

Greed is a malicious despoiler which ruins even the booty it
madly accumulates. **THOMAS CHALMERS (1780–1847)**

Those that much covet are with gain so fond,
That what they have not, that which they possess,
They scatter and unloose it from their bond,
And so, by hoping more, they have but less;
Or, gaining more, the profit of excess
Is but to surfeit, and such griefs sustain,
That they prove bankrupt in this poor-rich gain.
WILLIAM SHAKESPEARE (1564–1616)

The rich become useless, as they are oft grasping for more;
the poor become dangerous, as they are oft envying for more.
Greed does its best to do its worst on both ends of society's
spectrum. **EURIPIDES (c. 484–406 B.C.)**

Greed
Destroys

Self-serving greed is the animating power behind pride,
vengeance, and prejudice. Unchecked,
it wreaks havoc in the world.

A close friend of mine, an office furniture dealer, told me about a time when he visited Enron to consult with one of their executives about some furnishings. The executive showed him into a large, high-level boardroom in the Enron tower and said, "In this room are the controls for the axis on which the world turns." My friend remembers thinking, *Wow, what arrogance!*

The Bible says, "Pride goes before destruction, and a haughty spirit before a fall."[1] Within the tangle of the Enron debacle, there was certainly an element of pride and greed. And look at what that greed did to those it controlled and the innocent lives caught up in its deadly snare.

I once met with a highly successful entrepreneur who had built a sizable business from the ground up. When I commented on how much opportunity we have in America and how God has blessed us with such freedom, he said, "God didn't have a thing to do with my success. I had a tough life when I was young, I worked hard, and God gets no credit for what I've accomplished." Another executive who was in the room said, "I don't think I would be making that kind of statement. That sounds dangerous, even foolish." Later that year, that same entrepreneur—one of America's great success stories—was forced to declare bankruptcy. When I called to encourage him and to pray with him after his downfall, I discovered that his attitude had turned around completely. Years ago, I faced my own battle with greed, and I thank God He rescued me before I destroyed everything around me, including myself. Like the entrepreneur I mentioned above, I too had a tough life when I was young. I spent most of my growing-up years living with my mother in back alleys, dumps, and along riverbanks. I'll never forget the tears my foster mother, Mrs. Hale, cried the week before my wedding when she realized that the apartment I would have with my new wife would be my first real home. But once I became established, and once my ministry and reputation as an evangelist began to grow, I discovered the good life was intoxicating. When this unplanned and unwanted kid from Texas suddenly found himself in demand, it touched something deep inside me, and I was drawn to it. I became greedy for the praise, greedy for the recognition, greedy for the trappings of success. It seemed I couldn't get enough. But inside, my soul was shriveling.

Then one day God sent a humble man across my path, a pastor from a small church who told me he loved me and that his church prayed for me. This pastor was not well dressed; he didn't preach to thousands; he didn't have a lot of the perks of success; but he loved God and God used him to break my heart and break the hold that success had on me. It took some time, but I came to realize that what mattered was not the size of my ministry or its budget; it wasn't the size of the crowds that would listen to me speak; it wasn't the size of my house or my car or the things I could buy—it was my love for people that mattered, and I needed a transfusion of genuine love.

When we are self-centered and affected by greed, caring little for others, we inflict pain on those in our way; but in the end, we feel the sting of our own selfish pursuits.

Greed has an appetite that can never be satisfied and a thirst that can never be quenched. Its ambition can never be exhausted. It makes demands that can never be fulfilled and creates needs that can never be met. Greed always wants more. More money. More possessions. More power. More pleasure. More leisure. More prestige. More influence. More accomplishment. More food. More toys. More than the last guy. More than the next guy. More. More. More. Always more.

Greed is not only monetary—it desires everything. It is less about the things we have and more about the things that have us. I know men and women of great substance who are remarkably free of greed's entanglements, and I've met countless poor people who were so ensnared by greed that they were no longer able to function in any area of their lives. They hated everyone who had anything. Greed is less about dollars and cents than about discernment and good sense in how we use the resources we have.

When succumbing to greed, people invariably think that getting is better than having. Once they have something, they begin to take it for granted and eventually become bored by it. That is why greed perpetually compels us to get new things. It is a mad, unending, and vicious cycle.

Because greed is never satisfied, it is never gratified. Because it is never gratified, it is never thankful. Because it is never thankful, it is never at rest. And because it is never at rest, it never gains a sense of proportion, perspective, or purpose. Greed defeats every purpose, including its own.

Greed Has a Record

Greed is a particularly virulent and all-too-common vice. It consumes the lives of those it possesses. It is an equal-opportunity destroyer. Greed infects humanity in epidemic proportions. It brings down the great and the small. It causes the demise of men and nations. It undermines great ambitions. It squanders great opportunities.

The poisonous effect of greed is commonly referred to in legend and in literature. It plays a prominent role in the myths, proverbs, and stories of nearly every culture and every time throughout history. The Greek myth of King Midas is a well-known example. Midas had extraordinary wealth and opulence, but he was not content with it. He begged the gods for more. Dionysus, god of wine and feasting, granted Midas the fulfillment of any wish he might choose. Midas requested that anything he touched would turn to gold. The wish was granted, but it wasn't long before he realized his mistake. Everything he touched turned into cold, lifeless gold—his food, his wine, even his daughter. In the end, his greed defiled everything he needed to live and every natural pleasure he had ever had.

Such tales of woe abound. They show that the attempt to satisfy the cravings of greed is futile. Greed is certain to impose a smothering sadness and hopelessness upon the very people the world sees as the most accomplished and richly blessed. Successful actor Martin Sheen confessed that in all his years among the most glamorous and admired people in the world, "I never saw a satisfied rich man. They were never happy with themselves. They always wanted more."[2] In the 1987 blockbuster hit *Wall Street,* Sheen played a morally upright businessman at odds with a ruthless corporate shark whose motto was also the most famous line in the movie: "Greed is good."

The entire film was a profound demonstration of how wrong he was. But amazingly, that phrase endures while the real message is forgotten.

Such is the power and effect of greed.

Ideological Greed

Greed is not only dangerous to those like Midas and the Hollywood elite. Greed affects whole communities. The annals of history are strewn with the sad evidence that greed destroys. Its golden touch makes genuine fulfillment, satisfaction, and freedom unattainable.

Greed has no thought of justice. It gives no thought to the problems of social stability, cultural enhancement, or national security. It has no interest in the future—its concern is only for the moment. It does not seek to care for the needy, the poor, the despised, or the rejected. It is heedless of the victims strewn in its wake. It is entirely unconcerned about the people, the principles, or the prospects it tramples. It cares only for itself.

When greed and ideology come together, the results are devastating. Colonialism corrupted by greed became imperialism. Although exploration and expansion often led to great progress, when mixed with greed it became the leading edge of great oppression. Greed combined with socialism led to oppressive Communist governments like those in the U.S.S.R. and China and the genocidal purges carried out by Lenin, Stalin, Mao, and Pol Pot. Greed mixed with capitalism creates profit-driven commercialism, wherein corporations with no conscience pursue strictly bottom-line results; thus everyone and everything is defined and valued solely in terms of dollars and cents, giving rise to sweatshops and exploitative labor practices. It is greed run amok.

Guarding against Greed

Unfortunately, confronting and resisting greed is not as easy as simply identifying and condemning it. It is inherent to the human condition. It continually beckons to us, disguised as progress, ambition, diligence, accomplishment, or entrepreneurial zeal.

That is why greed must be resisted—not just in word but also in deed. We must wisely order our fiscal affairs, our consumption patterns, our work relationships, and our investment strategies to mitigate greed. We must take care to guard our eyes, our hearts, and our appetites. We must practice the healthy habits of gratitude, thanksgiving, charity, service, and giving. We must develop life plans, mission statements, and vision for our callings. In other words, we must not allow nature to take its course.

Thomas Chalmers, the nineteenth-century Scottish social reformer, argued that, "Our natural fallen inclination is to yield to the hearty tug of greed upon our affinities and affections. The power of greed is such that without great diligence we are all brought into its destructive thrall. Therefore free men and nations brace themselves to be perpetually vigilant, taking charge over it at every turn, in every way, at all times."[3] His stern counsel to all who cherish the privileges of a free and civil society was to "man the vanguard, the bulwark, the ramparts, the bastions, and the fortifications against the onslaught of greed."[4]

Gain Is Not Greed

Greed destroys. Greed is anything but good. But let's also be clear about what greed is not. Greed is not the same thing as being motivated by profit and the desire for gain. Greed is not the same as trying to maximize our return on investment, unless that return comes at the expense of other people rather than for their benefit, or it is unbalanced, unethical, or unfair.

The desire for gain is as natural and right as the autumn harvest. Every farmer who plants seed in the spring hopes for a bountiful return in the fall. Out of the produce of the fields, the farmer keeps some for himself, pays the wages of his helpers, sells some at a profit (if the markets are good), and sets some aside to be planted for the next year's crop. In the process, the farmer's immediate needs are met, he garners a return on his investment, and he perpetuates the success of his endeavor.

According to Scripture, the compassionate farmer also allows part of the harvest to be gleaned by those in need. "When you harvest the crops of your land, do not harvest the grain along the edges of your fields, and do not pick up what the harvesters drop. Leave it for the poor and the foreigners living among you."[5]

108

Just because we might have a big salary, a nice house and car, and are able to buy other nice things doesn't necessarily mean we're consumed by greed. It's all about priorities and perspective. I believe God wants us to utilize our gifts and abilities fully to maximize our return on investment, and then He wants us to be as generous as we can be with the proceeds of our success so that no one has to suffer hunger or live in dire need. He wants us to work together for the good of all humanity. Look at the example set by the early Christian church. They "began selling their property and possessions, and were sharing them with all, as anyone might have need."[6]

The Bible has a lot to say about "filthy lucre" and how the "love of money is the root of all sorts of evil"; and about thinking that "godliness is gain" and defining that gain materially; and about being careful in our wealth that our riches not take hold of us. Jesus spoke continually about releasing our resources to meet the needs of others—that we are to be like rivers and not storerooms. In fact, He said to the one who wanted to build bigger barns so he could store up his wealth, thinking only of himself, "You are a fool."

The legitimate, compelling desire for gain or financial success must not automatically be interpreted as greed. Achievement and healthy competition have a positive effect on society and the economy. But when other people's hopes and dreams (or savings and retirement accounts) are sacrificed on the altar of selfish pursuits; when human rights and the opportunity for people to advance are crushed by ruthless acts by those who love money more than people, then greed has begun its suffocating work. It is greed that causes corporate executives to look out for themselves while sacrificing the welfare of their employees and shareholders, as confirmed by the Enron scandal. This example of self-serving greed is but another picture of the awful effect it has on others. But the greedy never seem to notice.

The Cure for Greed

The antidote to greed is compassion. If you don't care, start with reforming your attitude toward other people and let love transform your thinking. Part of what makes us human is our ability to look beyond ourselves and care for others. It's the ability to see another person in need and to make a sacrificial decision to help that person at our own expense. It's the ability to differentiate levels of goodness and to choose the greater good. Gain is good. Giving is greater. Best of all, our giving does not negate our gain—it only adds to it in ways that cannot be captured on a balance sheet, but which are far more valuable than fiscal profits. Let me tell you from firsthand experience that when you see the gratitude in the eyes of someone you've helped, when you feel the hug and hear the sincere "thank you," you wouldn't sell that experience for a million dollars. It's priceless.

I had to learn how to care. In many ways, my eyes were opened a number of years ago when I went to South Africa to speak to local ministers. At the conference, I met missionary Peter Pretorius, who later became a partner in our mission outreaches. His testimony had a transforming effect on me. He told me of his life as a prestigious, successful tobacco farmer and race-car driver who lived life totally for himself. He explained how God had changed his life and how he decided to try to share God's message with people in neighboring Mozambique.

When he went to Mozambique to see if he could arrange for a series of public, evangelistic meetings, the individuals who transported him to the region failed to come back and get him at the appointed time. What was supposed to have been a brief, twenty-four- to forty-eight-hour trip ended up lasting more than a week. During his unexpected stay, Peter saw unimaginable suffering. He witnessed the heartbreaking sight of people literally dying at his feet. Every day another twenty to twenty-five malnourished adults and children were buried. Peter helped an elderly man find a resting place against a tree and went to get water for him. He wept when he came back and discovered that the man was already dead.

Peter told me that after he returned to his home in South Africa, he asked friends and neighbors to help buy and provide food for these people. He rented a truck to transport food back into Mozambique and began his first extensive feeding program. As he shared with me about the program—feeding children, providing crisis relief, and showing the love of God—I could clearly see that it was effective. Peter asked if I would come back later in the year to visit a refugee area in northern Mozambique on the border of Malawi.

I went—and I saw some of the most unbelievable scenes I had ever encountered. Families would walk forty-five to sixty-five miles, sometimes carrying children or others unable to walk—trying to get them food, help, and hope. What I saw I could never forget. I became like the Samaritan man in Jesus' parable who could not continue on his way without becoming involved. All the religious meetings could no longer hold me captive as I walked past suffering children and individuals whom I knew I could help in some way.

I believe in the blessings freedom brings and the potential for prosperity it affords. While enjoying life, however, I cannot look past others. I can say with everything in my being that I will live the rest of my life seeking to help every person I can and at the same time, trying to inspire others to help every suffering person on the face of this earth. I do not want there to be one child who is not fed or cared for. I can't do it all, but I can do something.

I believe that our business leaders should go to the countries where they're doing business to see firsthand how the people live and to begin the process of making a difference. If businesspeople will go with a heart of compassion to see how things really are "over there," it will change their life. No one will be able to go back to the office, or the boardroom, and not care about people in other places. They will want to make a difference.

One business can't do everything, but every business can do something. I'm not talking about just charity here; I'm talking about applying our business savvy and our experience in the following ways:

– raising capital
– training—"teaching the other person how to fish"
– putting systems and processes in place

111

– putting long-term, sustainable enterprises to work in disadvantaged areas

I'm not talking about imposing an American system on the rest of the world; I'm talking about applying American ingenuity to find and develop systems that will work in every country of the world. I'm also talking about partnering with others in a servant-cooperative effort, where we work with, instead of duplicating, ventures that are already on the ground and running.

Look Close, Look Far

I'm also not suggesting every opportunity to help must necessarily be in Africa, Asia, or Latin America. We have plenty of needs right here at home. One glaring opportunity that I cannot believe more businesses have not discovered is helping minority and disadvantaged enterprises to raise capital. As a white American whom God has gifted with the ability to speak well and persuade people, I've been able to raise funds for the projects we've undertaken, but I know dozens of leaders of worthwhile ministries and businesses who, because they are black or Hispanic have difficulty raising capital for their work. It shouldn't be that way, but that's the way it is. What we've done is to partner with these organizations to support them and try to help them find access to capital and to undergird their efforts to meet the needs in their communities. One example is a man named Freddie Garcia, a former drug addict who works directly with recovering addicts. Because of Freddie's background and perhaps because of the gritty nature of the work he does, he has a hard time raising money to support his mission. But, let me tell you, he's making a difference, and there are countless others like him across the country who are making a difference and could do more if they had adequate funding.

112

Regardless of where you live or do business, you won't have to look far to find a need. I recommend that you look within your existing spheres of operation. If you're doing business overseas, look overseas for opportunity. If your business is in a neighborhood, start there. Let me say this gently but firmly: Forsake all-consuming, self-serving interests and invest in something that matters. Focus on more than resource development; develop people and provide opportunities. Successful businesses provide jobs, produce profits, and when focused, help solve problems—anywhere in the world.

When as individuals and private organizations we get involved in meeting needs in our communities, we have several advantages over the government:

– Hands-on distribution of resources
– Firsthand accountability for how resources are deployed
– Ability to deliver a message of love with no political strings attached
– Personal interaction and encouragement that reveal true compassion

At Life Outreach International, when we have gone into countries where the government is corrupt, or the system is unstable, or where the needs are simply overwhelming, we have insisted on providing help directly to the place of greatest need. We don't just turn our resources over to government oversight and hope it goes to the right people—and we don't just send a check—but we agree to do specific things to meet specific needs. For example, in China, we agreed to install heating and cooling systems in orphanages, including some in Beijing, because that was a pressing need. We identified the kinds of resources that the children desperately needed and delivered

113

those things directly to them. We placed individuals with medical training in the orphanages. We have been careful not to release our resources to the government or allow them to end up in the black market. That's the advantage of private and faith-based initiatives: They can provide hands-on distribution of resources in an atmosphere of love and concern.

In the United States as private enterprise begins to make progress toward meeting the needs of our society directly, it can gradually replace some government programs with a more efficient and effective plan. As the government is released from the major role of provider—a role the founders never intended for it to play—and focuses on its legitimate responsibility to provide protection, we will be able to ask our representatives to give us our money back (the trillions now being poured into social welfare programs) in the form of lower taxes, which will pump even greater capital into the business sector and personal pocketbooks to be used for even greater good. Believe me, it's a win-win situation. It won't be easy, but it isn't just pie in the sky either. When individuals and businesses experience the benefit of a society where every person truly has an opportunity to succeed, there will be no turning back to the government dole. If private enterprise will get involved in helping the needy, we can see to it that no one is left out.

I'm not talking about simple solutions to complex problems. I'm talking about having the determination and setting the course to get these societal problems solved. I don't pretend to have all the answers, but I do want to be a catalyst to inspire the discussion. I hope to get individuals, businesses, churches, and governments talking about how to make the interests of people our highest priority—not greed, not politics, not personal power and influence. Let's channel our resources where they're going to be most effective.

Partnering for Progress

Look for groups that are already doing some good. Look for principled causes that you can wholeheartedly support. Bill and Melinda Gates are using their foundation to accomplish important work on behalf of the suffering. They've encouraged a caring response to the AIDS epidemic in Third World countries. And there are others who are putting their money into worthwhile charitable causes. I don't want to suggest that it's not already happening—but it needs to happen more. And it needs to spread out across the entire economy. You don't have to be the chairman of Microsoft in order to direct some of your resources to a worthy cause. You may not have millions of dollars at your disposal, but do you have thousands? hundreds? Even a few hundred dollars in the right place can do tremendous good. And you'll be surprised—once you start giving, it gets easier, and you'll start to see more opportunities than you have the resources to meet. Those who give will be blessed— Jesus guarantees it. "It is more blessed to give than to receive."[7] You may not necessarily be blessed with greater income or profits—although sometimes that happens—but without a doubt you'll be blessed with things money can't buy, such as joy, satisfaction, significance, and purpose. The supporters of our Life Outreach mission programs are among the happiest, most content people I've ever met. They thank us continually for the privilege of providing relief to those who suffer, and they rejoice in sharing life with those in need.

8

CHAPTER EIGHT

On the battlefield, when surrounded and cheered by pomp, excitement, and admiration of devoted comrades, and inspired by strains of martial music and the hope of future reward, it is comparatively easy to be a hero, to do heroic deeds. But to uphold honor in ordinary circumstances, to be a hero in common life, that is a genuine achievement meriting our highest admiration.
BOOKER T. WASHINGTON (1856–1915)

Character is always the most important issue in determining the outcome of human events, and character is revealed in what we actually do, not merely what we say or believe.
THEODORE ROOSEVELT (1858–1919)

Character cannot be made except by a steady, long continued process. **PHILLIPS BROOKS (1835–1893)**

Character
Counts

*More important than what we say or do in the public eye is
what we are like when no one else is around.*

Leadership expert John Maxwell has said, "Crisis doesn't make
character, but it certainly reveals it. Adversity is a crossroad
that makes a person choose one of two paths: character or compromise. Every time he chooses character, he becomes stronger, even if that choice brings negative consequences."[1]
Substantive character will always make us. The lack of it will just
as surely break us.

In *The Daniel Dilemma,* author Peggy Stanton talks about
Martin Luther King Jr. and the kind of character it takes to bring
about substantive changes in society:

> Signing on with Martin Luther King meant more than
> righting the wrongs against the black man in the South; it
> meant a total commitment to accomplishing those ends
> nonviolently, no matter the personal risk. As King wrote in

the book *Why We Can't Wait,* no one would be sent out "to demonstrate who had not convinced himself and us that he could accept and endure violence without retaliating." To this end, potential demonstrators were trained by [the Southern Christian Leadership Conference] to be prepared for the obstacles they would face: the verbal abuse, the beatings, the police dogs, fire hoses. If volunteers could not respond nonviolently to violent situations, they were not allowed to march. Finally, they were required to sign a ten-point pledge, which included among its *commandments* promises to:

1. Meditate daily on the teachings and life of Jesus.
2. Pray daily to be used by God in order that all men might be free.
3. Walk and talk in the manner of love, for God is love.
4. Sacrifice personal wishes in order that all men might be free.
5. Observe with both friend and foe the ordinary rules of courtesy.
6. Seek to perform regular service for others and for the world.
7. Refrain from the violence of fist, tongue, and heart. [Isn't that a great statement?]
8. Strive to be in good spiritual and bodily health.
9. Follow the directions of the movement and of the captain on a demonstration.[2]

It takes a lot of character to stand up to the kind of abuse endured by the civil-rights marchers, but it is precisely that kind of character that eventually broke down the walls of segregation and racial hatred in this country, and it's the same kind of character it will take to restore our nation to its proper course for the future.

Character in the Spotlight

If ever we had an opportunity to observe how adversity and crisis bring character to the forefront, that moment came on September 11, 2001, and in the days, weeks, and months that followed. We saw it in the actions of firefighters and rescue workers who worked tirelessly at great personal cost and risk. We saw it in the compassion, tenacity, forthrightness, resolve, and courage demonstrated by local, state, and national leaders. We heard it in the words of President Bush and others who reinvigorated our sense of purpose as a people and as a nation. We saw it in the real-life drama that pushed ordinary people into the spotlight at center stage—the heroes of Flight 93 and countless others who saved the lives of coworkers and friends at the Pentagon and the World Trade Center.

Even as the nation settled into a sense of normalcy again, public opinion polls indicated that President Bush's approval rating was holding strong at 86 percent.[3] According to the *Los Angeles Times,* it was "the highest job approval rating ever recorded" for a president.[4] Outside the poorer urban centers, the president's rating was an astonishing 97 percent, a figure the *Times* said was "approaching what legislators call unanimous consent."[5] Even among America's poorest urban and minority citizens, the president had a solid 70 percent approval rating.[6] Considering that just a few months earlier he had narrowly won the most hotly contested election in more than a century—and had garnered only about 8 percent of the African-American vote—the polls indicated one of the most remarkable turnarounds in American political history.

According to former White House staffer and speechwriter Peggy Noonan, the reason for this is not difficult to explain:

> In a president, character is everything. A president doesn't have to be brilliant; Harry Truman wasn't brilliant, and he helped save Western Europe from Stalin. He doesn't have to be clever; you can hire clever. White Houses are always full of quick-witted people with ready advice on how to flip a senator or implement a strategy. You can hire pragmatic, and you can buy and bring in policy wonks. But you can't buy courage and decency, you can't rent a strong moral sense. A president must bring those things with him. If he does, they will give meaning and animation to the great practical requirement of the presidency: He must know why he is there and what he wants to do. *He has to have thought it through.* He needs to have, in that much-maligned word, but a good one nonetheless, a vision of the future he wishes to create. . . . But a vision is worth little if a president doesn't have the character—the courage and heart—to see it through.[7]

In a transforming moment of crisis, President Bush manifested his character. As the nation watched him respond to the terrorist attacks, they saw a man who before had seemed uncomfortable reading from a TelePrompTer reveal himself as a man who didn't need to read a script—his moral steadfastness and steady resolve became evident through his calm demeanor and strong words.

Fictional Heroes, Real Character
Have you ever heard of Edward Stratemeyer? Believe it or not, he is among the more prolific and influential of American

authors. He wrote more books and sold more copies than almost any other writer who has ever lived—some 1,300 novels that have sold in excess of 500 million copies. He created more than 125 different series—many of them familiar and beloved American cultural icons.

If you are wracking your brain and can't remember ever hearing the name Edward Stratemeyer, perhaps you know him better by one of his pen names—Franklin W. Dixon, Victor Appleton, Carolyn Keene, Roy Rockwood, Laura Lee Hope, or Ralph Bonehill—or by some of his more famous characters, such as the Hardy Boys, Nancy Drew, Tom Swift, the Rover Boys, Jack Ranger, Bomba the Jungle Boy, the Dana Girls, the Bobbsey Twins, Dave Dashaway, or Don Sturdy. All of these characters and their series were invented by one very prolific writer: Edward Stratemeyer.

At the height of his career in the 1920s, Stratemeyer employed an entire syndicate of editors, copywriters, stenographers, coauthors, and secretaries just to keep up with his prodigious creativity. With their assistance, he was able to produce an astonishing array of stories, most of which were mysteries in which children or young adults upheld right and triumphed over wrong.

According to Stratemeyer, all of his books had a single unifying theme: the vital importance of moral character. He once said, "The history of the world, the outcome of great events, and the establishment of true heroism will always entirely depend upon [moral character]."[8] He attributed all his success and the enduring popularity of the numerous series he created to the fact that his commitment to character never wavered.

"Every story worth retelling," he said, "is the fruit of internal uprightness at work in the external world. Whenever any mystery appears, its solution will depend upon the exercise of ethics, first and foremost. Whenever any adventure arises, its resolution will depend upon the exertion of morals. Whenever any question emerges, its outcome will depend upon the establishment of standards. In every circumstance, character is the issue. It is the issue which underlies all other issues."[9]

Stratemeyer built his career on an absolute truth: Character counts! When push comes to shove, what matters most is not so much what we do as who we are. Whether we are writing a story for boys and girls, giving direction to a family or a community, marching in a demonstration, or leading an entire nation, character is the issue that supersedes all others.

Separating the Fruit from the Root

The issue of character isn't always a topic of discussion in the public forum. When things are going well, most people tend to take character for granted. Our awareness of it may get pushed to the back burner, as if it's not really all that important. When it appears that little is at risk, the economy is strong, and the world is at relative peace, we can easily become complacent about character. Before long, we start to forget the vital connection between a person's private character and his or her public accomplishments; we overlook the importance of our nation's social standards in determining our cultural progress. As long as things seem to be working all right, we may not be as concerned about what goes on behind the scenes or under the surface. We simply continue to eat the fruit of our success—until the fruit turns sour.

Drawing distinctions between an individual's private and personal choices and his or her public or civic actions may seem very modern and genteel, but the separation of these two very connected aspects of life constitutes an outright denial of one of life's most basic truths: A tree will be known by its fruit.

123

No good tree bears bad fruit, nor again does a bad tree bear good fruit; for each tree is known by its own fruit. Figs are not gathered from thorns, nor are grapes picked from a bramble bush. The good person out of the good treasure of the heart produces good, and the evil person out of evil treasure produces evil; for it is out of the abundance of the heart the mouth speaks.[10]

"Your character determines who you are," says John Maxwell. "Who you are determines what you see. What you see determines what you do. That's why you can never separate a leader's character from his actions."[11] The English historian and journalist Hilaire Belloc extends the argument further when he points out the connection between our character and our culture. He writes, "Biography always affords the greatest insights into sociology. To comprehend the history of a thing is to unlock the mysteries of its present, and more, to discover the profundities of its future."[12] In other words, by digging into the character of people, we can better understand the past and more reliably forecast the future.

Many of the most celebrated historians of our generation—including Paul Johnson, Niall Ferguson, Barbara Tuchman, Martin Gilbert, Edwin Morris, and Antonia Fraser—have approached their work primarily as the documentation of great lives rather than merely the reporting of great events. As social critic E. Michael Jones puts it, "Biography is destiny."[13]

Think of all the talented people whose lives and careers were ruined by a lack of character. How many actors and athletes have been brought low by a foolish lapse of judgment, a loss of self-control, or an erosion of integrity? How many gifted politicians and preachers have been undone by an inability to keep their lust at bay? Think of all the effective educators and administrators who've been tripped up by an inability to tell the truth—or the successful business executives who have succumbed to pride, ambition, and greed. The Bible says, "Those who plant trouble and cultivate evil will harvest the same."[14] You just can't separate the fruit from the root.

According to psychologist Steven Berglas of Harvard Medical School, people with extraordinary talent may achieve extraordinary success for a time. But, he says, success is often more dangerous for them than failure would have been. If they do not possess the bedrock character necessary to withstand success, they may be headed for disaster. In his book *The Success Syndrome,* Berglas argues that successful people run the risk of falling prey to one or more of "the four A's: arrogance, painful feelings of aloneness, destructive adventure-seeking, or adultery."[15] Each consequence is a terrible price to pay for weak character, and each has the capacity to undo whatever good the person may otherwise have accomplished.

125

Leaders cannot separate their private lives from their public performance. Who they are in the privacy of their own room will certainly affect who they are when they're out among the people. Ultimately, their character flaws will be revealed—either through success or adversity. Likewise, moral discrepancies in the heart of a nation will ultimately undermine its other advances and advantages.

For All Have Sinned

It's one thing to talk about the importance of strong character, but it's much more difficult to pursue it in the nitty-gritty details of life. Even as we expect—or demand—strong character in our leaders, our families, our friends, and ourselves, we must also practice compassionate concern for those who struggle— because every person sins, and every person will at some time struggle with temptation, lapses in judgment, and poor decisions.

In my own experience, I can see that some aspects of my character seem unshakably strong, whereas in other areas I find myself continually battling weaknesses and unbecoming tendencies. Even in the areas that I feel strong, I take seriously the Bible's warning: "Let him who thinks he stands take heed lest he fall."[16] I thank God for those around me with whom I can share my heart and my difficulties without feeling condemned—starting with my wife. Betty has such depth of character that she provides not only a shoulder on which I can lean, but strong arms that always seek to lift me up out of discouragement over my weaknesses. It would be easy to blame my struggles on my childhood, my parents, or my past, but looking for a scapegoat will not suffice. I must recognize—and we all must recognize—that we're in a continual battle against an enemy who wants to drag us down. Only by the grace of God can any of us continue to walk in integrity and character. We must support one another in this fight.

When we confront others in their wrongdoing, it should always be in a spirit of redemption. We should always seek to bring goodness out of bad situations. Friends who will help rather than merely accuse are a life-sustaining blessing. Sadly, members of the Christian community are sometimes the greatest accusers and the first to "throw stones." Although their intent might be to stand up for character, righteousness, and virtue, if they forget to temper their confrontation of wrong with a balance of forgiveness, mercy, and love, their best intentions can easily do more harm than good.

In order to properly discern another person's true character, we must understand the difference between weakness and wickedness. Those who battle weaknesses are aware of much-needed changes that should be made. On the other hand, some individuals are so given over to evil that the Bible says "their own conscience [is] seared with a hot iron" and "[their] god is their belly."[17] In Romans 1, the apostle Paul says their minds have become morally corrupt—unable to discern between good and evil. Individuals who have become so self-absorbed that they will go to any extreme to justify their practices rather than deal with their damaging acts have set their minds on the pursuit of their wicked ways. They have no intention of ever responding to the truth. As Christians, we're not to judge such people, but we should pray for them with the hope that they might repent. We can only hope that there will come a point when their conscience will be awakened and they will experience what the Bible refers to as passing from death to life.[18]

Because we all sin, many great people in the public eye struggle with recurring problems, disappointing practices, and unseemly habits. Sadly, many simply give in to their vices, revealing shallow character. Others do not seek help with their weaknesses, many times out of fear—fear of disappointing others, fear of being castigated and cast out, or fear of failure. Fear of consequences is certainly a reason that many religious, political, civic, and business leaders refuse to seek help.

Before Bill Clinton became president, we saw how his accusers lined up to reveal his failures and spread accusations in an attempt to bring him down. Were those who accused him motivated by a spirit of redemption—that is, a desire to help or heal—or by a spirit of destruction? Whenever confrontation arises, there is always a controlling spiritual force behind the action—and the fruit will reveal the root. Does the confrontation result in redemption and restoration or defamation and destruction?

Considering the difficulties that President Clinton subsequently faced while in the White House, it's easy to wonder whether strong people who would not be intimidated by his powerful presence and personality ever confronted him—in a spirit of compassion—about his weaknesses or failures. The rumors concerning his womanizing and related weaknesses had persisted for many years, from the time he was a young man in Arkansas. Did church leaders, civic leaders, or close friends ever intercede in an effort to help him and not merely shame him?

Through relationships I have with some of our nation's business and government leaders, I attempted to contact Mr. Clinton during the time of his much-publicized struggles, but to no avail. I still regret not being able to speak with him, because God has given me a genuine, deep concern for him as a person, and I felt led to reach out to him with compassion. As it was, I prayed for him and for those who were close to him.

Those who claim a relationship with God must offer loving assistance to all who struggle and are willing to admit it. Certainly there's risk involved in extending compassion—others may not understand or appreciate our efforts, but unless help is made available, there is little hope for overcoming our flaws.

People with great depth of character often have very real weaknesses. Consider such Old Testament heroes as Abraham, Moses, David, and Elijah; and in the New Testament, Peter, Thomas, and Paul. These men were doubters, rebels, adulterers, and murderers. But even as they struggled with their sinful natures, they desperately sought to please God. They battled and persevered to the end. Jesus said that those who endured to the end would be saved. This pertains to far more than eternal salvation. It refers also to the possibility of real, meaningful deliverance in this life. People all over the world desperately need to be delivered—set free from temptation, sin, and besetting weaknesses. Those who have been released from bondage need to share their freedom with compassion, love, and concern.

Safeguarding Character

Because I have seen and experienced firsthand how vulnerable a person becomes when he or she has achieved highly visible success according to the world's standards, I have been careful to caution other leaders. Over the years, I have shared my concerns in person and in writing. I believe I have a platform to speak to these issues with understanding and compassion because my own ministry and my life were nearly destroyed by some of the very same vulnerabilities I see in others. Unfortunately, there are not many who are willing to confront others when they see potential problems arising. Because others who were strong and full of love did not confront me for a while, I came very close to losing everything that was important in my life.

I know firsthand that an individual, even a truly gifted Christian, has never tasted the full impact of spiritual assault from the realm of darkness until he or she has experienced what this world calls "real success." When that almost indescribable sense of euphoria settles in and when the accolades, praise, and appreciation of other people are heaped on us, we are thrust into a conflict in which the subtleties and seductive potential of the enemy defies anything we can imagine. I have seen very few people, even among the godliest spiritual leaders, who have been able to survive the onslaught without some type of serious damage. When success is coupled with an undeniable gifting from God, a very special touch for His specific purposes, the battle then moves into realms very difficult to comprehend. I experienced such heady success in my early to midtwenties, and by the time I reached my early thirties, I had climbed so high on this ladder that I found myself being manipulated by well-intentioned others who were unknowingly seeking to use my gift for their own purposes. I was being exploited.

The exploitation was of course "for the benefit of other

129

Christians" or "to help reach the lost," and always "to further the kingdom of God." But the fact is, my intimacy with God had been interrupted, and I was literally blinded to what was taking place. My judgment was diminished, and my discernment ultimately short-circuited. I found myself defeated and held captive—until I reached a point at which I even despaired of life.

During this time, I learned some hard but good lessons. One was that people will manipulate, and it's often very difficult to realize when it's happening. I learned how crucial, how completely essential it is to maintain a humble, meek spirit before God, which is the only way to remain effective in ministry. I learned to be more sensitive, more cautious, more committed, and to walk even more intimately with God than ever before. I learned to seek out people who were courageous enough to confront and challenge me. I learned to love my enemies because they would tell me the "real" truth. While trying to hurt me, they actually helped me because I took their accusations to God in prayer.

Any person who longs to develop character that is strongly built on truth and on relationship with God can safeguard his or her character only by silencing, for a time, the sounds of the entire world so that he or she can clearly hear the voice of God. Jesus Himself had to do it! As a regular practice during His life on earth, Jesus pulled away from all the sounds of the world, from the suggestions of men and the counsel of His closest associates, and spent time totally alone with God. He went out into the wilderness or to a hillside and prayed.

If Jesus did it, we must do it, too. I have encouraged President Bush to make time in his schedule—in the midst of all the concerns of his office—to pray alone, away from the pressure exerted by others. I've had the privilege of praying with the president on a number of occasions, and one time when I visited him at his Crawford, Texas, ranch, he took me to a hillside over-looking a riverbed to show me one of the places he goes to spend time in prayerful meditation. He was simply affirming his belief in the importance of time alone praying. We all need to find that quiet place where we can hear the voice of God. Character can be safeguarded only by continually aligning our thinking and vision with that which is ultimately true and right. The best way to safeguard our character is through consistent time spent with God, reading His Word—the Bible—and with others of godly character who will hold us accountable.

True Leadership

What is it exactly that makes someone a leader? What distin-guishes one person over another? What character traits are nec-essary to steer people in the way they should go? What constitutes genuine leadership? Samuel Johnson, the great eighteenth century English author, defined a leader as "a man who bears in his life both the most tangible and intangible qualities of heart and mind and flesh."

131

Those most "tangible and intangible qualities" are princi-ples or moral standards. They are the component parts of genu-ine and substantive character, founded on the absolute truths we've been talking about in these pages.

Again and again, history bears out the truth that those with great moral character drive the great moments of history. Con-sider George Washington, for example. Washington was not a particularly great general—during the War for Independence he spent most of his time escaping from the better armed, better positioned, and better prepared British. He was a quiet and dig-nified man of few and simple words—not an enthralling speaker. He was not a profound or deep thinker—he relied on Alexander Hamilton, James Madison, John Jay, and Thomas

Jefferson to formulate and implement American policy. Nevertheless, he was one of the greatest leaders America has ever known. Why? Because he was a man of unwavering character. He had the full confidence of his men on the battlefield and of his fellow citizens in the political arena, precisely because they knew they could trust his integrity and fortitude. He was a man of vision, and others knew they could depend on him to live in accordance with that vision, no matter what.

Teddy Roosevelt was not a particularly adept politician. In fact, he very nearly destroyed his career half-a-dozen times because of his unwillingness to do what was expected of him. He was usually "too young" for the positions he held—after all, before his fiftieth birthday he had served as a New York state legislator, undersecretary of the navy, police commissioner of New York City, a federal civil service commissioner, governor of the state of New York, vice president under William McKinley, a colonel in the army during the Spanish-American War, and two terms as president of the United States. He was the most controversial American politician of the twentieth century—both at home and abroad. Nevertheless, even his ideological adversaries admitted that he was the greatest leader the nation had known since Lincoln, perhaps even since Washington.[19] How could that be? Roosevelt was a man of sterling character. He was able to achieve so much and lead so well because he was well grounded.

Like Roosevelt, Winston Churchill was a volatile politician, hot tempered, outspoken, and bookishly intellectual—hardly the sort of personality suited for life in the public eye. He was often ill, suffering from poor circulation and a bad heart, conditions that were only intensified by a slew of unhealthy habits, and he was hampered by a speech impediment. In his political career, he changed parties three times and was marginalized by his peers. By the time World War II broke out, he was considered a political has-been. Nevertheless, despite all his liabilities, Churchill was the man to whom the entire free world looked during the time of the Nazi terror. He had the courage to stand up to Hitler and prevailed against all odds. How was this possible? Very simply, he was a man of tremendous moral reserves. He was driven by a clearheaded sense of right and wrong. He was a man of deep and abiding character.

The stories of Patrick Henry, Samuel Adams, John Quincy Adams, Harriet Beecher Stowe, Andrew Jackson, Robert E. Lee, Harriet Tubman, Booker T. Washington, George Washington Carver, and Jane Addams tell a similar tale. These remarkable men and women did not make their mark on history because they were more talented, had better opportunities, or got better breaks than their contemporaries. They made their mark on history because they manifested solid and substantive character. They were living demonstrations of the truth that leadership develops from the inside out.

133

Industrialist G. Alan Bernard said, "The respect that leadership must have requires that one's ethics be without question. A leader not only stays above the line between right and wrong, he stays well clear of the gray areas too."[20] Without such character, no one will be able to sustain success. Likewise, no nation has been able to preserve freedom, advance material progress, or establish social harmony or security without strong character.

Leaving the Past Behind and Moving Forward

How do we deal with our past failures? It is not a question of whether or not we have failed. Everyone has failed. Perhaps some would refuse to admit it, but we all have failed. The question is, have we learned from our failures? Have they strengthened our lives and our character? Has failure caused us to refocus in a positive and meaningful way? If we learn from our failures and find ways not to repeat them, we can move forward—and help others to move forward as well.

Great character does not imply an absence of weakness or personal struggle. In fact, humility in the face of our weakness is yet another indication of our character. Great character is formed by our consistent response to pressure, problems, and difficult circumstances. Like the apostle Paul, we must move forward, "forgetting the past and looking forward to what lies ahead." We must strive "to reach the end of the race and receive the prize for which God, through Christ Jesus, is calling us up to heaven."[21]

9

CHAPTER NINE

Even the greatest of delights without the least of restrictions will quickly cease to satisfy. A pristine joy, like sex, made common and base is merely a defiled and repulsive thing.
ROBERT LOUIS STEVENSON (1850–1894)

Sex is ruled by a peculiar version of supply and demand— our desire for it can only be spoiled by promiscuity.
CHARLES DE GAULLE (1890–1970)

Purity is the beginning of all passion. Thus, faithful marriage is the only guarantee of unbridled sexual pleasure.
HENRY WADSWORTH LONGFELLOW (1807–1882)

Sex Is a Great Gift That Must Be Protected

*The breakdown in sexual standards and practices
has hurt or destroyed countless people. This is one
of the most compelling evidences of the impact
of our ideas and beliefs on our quality of life.*

Rachael Yarborough came home from school one day very upset. Along with the other junior high school students in her Family Life Skills class, she had been shown an explicit film depicting four couples, two homosexual and two heterosexual, performing a variety of graphic sexual acts.

At first her mother, Marjorie, thought Rachael was exaggerating about the explicit nature of the film. "I have worked very hard to teach all of my children to be tolerant and open-minded about things," she said. "So I just assumed that Rachael was simply overreacting to a legitimate classroom exercise." Even so, her daughter was so upset that Marjorie decided she should get all the facts. When she made an appointment to visit the school's guidance counselor, she was entirely unprepared for the cultural melee over sex she was about to walk into. "I actually went in," she said, "in an effort to better understand how I could help Rachael accept things. But, I was quickly put on the defensive."

The counselor initially refused to answer any questions about the curriculum. "She told me that it would be inappropriate to discuss the material outside of its fuller classroom context." When Marjorie pressed her on the issue, the counselor became irate. "She accused me of being overly protective. She accused me of being a fundamentalist and [said] that it was probably my narrow sectarianism that was causing my daughter's trauma." But Marjorie was not a fundamentalist with narrow sectarian views at all. At the time, she did not even attend a church—and hadn't since her college days. She was simply a concerned parent.

Because she could not get any answers from the guidance counselor, Marjorie decided to take up the issue at the next school board meeting. Again she was stonewalled—and again she was denounced as a "right-wing extremist," even though she was in fact a lifelong liberal Democrat. It was not until much later that she discovered the curriculum was accompanied by a cautionary note instructing teachers not to allow parents to have any access to the material whatsoever. The caution read, in part: *Many of the materials of this program shown to people outside the context of the program itself can evoke misunderstanding and difficulties.*

"It was difficult for me to fathom how or why the school could justify keeping parents in the dark about the programs their children are exposed to every day," Marjorie said. "But I guess they have their reasons."

Hijacking Our Children's Innocence
It turns out that one reason school officials, counselors, teachers, and the providers of the curriculum want to keep parents

in the dark about their sex education programs is because the materials are mind-bogglingly shocking. These programs seem to be designed precisely for the purpose of breaking down any and all sexual inhibitions, invalidating sexual taboos, and undermining normal sexual values. They deliberately betray the trust of parents and incite an emotional and sexual upheaval in the children.

Spawned in the miasma of the sexual revolution that took hold during the twentieth century—led by the radical opinions of writers such as Sigmund Freud, Margaret Sanger, Bertrand Russell, Alfred Kinsey, Shere Hite, and Ruth Westheimer—most contemporary sex education materials are uniformly brazen and perverse.[1] Often they are peppered with crudely obscene four-letter words and illustrated by explicit nudity.[2] They openly endorse aberrant behavior—including homosexuality, bisexuality, incest, and even bestiality—often described in excruciating detail.[3]

This, the most crass brand of moral hedonism and sexual relativism, is consistently presented to millions of public school children under the guise of academic objectivity and neutrality. Any resistance their young and impressionable consciences might offer is slowly but surely overwhelmed.

"Our goal," one curriculum writer says, "is to be ready as educators and parents to help young people obtain sex satisfaction before marriage. By sanctioning sex before marriage, we will prevent fear and guilt."[4]

According to a Planned Parenthood pamphlet for teens, "Sex is too important to glop up with sentiment. If you feel sexy, for heaven's sake, admit it to yourself. If the feeling and the tension bother you, you can masturbate. Masturbation cannot hurt you and it will make you feel more relaxed."[5] Another of the organization's publications for teens asserts: "There are only two kinds of sex: sex with victims and sex without. Sex with victims is always wrong. Sex without is always right."[6] "Relax about loving," admonishes yet another booklet. "Sex is fun and joyful, and courting is fun and joyful, and it comes in all types and styles, all of which are okay. Do what gives pleasure, and enjoy what gives pleasure. Don't rob yourself of joy by focusing on old-fashioned ideas about what's normal or nice. Just communicate and enjoy."[7]

"It's up to you alone—as long as you feel comfortable" is the amoral message repeated again and again in modern sex education materials and on teen-oriented Web sites such as teenwire.com. "Whatever you choose to do—it's your decision," they say, because "there are no 'right' or 'wrong' answers—just *your* answers."[8] Sexuality is simply a matter of personal preference. Thus, for instance, Planned Parenthood argues:

> You have noticed how the kinds of food you like and
> dislike are different from some of those other people like
> and dislike. It is much the same with the sexual appetites
> of human beings.[9]

Sociologist Thomas Sowell pointed out the alarming extremes to which this valueless logic has gone:

> Concepts of "normal" or "healthy" sex are dismissed
> because "each of us has his or her own legitimate set
> of sexual attitudes and feelings." Homosexuality is a
> matter of "preferences." Sadomasochism may be "very
> acceptable and safe for some people." Although it is illegal
> and "exploitation" for adults to "take advantage" of chil-
> dren sexually, "there may be no permanent emotional
> harm."[10]

139

The Covert Realignment of Our Children's Values

The kind of aggressive relativism found in much of the sex education material available today is a far cry from simply dispelling childish myths about storks and cabbage patches. These programs are not merely designed to provide accurate biological information. Instead, they are calculated to change the minds, morals, and motivations of an entire generation. They are designed to completely reshape the perspectives and personalities of children everywhere—including yours. One former Planned Parenthood medical director, Mary Calderone, has forthrightly admitted that in sex education, "Mere facts and discussion are not enough. They need to be undergirded by a set of values."[11]

But whose values? Certainly not those of parents. According to Randy Alcorn in his book *ProLife Answers to ProChoice Arguments,* the values presented in schools are those of Planned Parenthood:

> When Planned Parenthood comes to school classrooms, it typically passes out birth control samples and instructs students in how each is used. It tells students where the local clinic is located, its phone number, and hours of operation. Children are continuously reassured that their parents will never know. After thorough investigation, one magazine claims that "parental non-involvement is the cornerstone of [Planned Parenthood's] youth marketing strategy."[12]

Another reason that some education and health officials want to keep parents in the dark about the true nature of their sex education programs is that the multimillion-dollar, tax-funded efforts have proven to be anything but effective. In fact, they have backfired, actually increasing teen pregnancies and the incidence of sexually transmitted diseases. The reason for this is clear, according to Randy Alcorn:

> The cause of unwanted pregnancies is *not* the absence of birth control. It is the presence of teenage sexual activity. Planned Parenthood has had a profound influence on the young people of America for two decades, yet the rate of teen pregnancy has skyrocketed in that time. Why? Largely because of the philosophy stated by former Planned Parenthood president Faye Wattleton: "We are not going to be an organization promoting celibacy or chastity."[13]

Planned Parenthood's own survey, conducted by the Louis Harris pollsters, showed that teenagers who have taken "comprehensive" sex education courses from Planned Parenthood have a 50 percent higher rate of sexual activity than their "unenlightened" peers.[14] At the same time, the courses had no significant effect on their contraceptive usage.[15] The conclusion, one that even the most ardent sex education researchers have been unable to escape, is that "value-free sex education courses only exacerbate the teenage pregnancy problem."[16]

In 1970, fewer than half of the nation's school districts offered sex education courses and none had school-based birth-control clinics.[17] Today more than 75 percent of the districts teach sex education and there are more than three hundred school-based clinics in operation.[18] During that time, the percentage of illegitimate births increased from 15 percent to an astonishing 51 percent.[19] In California, the public schools have required sex education for nearly forty years, yet the state has maintained one of the highest rates of teen pregnancy in the nation.[20]

According to the Harris poll, the only things that influence the teenage pregnancy problem positively are frequent church attendance and parental oversight, the very things that sex education courses are carefully designed to circumvent.[21]

What Price Freedom?

You would think that we would know better than to suggest that something as intimate and volatile as our sexuality could be "liberated" from standards of morality without dire consequences. And yet misguided individuals continue to play with fire and get burned. History is replete with stories of men and women of great promise who abused sex for power or pleasure only to suffer calamity as a result. From Cleopatra and Mark Antony, to Guinevere and Lancelot, to Bill Clinton and Monica Lewinsky, sad tales abound of remarkable men and women hurt by their abuse of sex. Nevertheless, in our schools, we don't talk about the consequences of "sexual freedom" beyond the physical issues of sexually transmitted diseases and pregnancy.

When I was growing up, like many young boys, I was exposed to explicit sexual images and the national preoccupation with this powerful temptation. Were it not for some defining positive influences in my life, I could easily have been trapped, overwhelmed, and controlled by the captivating power of sex. These are the issues that ought to be addressed in the sex education courses in our schools!

Because human sexuality is one of the most beautiful, mysterious, complex, and satisfying experiences in life, it is also one of the most dangerous. During my forty years in public ministry, I have listened to the stories of defeated national and spiritual leaders, both men and women, including more ministers than I would care to count, whose careers and lives were in a shambles because of sexual sins. No one is immune to the allure and the destructive potential of misguided sex. In fact, with the prevalence of sexual images in the media, the mailbox, and the mall, we're all adversely affected to some degree.

The Bible helps us to understand the impact of immorality on our spirits: "Run away from sexual sin! No other sin so clearly affects the body as this one does. For sexual immorality is a sin against your own body."[22] Any form of sexual impurity inflicts damage on the human psyche and emotions. The Bible clearly indicates that when we compromise sexually, we are engaging in self-destructive behavior. Whether we believe it or not, we inflict damage on ourselves that ultimately could destroy us. It is comparable to the way drug addiction destroys an addict's body, mind, spirit, and soul.

In his counseling practice, psychologist Doug Weiss has heard countless stories of twisted and perverse sexual experiences. Weiss wrote a best-selling book titled *Women Who Love Sex Addicts*, in which he shares his own testimony and the stories of others whom he has counseled, many of whom had become so desensitized that they could no longer find a source of arousal. The staff in our prayer center at Life Outreach is often shocked and dismayed by the testimonies they hear about damage inflicted by inappropriate sexual activity.

Sex has an addictive potential, and sexual relationships outside of marriage create cravings that never should have been stirred up. According to recent surveys and the testimonies of thousands of individuals who have contacted our ministry, sexual images presented through the entertainment media— everything from suggestive prime-time television programs to explicit, hard-core pornography—are taking a toll on families, marriages, and single adults. So many women have been devas-

143

tated, humiliated, devalued, and made into objects of lust by purveyors of sensuality. Disheartened wives have expressed their pain, frustration, and anger as they cry out for help. They say, "How can I compete with all the images, the "perfect" bodies, and the never-ending emphasis on explicit, unrestricted sex? My husband's brain is twisted by lust."

Responding with Compassion

I am convinced that counselors, religious leaders, and the entire Christian community must become very focused on helping people be restored to normal sexual relationships. With so much emphasis on self-centered gratification in our society, the challenge before us looms large. Christians must demonstrate God's love and concern for those who have experienced the pain of sexual immorality. Any individual who desires restoration must be encouraged to move forward in wholehearted commitment to God's ordained boundaries for sexuality. Those who are attempting to help in the restoration process, including spouses who desire reconciliation in their marriage relationship, must avoid shaming the one who is struggling. Anyone who has failed already feels ashamed. I'm convinced that one reason many church leaders and national leaders do not seek help is the fear of being shamed. They are already embarrassed by their mistakes, and they do not want to disappoint people who respect and trust them. Somehow we must create a way for people who have fallen to seek help (and find it!) without the fear of being destroyed in the process.

Before we tape our nationally televised program, *Life Today*, each week, we have a dinner meeting with our guests. During one of these gatherings, a well-known Christian man blurted out, "I have really drifted. Just recently I started watching pornography again. I feel so bad." In a matter of moments, all of us as a group had gathered around this man in a spirit of love to pray for him and administer forgiveness, restoration, and redirection. We were inspired by his openness and honesty. I later commented to one of our staff leaders, "That gentleman paid us one of the highest compliments we'll ever be paid. By confessing to us, he said, 'I can trust my life and my pain to you. I know you love me. You do not want to hurt or destroy me. You are my friends. You want to help.' " This same message of love, concern, and compassion must be communicated to everyone who struggles and to those hurt by defeat.

The news of inappropriate sexual activity on the part of some Catholic priests—and the decades-long cover-up by some members of the Catholic hierarchy—was understandably shocking. But one of the things that distressed me most was the fact that we never heard any priest or guilty party openly admit that his actions were wrong. We never heard of any priest who cried out for help. Perhaps some did, but such acts of repentance and expressions of desire for restoration had not been made public as of this writing. If such criminal acts involving the clergy and children or other parishioners ever become tolerated by the general public or excused by those who practice such despicable behavior, then our society will have reaped the dehumanizing and destructive consequences of refusing to abide by moral absolutes.

When I hear the stories of individuals and couples who have been crushed by sexual failure, my heart aches, and I cry out to God on their behalf. At Life Outreach, we diligently seek to direct people who are hurting to the most effective, able, and compassionate counselors. I always emphasize the importance of couples seeking help together. As Christians, we should give our support with broken and contrite hearts, offering hope and practical help to those who are so obviously defeated. I could share many true life stories of individuals who have been gloriously delivered from sexual sin and temptation and who now walk in joyful victory while experiencing new, restored, and beautiful intimacy with their spouse. Many of those who have been restored are now effectively working in national and spiritual leadership roles.

The message of hope and forgiveness must be communicated in a spirit of compassion to all who have been wounded by sexual sin. No amount of pain and damage is too great for the healing hand and heart of God. If you're presently suffering, seek hope and seek help. I believe it can be found. Somehow, in love, we must make compassionate help even more accessible and inviting.

God's Perfect Plan

How do you adequately describe an experience as explosively stimulating, as exhilarating, as potentially fulfilling and satisfying as sex? You can't. It is miraculous and supernatural. It is an experience so incomparable that many throughout history have placed it in the category of something eternal, holy, and divine. In Judeo-Christian belief, God gives woman to man for their mutual fulfillment and benefit. Only a great and loving God would create such a wonderful gift for His creatures, a gift that is a reflection of the love God enjoys in the Trinity with the Son and the Holy Spirit.

From the beginning of time, God intended sexual relations to be good. In fact, according to the account in Genesis, He intended for sexual intimacy to be very good, pleasurable, and beautiful. It was designed to be a passionate and pure expression of love between a man and a woman who are joined in a lifelong, covenantal commitment. Reflecting something of the mystery of our intimate relationship with God, sexual intercourse expresses our ultimate vulnerability, commitment, and connection with our spouse. Whatever happens between a married couple that has reached a point of understanding and openness, where they can share their most intimate feelings and desires and seek with joy to satisfy each other is proper. We needn't suggest what they should or shouldn't do. We do need, however, to encourage them to build their relationship in a stable, loving, and unselfish manner. Marital relationships are not only the means by which the future of the human race is ensured, they are also the means by which the bonds of family and community are preserved. Individuals who have a healthy, monogamous sex life generally have more emotional, psychological, and financial stability as well. The children of active, faithful parents generally have a more positive outlook on life. Proper sex brings happiness! Improper sex brings misery. Such a precious gift is not to be taken lightly.

One of the more influential thinkers during the waning days of the Roman Empire, Clement of Alexandria, argued that "pure, protected, and passionate marriage between one man and one woman is the only possible environment in which the full potential for sexual pleasure, sexual satisfaction, and sexual fulfillment may actually be had." Tragically, for many people, sex has become a substitute for love. Although sex is a beautiful expression between two people who are committed to one another and therefore one in body, mind, spirit, and emotion, it was never intended to become an end in itself. Sex is an expression of love, not a substitute for love. We often wrongly refer to sexual relations as "making love." But love goes far beyond the act of sexual intimacy.

The physiology of sexual relations is more than a little obvious. Any discussion, therefore, about sexual orientation and desire is rather disingenuous. All moral arguments aside, the

147

basic physiology of homosexuality ought to be evidence enough of its perversity. It defies reason how otherwise rational people can defend it as simply a lifestyle decision—one of several equal and natural options. What God intended as the ultimate expression of love becomes, in many instances, an outlet of the most profound self-hatred and exploitation.

Sexual Intimacy as a Spiritual Battleground
Why all the uproar in our society over sex? Because we all know, without being told, that our sexuality is central to our humanity. Beyond its obvious importance for procreation, sex embodies our deepest desires for intimacy with and knowledge of our spouse as well as our Creator. It only makes sense that the enemy—the forces of darkness—would focus their attack on that which is most central to who we are as human beings created in the image of God.

148   In the fallenness of our humanity, the precious gift of sexuality can become a tool of the enemy. When broken and used inappropriately, this powerful connection between men and women can inflict great harm. We must safeguard this indescribable gift with its marvelous creative potential, or else its harmful and overwhelming potential can destroy lives, relationships, and families, as well as undermine the well-being of individuals and nations. Just as freedom's survival depends on the responsible actions of a nation's citizens, so too does sexual liberty require responsibility, restraint, and personal commitment. Sadly, in our society, this priceless treasure has largely been stolen from the carefully protected shrine of committed, responsible, and unselfish service.

Hugh Hefner's playboy philosophy—which unfortunately has met with great public acceptance—advocates sexual freedom as a license for lust-controlled living. However, the attempt to justify selfish sexual gratification, making it an ultimate pursuit for many people, leads to sexual addiction or the abuse of sex by those caught in the web of deceit. Thus, the modern erosion of sexual morality has opened a Pandora's box of social, cultural, and personal ills. Families have been devastated. Children have been defiled. Crime statistics have skyrocketed, along with rates of unwanted pregnancies, sexually transmitted diseases (including AIDS), abortion, rape, and pornography.

With the emerging technology of the Internet, hard-core pornography and illicit—and often illegal—images are available on demand anywhere a computer is found. Wives have caught husbands browsing perverse sites; vast collections of porn have been found on pastors' hard drives, employees have been summarily dismissed for violating "acceptable usage policies"; and children have found themselves exposed to a bizarre, often frightening, underworld of sexual depravity. The effect of pornography and its easy access is creating relationship problems that demand the serious and compassionate focus of all churches, religious leaders, and counselors. Porn has "gone mainstream" and upscale, presenting Hollywood's best in all their seductive power. Millions are being taken captive, even within the Christian church and its leadership. About 90 percent of the participants at Promise Keepers' men's conferences, most of whom were regular church attenders, said they were adversely affected by pornography.

Many individuals, both men and women, feel trapped by such personal shame that they seldom seek help. Unless the community of compassion and those claiming a relationship with Christ meet this challenge head-on, there is little hope for recovery on the part of these victims. If you or someone you know needs help with overcoming sexual addiction or other sexual sin, I suggest you visit the Web site of Pure Life Minis-

149

tries (www.purelifeministries.org) or Heart to Heart (www.intimatematters.com). These organizations and others with similar goals can help you get onto the road to recovery and restoration. Many local churches also offer counseling and pastoral care.

Renewing Our Commitment to Purity

Sex within the boundaries set by God is healthy, invigorating, and joyous. Outside those bounds, it becomes twisted, manipulative, and dirty. The marriage bed is the source of liberating happiness. Promiscuity, on the other hand—whether heterosexual or homosexual—is the source of humiliating exploitation. It always has been. Sex outside of God's intended context is always destructive. Just ask any man who has lost his wife because of his infidelity. Ask the woman who is dying of AIDS. Ask the scarred adult who was molested as a child. Ask the children who are growing up with one parent in the home because of the other's promiscuity. Nearly every indicator of civility in society is in some way undermined by sexual promiscuity—or what some modern commentators prefer to call "sexual liberation." As it turns out, the age-old traditions of faithfulness, honesty, purity, and integrity became traditions for a very good reason: they ensure that the good and true and beautiful remain good and true and beautiful.

This marvelous treasure with its wonderfully sublime potential obligates us to be prudent. The temptation to violate God's purpose and design is too great without the safeguards of self-control, discipline, and wisdom. We've already seen too many lives destroyed, relationships shattered, and families split in our nation. If our marriages, our families, and our nation are to survive, we must renew our commitment to purity, virtue, righteousness, and modesty.

CHAPTER TEN

There is no other place where the human spirit can be so nurtured as to prosper spiritually, intellectually, and temporally, than in the bosom of the family's rightful relation.
JOHN CHRYSOSTOM (347–407)

The family is the only means by which real and substantial change for good might truly be effected.
JAMES STUART (1849–1901)

The longing for home is woven into the fabric of our lives and is profoundly affected by our inescapable connection to places, persons, and principles: the incremental parts of community. **JONATHAN JELLISTON (1891–1977)**

Strong Families Are the Cornerstone of Society

When families break down, so do people. We must be
diligent to keep our families solid and strong.

I grew up without a father—except for a brief period early in my life when I lived in the foster care of the Reverend and Mrs. Hale. During those years, I saw what living with a caring mother and father could be. I knew I was loved. I felt a sense of security.

Although I lived with the Hales for a fairly short time, their family had a profound impact on me, and I determined that I would someday have a stable family of my own. I overcame rejection, poverty, and extreme circumstances to marry the most awesome woman and raise three children, including our adopted son. Our kids have been some of the greatest sources of joy in our lives and have provided Betty and me with a sense of personal achievement and success. Now that they're grown and have families of their own, I can say that I feel honored to know these great people.

As our children grew up, they witnessed the sad home situations of their peers and saw the problems that arose from dysfunctional families. At some point in their young adult years, they each said to us in their own words, "Mom and Dad, we want what you gave us: a family and a home." And they pursued their goals with diligence and resolve. Betty and I are inspired by our children's love for their spouses and their dedication to parenting their children with love. Parents who have had similar experiences would no doubt agree that there are few greater joys in this life.

What is a family? When God created humans, He made them male and female. He gave them the ability to procreate and told them to populate the earth. Thus, the first family emerged.

The family starts with a man and woman coming together in marriage, a lifelong commitment to live in love and unity. A family grows when this union produces precious children. The parent-child bond enables children to grow up in a stable, secure environment, providing them with the basis for a positive, productive life.

Nothing can replace the family. Government services can't replace a mother and father's love and nurture. Social services can't replace a sibling's support and devotion. Small groups can't replace a family's loyalty and comfort. A family is a one-of-a-kind relationship.

The longing and need for family connection is woven into the fabric of the life of every man, woman, and child. We were created to be relational beings, to find a sense of belonging in our primary relationships: husband to wife, parent to child, brother to sister.

Unfortunately, the institution of the family is under siege in our society. The prevalence of divorce, the incidence of babies born out of wedlock, and the natural consequences of disease and disaster have forced many parents and grandparents to raise children in less than ideal circumstances. When I was placed in a temporary foster home, it was family to my foster parents and me. It was also family when my mother took me into a dysfunctional home with a stepfather. I later lived alone with my mother in another family arrangement before my alcoholic birth father reentered our lives, producing a form of family that was hell on earth. Although none of these situations would qualify as a model, they all represent family circumstances that many people endure today.

We must find ways to support and offer encouragement to single-parent families and to those who are struggling to provide stable homes for their children. And we must work together as a community to solve the underlying problems. Families—fathers and mothers, brothers and sisters, aunts and uncles and cousins, grandparents and grandchildren—are the cornerstone of society. Amid the pressures and problems of life, the family unit has always been recognized as the glue that holds society together. When the family begins to break down, the rest of society disintegrates along with it.

The Value of Families

What makes the family so valuable? At its best, the family is the place of nurture, protection, support, and encouragement necessary to successfully navigate the hazards of daily life. In the midst of our homes, we can know and be known. We can taste the joys and sorrows of genuine intimacy. We can gain a vision of life that is sober and sure. We can be bolstered by a family's love. We can be strengthened by its confidence. We can be emboldened by its legacy. And we can be stabilized by its objectivity. Everyone desperately needs the kind of perspective that comes from living with a close-knit family.

The family is a safe place for children to explore who they are as they probe their intellectual, emotional, physical, and spiritual dimensions. In the context of a family's unwavering love, children test out their personalities and learn relationship skills. They explore their gifts and interests.

The home is a child's first classroom. In the natural interaction with parents and siblings, children learn about love, security, and play. They learn that actions have consequences, both positive and negative. For centuries, people have viewed the home as the center of religious education. The Old Testament instructs parents: "And you must love the Lord your God with all your heart, all your soul, and all your strength. And you must commit yourselves wholeheartedly to these commands I am giving you today. Repeat them again and again to your children. Talk about them when you are at home and when you are away on a journey, when you are lying down and when you are getting up again."[1]

Parents are not only their children's first teachers but also their first mentors and models. Most of us have felt the satisfaction of watching our children emulate our positive traits, but we also know the embarrassment of watching our children imitate our selfishness or impatience. In the context of family life, parents have unparalleled opportunities to practice what they preach and live out their beliefs.

The home is an incubator for sound values. It reinforces the principles of authority, structure, obedience, and selflessness. In the nurturing environment of the family, children learn right from wrong, the need for telling the truth, the joy of being forgiven, and the strength that comes from being loved unconditionally.

Let me say here that children *must* have direction, which in many ways comes through appropriate discipline. Unfortunately, the rise in reported incidents of child abuse has caused a backlash against physical discipline. But when physical discipline is applied in love (and never in anger), it is very effective and establishes the boundaries that children need in order to feel fully secure.

A healthy, stable family life provides us with a genuine social security. Those who know us best and love us most will always be our greatest resource in times of trouble. Because family members share with us a common sense of destiny and a bond of intimacy, we can—and we will—rush to one another's sides when needed. Most parents, without thinking twice about it, would willingly risk their lives in order to save one of their children. While in most circumstances this human act would be regarded as heroic, for parents it is only ordinary.

Many other cultures share our vision that the family is one of society's most precious resources. In fact, some cultures value the family so highly that multiple generations live together, and adult children would never consider moving away from their extended family.

Threats to the Stability of the Family
Most cultures also agree that when the family unit is threatened, the results are catastrophic. When families break down, so do people.

Today's families face many pressures. We face the normal stresses of work and financial obligations. But we face unique stresses as well: time pressure, fast-paced living, information explosion, decision stress, dizzying opportunities that result from our relative wealth, and separation caused by our mobility, to name just a few. Many families echo the lament of a couple I talked with recently: "The hardest thing for our family is dealing with the disruption caused by keeping up with everybody's activity schedule. The two of us have church committee meetings three nights a month plus our small-group meetings once a week. Add to that our teenagers' sports, choir, and youth-group activities, and we barely have a meal together during the week. Our youngest child has just signed up for a soccer program, and we are dreading the consequences. Something has to give—and we don't want it to be our family. All of these are good things, but we sometimes feel that we don't have any time or energy left for other things that really matter to us." Many of us can empathize with this couple.

However, perhaps the two greatest threats to the stability of the family are the brokenness that results from divorce and the devaluation of the family.

Fractured Families

No couple begins a marriage with the intention of getting a divorce. Most people agree that divorce puts family relationships in danger. But divorce happens. Infidelity, abuse, and addictions often lead to a breakup of a marriage. And the results? Brokenness, grief, anger, hurt, loneliness, added financial pressure, added time pressure, and more.

Despite what many couples think, children always suffer as a result of the divorce of their parents. In the book *The Unexpected Legacy of Divorce,* social science researcher Judith Wallerstein and her coauthors conclude that the effects of divorce on children are far more serious than we thought a decade ago. Wallerstein finds that the children of divorce suffer in significant ways: missing role models of a healthy marriage partnership; prolonged adolescence; more at-risk behavior, including drug and alcohol use as well as earlier sexual experimentation; fewer opportunities because of financial pressures; difficulty blending in to stepfamilies if parents remarry; less social competence.[2]

I have heard several young adults express hesitance about getting married because of what they experienced after their parents divorced. One twenty-six-year-old said it this way: "I really love the man I'm dating right now, and I know he loves me, too. But frankly, I'm scared. My parents have no idea of the damage they did to my siblings and me when they divorced a decade ago, but I know I will never put children through that hell. I'm almost convinced not to get married if that's what it would take to avoid hurting children the way my parents hurt us." Pretty sobering.

Devaluation of the Family

The second major threat to stable families is what I call the devaluation of the family, and I see it happening in two arenas: in the media and in the attempt to redefine the family.

If you were to watch any six prime-time sitcoms on television, you probably wouldn't find a healthy marriage relationship portrayed. Couples on television fight with each other, deceive each another, and demean each other. Infidelity is the norm—for parents and children. We are supposed to laugh, and many do. Movies often offer even worse fare, complete with profanities, obscenities, and scandalous visual detail.

Where are our children finding their role models for healthy marriages and family life? If more than 40 percent of first marriages and 60 percent of remarriages in our country end in divorce, the number of healthy models is dwindling.[3] And the media are certainly not helping.

Significant books also have devalued marriage and family life. Betty Friedan's 1960s blockbuster *The Feminine Mystique* disparaged women who chose to invest in their homes and marginalized the family as a barbaric institution of oppression. Friedan's rhetoric contributed significantly to the editorial profile of virtually all the women's magazines during the succeeding decades, from *Cosmopolitan, Mirabella, Ms.* and *Vogue* to *Ladies' Home Journal, Good Housekeeping, Family Circle,* and *Redbook.*

In an extension of the thinking begun in the 1980s, social scientists are attempting to redefine the family, trivializing the nuclear family as the bedrock of society. According to sociologist and educator Judith Stacey, "Family sociologists should take the lead in burying the ideology of the nuclear family and in rebuilding a social environment in which diverse family forms can sustain themselves with dignity and mutual respect."[4] She boldly advocates rewriting the concept of "family."

In his book *The New Absolutes*, William D. Watkins accurately observes: "The new American family . . . doesn't need parents. It doesn't require children. Marriage is optional, too. Family is whatever you want to call it, whatever you come home to. This is the norm we are supposed to accept. This is the emerging absolute. This is decadent Rome reborn."[5]

The family has been redefined in our society as someone you come home to or any grouping of two or more individuals with or without children. Live-in couples and same-sex marriages with children can be called "family." While these arrangements may have a level of commitment, affection, and harmony, they can never replace the nuclear family unit.

Certainly, we can live as a family in churches or communities. We can have a family spirit in the workplace, where there is harmony, unity, and the same purpose—but this is not "family" in the true sense of the word. If we move away from the foundation of the nuclear family as it has been preserved since the beginning of humanity, we are building our houses on sand, and they will not stand.

Turning the Tide

How can we undergird the family, making it once again a strong foundation of our society? Start with your own family. If you are a parent, remember that although other adults will have an impact on your children's growth and development, no one else can be their father or mother. You have a singular, unique role to fill. Make your family environment as safe and nurturing as you can. If you are a grandparent, realize that your influence is not over just because your children are grown and have children of their own. Invest in your children's marriages and nurture your grandchildren. Parents and grandparents, remember that you are a mirror, a model, and a mentor.

You are a mirror. Your marriage represents not only the love you and your spouse have for each other but also something far greater. The New Testament tells us that the relationship between a husband and wife is a mirror of the lavish love Christ has for His bride, the Church.[6] Every time you are faithful, you mirror God's faithfulness to his people. Every time you are gracious, you mirror God's grace to us. Seeing yourself as that mirror can inspire you to take your relationship seriously. Your Christlike marriage will have a stabilizing effect on your own family as well as on the families in your sphere of influence.

You are a model. I did not learn how to be a father by observing my own dad. And apart from the few years during my childhood when Reverend Hale was my foster father, I didn't have a consistent example of fatherhood in my life. It was only by the grace of God that I learned how to be the husband and father that my family needed. I diligently sought God's direction, and He granted me insight and wisdom that produced some very favorable results. Words cannot convey the joy I felt when one of my daughters, in a Father's Day card she sent a few years ago, affirmed the efforts I had made to set a good example while she was growing up. She said, in part,

> I never desired to walk away from God and the values you taught, because I saw them as real and the true joy in a

relationship with Him by your example. I also knew that as humans we do fail, but God is so gracious! You never made me think you were perfect—which made it easier to share my failures with ya'll and grow from them! So, thank you! I love you very much.

Educators tell us that we learn far more effectively when we see something demonstrated than when we are merely told how to do it. Your children need to *see* what it looks like to live an upright and godly life. You can tell people that your family is important, but does the way you live your life support what you say? You can tell your children and grandchildren to respect others, but do they see you modeling respect for others? You can tell your children and grandchildren that they need to tell the truth and own up to their personal failings, but do you confess your offenses to them, asking for their forgiveness? As parents and grandparents, we have an invaluable opportunity to show the people around us what a strong marriage and family looks like. And it's not only our own families who are watching. Remember the twenty-six-year-old woman who is afraid to marry? She—and dozens like her—may be watching you, too.

You are a mentor. Be willing to move beyond just modeling a healthy marriage and family. If your children are married, they may want to know more about the behind-the-scenes reality of your marriage and what makes it work. Be vulnerable with them, willing to discuss your discouragements and joys, temptations and victories. Allow God to use the wealth of your years to be a positive resource to guide your adult children in their marriages.

Then move beyond your family to people who need the support and encouragement your marriage and family can give. Extend your ability to mirror, model, and mentor to your com-

161

munity. Be especially sensitive to the needs of people who come from fractured families. Rather than clucking your tongues about how awful divorce or abuse or infidelity is, get to work supporting others in their marriages.

The divorce statistics suggest that many young people who marry today are the children of divorce. Their parents did not give them positive marriage models, but many of these young couples are open to learning from older husbands and wives who have enduring, vibrant marriages and families. Be open to becoming a marriage-mentor couple for a younger couple in your church or community. Invest in their relationship. Invite them into your home.

Men, you are in regular contact with other men who face sexual temptation. What can you do to help them stay faithful and pure? Women, how can you model purity and modesty and encourage other women to stay modest and pure?

We all know children whose fathers have abandoned them. Dads, invite these children into your family's life. Allow them to feel your love and care and protection.

Consider becoming a foster family or adoptive family. I owe incalculable thanks to the foster parents who looked after me and gave me the opportunity to grow. In fact, it was my foster mother, Mrs. Hale, who encouraged me to go forward at Memorial Baptist Church in Pasadena, Texas, and give my heart to Jesus when I was a teenager. She even walked the aisle with me to lend her support.

As I witnessed firsthand while growing up, single parents face tremendous stresses. Consider coming alongside a single parent you know and providing whatever support you can—financial, emotional, and spiritual as well as the physical help of assisting with household chores, such as repairs. Again, your own family is one of your most precious resources. Invite single-parent families to be a part of your family, sharing your outings and celebrations with them.

If you know people who have been or are being abused, commit to walking with them on their journey to protection and healing. Help find support groups or professional help for people who have been wounded by verbal, physical, or sexual abuse.

Everyone needs these essential benefits, but the poor and the oppressed particularly need them. A full 75 percent of men, women, and children who live below the poverty line in this country live in broken homes.[7] If your church does not have a program to reach out to the poor, join the efforts of the Salvation Army or another social service agency that compassionately works to restore men and women to wholeness. Find an effective outreach to the suffering, and support it financially and with your time, if possible.

If the movement to redefine the family upsets you, become involved in the issues. Become knowledgeable about what people who oppose the nuclear family are saying, and then engage in the dialogue. Become an advocate for the family socially and politically.

No culture, society, or civilization has ever survived—much less prospered—when the family was not honored, protected, and firmly established as the basis of human relations. Think of all the communal endeavors, the ideological trials, and social experiments that have attempted to replace the family with some new and efficient alternative. Each has failed—and failed miserably.

We will find no replacement for the family. There *is* no substitute. There *is* no alternative. The family always will be the cornerstone of society. We must be diligent to keep that cornerstone solid and strong.

CHAPTER ELEVEN

To recognize and celebrate the differences among us is not only true sanity, it is true compassion. We are equal only in this: our opportunity to see that our innate inequalities never stand in the way of our progress toward justice, happiness, and liberty. **THEODORE ROOSEVELT (1858–1919)**

Not all beings are equal. . . . One need only visit a junior high school gym class, sample the range of college entrance examinations, taste your mother-in-law's cooking, or witness the madness of a Friday evening commute on a modern motorway to see such disparities. **HILAIRE BELLOC (1870–1953)**

Discrimination is evil and destructive because it is rooted in prejudice but discernment is just and constructive because it is rooted in compassion—to treat everyone exactly the same is as cruel as arbitrarily treating everyone entirely differently. **BOOKER T. WASHINGTON (1856–1915)**

11

Equality Is
Not Sameness

The cause of justice is made all the more essential by our differences in aptitude, motivation, and ability.

Betty and I have eleven beautiful grandchildren. We love them all dearly and equally, but that doesn't mean they are all the same. It doesn't take more than a glance to see that they are different ages and sizes and that they don't all have the same eye color, hair color, or complexion. Also, some are athletic and competitive, whereas others are more musically and artistically inclined. Some share the same interests but not the same abilities. Some are very focused; others seem continually distracted. Some seek out the company of others, whereas others enjoy being alone. Despite their many differences, all eleven kids have at least one thing in common: Papaw wouldn't trade a single one of them for anything.

Every parent and grandparent understands the truth of what I'm saying. We know that all of our children and grandchildren are beautiful and special, but we do not deny the distinct differences among them. To force an artificial "equality" on them would be to quell their natural gifts and abilities. In order to help them reach their full potential, they must be encouraged and challenged to become the individuals they are capable of being. If we understand that equality is not sameness as it pertains to our children and grandchildren, why can't we extend the same principle to guide our understanding of other people in our nation and around the world?

Through the years, there has been much misapplication of that greatly admired phrase in our Declaration of Independence: "All men are created equal." Does that mean we've all been blessed with the athletic ability of a Tiger Woods, Michael Jordan, or Mark McGwire? Does it mean that we all have the mental genius of an Albert Einstein or the ingenuity of a Thomas Edison? Of course not. All men are *not* created equal when it comes to interests, aptitudes, abilities, strengths, weaknesses, opportunities, or privileges—nor would we want them to be. It takes all kinds to make our world such a beautiful, diverse, and interesting place.

Equal Rights, Not Equal Outcomes

Our nation's founders defined what they meant by "equality" when they said that we are all "endowed by [our] Creator with certain unalienable rights." The point they were trying to emphasize was *equal rights under the law,* not equal outcomes for every individual. And notice that the three rights they enumerated as examples were the rights to life, liberty, and the *pursuit* of happiness. Happiness is not a guaranteed right, and even our right to pursue it implies some *action* and *effort* on our part. Any attempt, therefore, to legislate equality of outcomes or to impose a one-size-fits-all standard on society is misguided and simply will not work. It should be obvious that the differences between people and the unequal distribution of abilities, motivation, and aptitudes make it unlikely that the playing field will ever truly be "leveled." But that's no excuse for people not achieving their maximum potential. As a nation, we should be doing everything we can to remove barriers that hold people back, but it will always be the responsibility of the individual to make the most of his or her opportunities. I endured tough circumstances as a child, but I saw my situation as a challenge to overcome, not an excuse for not working to better myself. There will always be obstacles to freedom, success, and advancement, but therein lies the challenge—and the opportunity.

The Legacy of Booker T. Washington

As the first great leader to work for the civil rights of all Americans, Booker T. Washington emphasized the importance of education, hard work, and self-discipline for the advancement of every man or woman, regardless of race. He never tried to overlook the differences between people. He did not expect to make everyone the same, but he wanted to remove unnecessary obstacles—such as prejudice, lack of education, and lack of cooperation between the races—so that everyone would have an opportunity for advancement and success.

A remarkable bronze sculpture of Washington stands in the center of the Tuskegee University campus in southern Alabama. Sculptor Charles Keck portrays him as a stately, dignified figure standing with eyes set on the horizon and one hand extended toward the future. With his other hand, he is pulling back a thick veil from the brow of a young man crouched at his side. The younger man is obviously poor—he is only half-clothed, in stark contrast to Washington's dapper appearance—and is sitting upon the symbols of his labor, an anvil and a plow. But he, too, is gazing off into the distance while grasping a massive academic textbook. The inscription beneath this arresting image says, "He lifted the veil of ignorance from his people and pointed the way to progress through education and industry."[1]

The monument is a perfect tribute to the man. Although Washington's life story—his long and difficult journey up from the obscurity of slavery to the heights of national influence and renown—is a remarkable testimony of individual achievement and personal sacrifice, his greatest legacy was not in what he accomplished for himself, but in what he helped thousands of others—both black and white—to accomplish.

Born in 1856 on a small tobacco plantation in Franklin County, Virginia, Washington spent his first nine years in slavery and abject poverty. Even after emancipation, his family faced a meager existence. When Washington was sixteen, he gained admission to the Hampton Institute—one of the first schools established for former slaves. He worked full-time as a janitor in order to pay his tuition yet was able to graduate with honors in only three years. After graduation, he returned to his family and taught in a local grammar school. Before long, he returned to Hampton as an instructor and later became assistant to the president. When the state of Alabama contacted Hampton about the possibility of establishing a similar college, Washington was recommended for the job. On July 4, 1881, at the age of twenty-five, he founded the Tuskegee Institute.

169

In the early days, he faced enormous obstacles: no money, no faculty, no campus, no land, and no students. He had nothing except Alabama's resolution to launch the school and his own determination to raise a generation of leaders from the ruins of the postwar South and the legacy of slavery. Eventually, he was able to instill his philosophy of competence and community-mindedness in thousands of students, many of whom went on to make a substantive difference in the welfare of African-American families, churches, neighborhoods, and businesses. By the time Washington died in 1915, the Tuskegee Institute had grown to encompass a 2,000-acre campus of 107 buildings with more than 1,500 students and nearly 200 faculty members.

Boldly and wisely, Booker T. Washington built his legacy on the basic truth that all human beings "are endowed by our Creator with certain unalienable rights." Because of his firm conviction that the founding principles of freedom ought to be applied to everyone in our nation, he became a prominent spokesman for the plight of former slaves. In 1895, when he was asked to speak at the Cotton States and International Exposition, his remarks received wide attention throughout the country, galvanizing public opinion in favor of black self-improvement:

> In all things that are purely social we can be as separate as the fingers, yet one as the hand in all things essential to mutual progress. There is no defense or security for any of us except in the highest intelligence and development of all. If anywhere there are efforts tending to curtail the fullest growth of the Negro, let these efforts be turned into stimulating, encouraging, and making him the most useful and intelligent citizen. Effort or means so invested will pay a thousand percent interest. These efforts will be twice blessed—blessing him that gives and him that takes. There is no escape through law of man or God from the inevitable: The laws of changeless justice bind oppressor with oppressed; and close as sin and suffering joined, we march to fate abreast.[2]

Whether we care to admit it or not, said Washington, we're all in this together—and life would be much better for everyone if we would look out for the best interests of all our citizens.

The Advantages of Diversity

Booker T. Washington saw advantages rather than liabilities in the great diversity of the United States. Consequently, he was able to lay the philosophical groundwork for a workable civil rights reform movement that rested not on utopian ideals but was grounded in the hard-edged reality of practical, everyday living. No one would claim, for example, that Washington and the young scholar with whom he is depicted in the bronze sculpture were equally gifted in vision, ambition, or personality. Although both men deserved equal protection under the law and the right to life, liberty, and the pursuit of happiness, we wouldn't expect the outcome of their pursuits to be exactly the same. It would seem that this principle would be self-evident, but nevertheless, over the past several decades, ongoing attempts have been made in our country to "level the playing field" through taxation, legislation, and government programs to compensate for the disadvantages that some people face. As well-intentioned as these efforts have been, many of these programs have not accomplished their intended purpose. We can pass laws to limit certain behaviors and guard against overt discrimination, but we cannot legislate equality. True equality is only possible through a fundamental change in the human heart, which can only happen by surrendering our lives to Jesus Christ. In order for us to treat all people as Jesus would have us do, we must see people through the eyes of Christ.

In our society, as much as we might talk about "balancing the scales" and "achieving parity" as desirable outcomes, in the practical realm of everyday life, we're much more likely to favor the imbalances—and the strengths—inherent in diversity. In professional sports, for example, there is talk about wanting "parity" between teams—but what does every coach and general manager try to do? They try to stock their rosters with play-

171

ers who have a distinct advantage over any of their competitors. Any coach who would attempt to fill positions on the field without exercising discernment or discretion about his players' abilities, aptitudes, and attitudes would likely be in for a very long and difficult season. A wise and discerning coach evaluates his players' relative strengths and weaknesses and devises a game plan to optimize his team's chances of winning. So, for example, in the NBA, when teams play the Los Angeles Lakers, they don't try to level the playing field by insisting that Shaquille O'Neal not play—because of how unfair it would be to allow such a massive, agile, and talented athlete to offset the balance of the game. Instead, many coaches devise double-teaming strategies, or instruct their players to intentionally foul O'Neal (a notoriously erratic free-throw shooter), or otherwise work to disrupt his game, while at the same time looking for ways to create mismatches with their own players in order to score more points.

In the same way that a coach might level the playing field by inspiring his team to elevate their intensity and their focus and their determination to overcome, we ought to encourage those in our society who face difficult challenges not to use their circumstances as an excuse but to elevate their ambition, desire, and dedication to climb out of the pit of despair. I believe that's what Booker T. Washington did.

Equal Opportunity in America

Despite our high ideals as a nation, we have not always done a good job of protecting equality of rights in America. The history of the various amendments to the Constitution—which reflect increasingly specific protections for people of different races and gender—shows that we still have some work to do to ensure equal protection under the law. Almost fifty years after the death of Booker T. Washington, and a century after the Emancipation

Proclamation was issued, the 1963 March on Washington once again brought the issue of civil rights to the forefront in our society. Far larger than any previous demonstration for any other cause, the march had an obvious and immediate impact, both on the passage of civil rights legislation and on nationwide public opinion. It illustrated the power of mass appeal and inspired imitators in other social movements.

By midday on the day of the march, more than 200,000 people had gathered near the Washington Monument. It was a diverse crowd—black and white, rich and poor, young and old. Despite fears that had prompted extraordinary precautions—including executive orders authorizing military intervention in the case of rioting—the marchers walked peacefully to the Lincoln Memorial.

Televised live to an audience of millions, the march provided a number of dramatic moments, but the most memorable was Dr. Martin Luther King Jr.'s stirring "I Have a Dream" speech. Dr. King, who was introduced as "the moral leader of our nation," electrified the crowd with his passionate and poetic assertion that the audience's great diversity was not a hindrance to full and just freedom. It was not an obstacle to equality of opportunity, access, and treatment. Instead, it was liberty's most obvious inducement. Dr. King was able to see the inherent strength in our differences. He was able to envision America's diversity of strengths and weaknesses, gifts and faults, and prizes and defects all working together for good.

By all accounts, the March on Washington was a success—but it was only the beginning of a long and arduous process. Many more battles would be fought in the days ahead. Many of those battles must still be fought, but the hope of equal opportunity in the midst of a distinctly unequal world was raised for us all.

Diversity Was God's Idea

When we come to realize that our differences are valuable, we begin to see how diversity can be a force for good in the world. The apostle Paul explained the natural strength of diverse parts working together for a common purpose in his discussion of spiritual gifts in the fledgling Church. Writing to the Church in Corinth, he said,

> The body has many different parts, not just one part. If the foot says, "I am not a part of the body because I am not a hand," that does not make it any less a part of the body. And if the ear says, "I am not part of the body because I am only an ear and not an eye," would that make it any less a part of the body? Suppose the whole body were an eye—then how would you hear? Or if your whole body were just one big ear, how could you smell anything?
>
> But God made our bodies with many parts, and he has put each part just where he wants it. What a strange thing a body would be if it had only one part! Yes, there are many parts, but only one body. The eye can never say to the hand, "I don't need you." The head can't say to the feet, "I don't need you."
>
> In fact, some of the parts that seem weakest and least important are really the most necessary. And the parts we regard as less honorable are those we clothe with the greatest care. So we carefully protect from the eyes of others those parts that should not be seen, while other parts do not require this special care. So God has put the body together in such a way that extra honor and care are given to those parts that have less dignity. This makes for harmony among the members, so that all the members

care for each other equally. If one part suffers, all the parts suffer with it, and if one part is honored, all the parts are glad.[3]

The New Testament says we are "living stones" that God is using to build a spiritual house.[4] The idea of stones suggests unique shapes, sizes, and colors—not uniformly shaped bricks. The fireplace in my house is made of stones quarried from the rocky beds of mountain streams, and I like the fact that no two stones are the same. Even though Betty and I have lived in our home for more than twenty-five years, I never get tired of looking at the fireplace and admiring all the unique shapes, qualities, and colors of the stones.

I have been blessed to work with people all over the world, from different cultures, religions, and levels of prosperity. I've been amazed at the wonder of God's diverse creation. People are so different, yet every one of us expresses the character of God in unique and defined ways. Diversity was God's idea, which He incorporated into His creation of the earth and everything in it. And when we allow diversity to work for us, we can achieve unity in spite of our differences, we can tolerate distinctions in others, we can work together to accomplish what is good and right and true, and we can promote beauty, justice, and freedom.

When we as humans come along and try to make everything uniform—in our communities, denominations, political parties, and social movements—in a sense we're "stacking bricks," and in the process we overlook the distinctive beauty of what God created and intended for us. If we are to succeed—as a nation, a church, a community, or a family—we must recognize and respect our differences, learn to utilize our strengths, and overcome our weaknesses. Only when the "living stones" of our society learn to fit and function together will we be able to stay strong, coexist in peace, and fulfill the dream of freedom and opportunity.

The Greater Shall Serve the Lesser

How do we go about ensuring equal protection under the law and equal opportunity for all? We need to start by confronting the prejudice in our own hearts and in those around us that would keep us from extending the privileges of equality to everyone. The institution of government cannot achieve this, but we the people can. When we see all of the opportunities afforded us in America, it should inspire in us a greater appreciation for our freedom and motivate us not only to dedicate our lives to guarding these privileges, but also to developing the underprivileged in every possible way. Jesus said, "Much is required from those to whom much is given, and much more is required from those to whom much more is given."[5]

When those of us with greater privileges, greater advantages, greater resources, and greater opportunities offer the advantage of those resources to others less fortunate, in effect we extend equality to them. We need to do this in all areas. When we see others who are struggling and who have fewer opportunities for advancement, we ought to pour ourselves into trying to help them find more opportunity and achieve beyond their wildest dreams. Somewhere in our local communities, in our nation, and in the global community, we must unleash a spirit of harmony that says, "We're in this together, and I must build you up to make us both strong; I must work to help you overcome the limitations that are holding you down." Whether those limitations are due to poverty, prejudice, lack of opportunity, lack of education, or lack of resources, we must take responsibility for tearing down the walls of bondage and oppression.

Just because one person has a greater capacity for learning or a greater ability to succeed than someone else doesn't diminish the value or importance of the one less gifted. In fact, if we would really pay attention to what Jesus said about the greater serving the lesser, we would see our advantages as opportunities to serve the less fortunate.[6]

Jesus said that when we feed the hungry, offer a glass of water to someone who is thirsty, show hospitality to a stranger, clothe the needy, visit the sick and those in prison, it's the same as if we had offered that food, water, clothing, hospitality, and compassion directly to Him.[7] If people in the Church would apply the principle of serving the less fortunate with the same zeal that they use to defend their theological positions, if Churches competed to outserve each other instead of competing for new members, there wouldn't be so many hungry, thirsty, homeless, suffering people in the world. There wouldn't be such inequality in our society, because a service-oriented Church would eradicate it.

True justice—the principle of right action in conformity to truth—is the model for how we can deal with poverty issues in our country. It's the model for how we can deal with minority issues. Right action can only be sustained by right motives. We need to genuinely care about people who are in need—not as a political strategy to advance the agenda of our party, nor as a church-building strategy to get people to join our congregation—but because it's the right thing to do. In the book of Isaiah, God tells us how to overcome inequality and preserve the foundations of freedom and opportunity:

> Free those who are wrongly imprisoned and . . . stop
> oppressing those who work for you. Treat them fairly and
> give them what they earn. I want you to share your food

with the hungry and to welcome poor wanderers into your homes. Give clothes to those who need them, and do not hide from relatives who need your help.

If you do these things, your salvation will come like the dawn. Yes, your healing will come quickly. Your godliness will lead you forward, and the glory of the Lord will protect you from behind. Then when you call, the Lord will answer. "Yes, I am here," he will quickly reply.

Stop oppressing the helpless and stop making false accusations and spreading vicious rumors! Feed the hungry and help those in trouble. Then your light will shine out from the darkness, and the darkness around you will be as bright as day. The Lord will guide you continually, watering your life when you are dry and keeping you healthy, too. You will be like a well-watered garden, like an ever-flowing spring. Your children will rebuild the deserted ruins of your cities. Then you will be known as the people who rebuild their walls and cities.[8]

12
CHAPTER TWELVE

The most terrifying words in the English language are, "I'm from the government and I'm here to help."
RONALD REAGAN (1911–)

We have staked the whole future of American civilization, not upon the power of government, far from it. We have staked the future upon the capacity of each and every one of us to govern ourselves, to sustain ourselves, in accordance with the Ten Commandments of God.
JAMES MADISON (1751–1836)

I tell you true, liberty is the best of all things; never live beneath the noose of a servile halter.
WILLIAM WALLACE (1270–1305)

12

If Government Doesn't Serve, It Will Enslave

We must be vigilant to keep the blessings of government within their proper bounds lest they come to dominate the whole of our lives.

Government was never meant to save people. That's God's job. The government's role is to protect and preserve freedom so that people can live their lives freely and securely. Abraham Lincoln understood the importance of limiting government, as he expressed in the following excerpt from a letter he wrote to his brother in 1859:

> You cannot bring about prosperity by discouraging thrift.
> You cannot strengthen the weak by weakening the strong.
> You cannot help the wage earner by pulling down the wage payer.
> You cannot help the poor by destroying the rich.
> You cannot establish sound security on borrowed money.
> You cannot keep out of trouble by spending more than you earn.

> You cannot build character and courage by taking away
> man's initiative and independence.
> You cannot help man permanently by doing for them
> what they would and should do for themselves.[1]

Americans historically have shared a profound distrust of government's ability to solve society's problems. Although we recognize the need for a strong and active civil authority, it must operate within a strictly limited sphere. To paraphrase the great twentieth-century statesman Henry Cabot Lodge: If we fail to remember that government is only a tool suited for certain limited purposes, and if we allow the tool to begin to dictate what jobs we can and cannot do (and how), we will steadily forfeit our freedoms.

Most observers and serious students of history would openly agree that America is without a doubt the greatest nation the world has ever known. The freedom, opportunities, prosperity, and peacefulness that we enjoy are noted and envied all around the world. Let me ask you a question, though: Are you concerned about the level of poverty in our country and around the world? Are you satisfied with how we care for the fatherless, the homeless, and the hopeless in our society? Are you disturbed by the level of drug addiction in our nation or with the divorce rate? Are you happy with the way minorities still have to fight to be treated equally, even as thousands of illegal immigrants pour across our borders every year? I'm not! Somehow we must focus on solving these problems and not just cast them aside as though they were unimportant to the future of our country. But how?

As we look around at our world, we see much that is not perfect. There is pain, suffering, and heartache. Too often, we rush to the conclusion that our government should rise up and confront these problems head-on. Our government should make our lives better. But there's a problem: No government, by itself, can ever be the ultimate hope and provider. No government alone can ever solve the world's problems. In fact, there is really only one answer to the world's imperfections, and it is the true and living God, not government. Any community or nation that desires stability and peace must accept and commit itself to a source of supreme authority. However, any attempt to impose this system on its citizens, whether for religious or political purposes, will drastically limit freedom. So then, what is the purpose of government? Government should care about the people and should protect their freedom and their rights. But government can never take God's place. If we look to government primarily or exclusively to solve the world's problems, we will be bitterly disappointed time and time again.

In a sense, excessive government is a form of judgment through natural consequences on a population for their lack of compassion and personal responsibility, their indifference to the less fortunate, and their self-centered focus on individual achievement and personal comfort. Politicians will always step up to offer promises of assistance to those who have been neglected, if only for the purpose of gaining their political support. Even if elected officials are motivated by legitimate concern for the needy, if their involvement results in more laws being passed, their actions will still fail to provide effective solutions, because no amount of legislation can replace the genuine love and care that God can supply through the direct action of His people.

The Purpose of Government

Marxists believe that all people are subjects of the state; that all people are basically the same; and that individual freedom and expression is purposeless and should be discouraged. Sadly, this ideology still holds sway in some parts of the world, and we see similar tendencies in our own social and political systems that pit brother against brother, party against party, person against person, race against race. This is not what God intended for people, and we've got to see it stop. How? Simple—we must see people as God sees them, as creatures of eternal value and significance. The tendency to believe that people are valuable only as subjects of the state dissolves when people act in ways that honor God. Only through living as God intends can we hope to overcome the evils in our world. It is also only with God's help that we will find the strength to win our own personal battles.

How Does Change Occur?

Change—real, lasting change—is not going to come from the government. If we want to see our nation change, we will have to look someplace else. The only true hope for change lies in what I call the "Principle Equation": Our nation is ruled by constitutional principles that were put in place by principled men, and we can only preserve our freedoms and effect positive change if people choose to live according to those principles.

183

Politicians, with their programs and platitudes, will never accomplish lasting, positive change. It's not going to be done by arguing about special interests, pork-barrel legislation, and logrolling. Instead, we must have principled leadership that transcends party politics and special interests—leadership that puts the interests of people first in a spirit of love, compassion, and concern. Let's not continually discuss conservatives and liberals, Democrats and Republicans—principled leadership can come from both sides of the aisle—let's talk about what's right. And let's base our leadership on the absolutes: principles that have stood—and will stand—the test of time.

Ultimately, however, even leadership that is solidly based on the absolutes will not be able to effect change on its own. We have a government of the people, by the people, and for the people, and it's only *by* the people that change for the better will occur. It's going to take a foundation of genuine love. As long as we pursue our own selfish interests, radical change is not going to happen. Only when we put the interests of others above our own will we have the kind of impact we desire. It's going to take open and honest debate, not filtered through the agenda of some media company—whether conservative or liberal, it doesn't matter. We must foster debate that allows for ideas to be fairly and completely communicated so that we the people can decide between what is good and what is better, between what is right and what is wrong, between what is helpful and what is unhelpful, between what is effective for change and what is a waste of time and energy.

184

The Place of Government

What, then, is the place of government? Surely no reasonable person would suggest that a civilized nation could be improved by completely ridding itself of its leadership. To the contrary, such an action would certainly result in the collapse of that nation altogether. The Bible declares, "Whoever has no rule over his own spirit is like a city broken down, without walls."[2] Indeed, government plays an important role in any successful society. But government can be truly successful only when it does not attempt to overextend itself, to influence policies and events that lie outside its proper sphere. It is when governments overreach that they fail or become dangerous.

There is no question that governing the civic affairs of our society is important. When it is working at its best, government can help to "form a more perfect union, establish justice, insure domestic tranquility, provide for the common defense, promote the general welfare, and secure the blessings of liberty to ourselves and our posterity."[3] Government is one of the primary means by which we define our values and priorities as a people. It is a chief indicator of our moral resolve. It is a central feature of our aspiration for equality, justice, and goodness. It is a reflection of our moral principles and our community standards. But as important as government is, it is not all-important. It should never come to dominate our lives or concerns.

In its proper role, government is practically invisible. It quietly goes about its unobtrusive business so that we can go about ours. It serves us in such a way as to enable us to simply live our lives—caring for our families, building our careers, pursuing our interests, participating in our churches, and developing friendships in our communities and neighborhoods. And because as citizens we are occupied first and foremost with living our lives to the utmost, government finds its place on the periphery.

Senator Ted Kennedy once said, "The ballot box is the place where change begins in America."[4] I could not disagree more strongly! As George Will has argued, "There is hardly a page of American history that does not refute that insistence, so characteristic of the political class, on the primacy of politics in the making of history."[5] In fact, says Will, "Almost nothing is as important as almost everything in Washington is made to appear. And the importance of a Washington event is apt to be inversely proportional to the attention it receives."[6]

Does that mean we shouldn't bother to vote or try to pass good legislation? No, of course we should. But our goal in doing these important things is not to enable government to provide; it is to enable government to enable people.

How Government Is Perceived

According to political analyst E. J. Dionne, "Americans view politics with boredom and detachment. For most of us, politics is increasingly abstract, a spectator sport barely worth watching." He says that because the average voter "believes that politics will do little to improve his life or that of his community, he votes defensively," if at all.[7]

Recent surveys found that more than 54 percent of all Americans actually wanted less government and fewer taxes. They wanted less bureaucracy, less intrusion, and less spending. They wanted fiscal responsibility and legislative accountability. They wanted decentralization and deregulation. They wanted efficiency, not entitlements. They wanted principled leaders, not pork-barrel legislators.[8]

This apparent populist shift was more than just a pocketbook reaction to a recessionary economy. Not only did the majority of Americans express support for getting things like budgets, taxes, and appropriations in line, they also demonstrated widespread support for upholding strong and principled convictions on moral and social issues. A surprising 68 percent claimed to prefer "a government that encouraged traditional values."[9] Nearly 87 percent favored some kind of legal restrictions on abortion-on-demand.[10] An overwhelming 89 percent opposed relaxing the behavioral restrictions on homosexuals in the military. And some 62 percent opposed conferring on homosexuals preferential minority status.[11]

When asked to identify the most important issues facing the nation, "reducing taxes and government spending" was selected by more than a 2 to 1 margin over any other concern except "protecting Americans at home and abroad from terrorism."[12] Reinforcing "traditional family values" came in next—

followed closely by "promoting freedom and democracy" and "eliminating intrusive government regulations."[13]

That is not just a modern phenomenon; it has always been a fact of life. Many who live and die by the electoral sword may well be shocked to discover that most of today's grand and glorious headline-making political events will go down in history as a mere backdrop to the real drama of everyday activities. But it is rightly so. As much emphasis as the media and politicians place on campaigns, polls, and trends these days, most of us know full well that the lives and interests of our fellow workers, next door neighbors, close friends, and family members are far more important—just like they've always been.

Our Government Was Created to Serve, Not to Rule

As odd as it may seem, this kind of robust detachment from government is actually close to what the founders of our nation originally intended. They feared ongoing political passions and thus tried to construct a system that minimized the impact of factions, parties, and activists.[14] Citizens of the republic were expected to turn out at the polls to vote for men of good character and broad vision—and then pretty much forget about politics until the next election.[15]

Gouverneur Morris, who wrote the first draft of the Constitution and was instrumental in its acceptance, said, "The Constitution is not an instrument for government to restrain the people, it is an instrument for the people to restrain the government—lest it come to dominate our lives and interests."[16]

Similarly, Patrick Henry said, "Liberty necessitates the diminutization of political ambition and concern. Liberty necessitates concentration on other matters than mere civil governance. Rather, whatsoever things are true, whatsoever things are honest, whatsoever things are just, whatsoever things are pure, whatsoever things are lovely, whatsoever things are of good report; if there be any virtue, and if there be any praise, freemen must think on these things."[17]

Suspicious of professional politicians and unfettered lobbyists and special interests, the founders established a system of severe checks and balances designed to depoliticize the arena of government.[18]

Though there was disagreement between Federalists and Anti-Federalists about how much "energy" or "lack thereof" government ought to exercise, there was universal agreement about what was then called the "peripheral importance of institutional action to the actual liberties of daily life."[19]

Thus the founders worked together to ensure that the republican confederation of states was free from ideological or partisan strife.[20] They wanted to make sure that government stayed in its place. They wanted to make sure that it served so that it would never be tempted to enslave.

188

Although our government has not always stayed entirely in its place, for much of our history, American life has been marked by the distinct conviction that what goes on next door is of greater immediate concern than what goes on in Washington.

Ordinary People

One of the great lessons of history is simply that it is ordinary people—not kings and princes, not masters and tyrants—who ultimately determine the outcome of human events. It is laborers and workmen—plain folks, simple people—who change the course of history, because they are the stuff of which history is made. They are the ones who make the world go round. As G. K. Chesterton said, "The most extraordinary thing in the world is an ordinary man and an ordinary woman and their ordinary children."[21]

Ultimately, that is why government needs to serve us in our everyday pursuits rather than intrude on them. If it impedes us from focusing on the things that really matter—family and home, community and culture—then it ceases to benefit us. If government does not serve, it will enslave. This fact should inspire all the wonderful, ordinary people of our great nation to actively participate in the political process. Failure to do so is an invitation to a slave master to come and take citizens captive.

The Welfare Myth

One of the great fallacies of our time is that it is somehow the responsibility of the government to act as savior. Just look at the numbers of American citizens on welfare, receiving money from the government each month. The founders of the United States designed a limited government whose primary purpose was to protect and to serve the people. But over time we have allowed socialist ideas to creep into the equation, gradually skewing our view of government from protector to great and powerful provider. Dan Smoot, who founded the *Dan Smoot Report* in 1955 to document the truth about the American Constitution as a yardstick by which to measure liberty, described the limitations of government this way:

189

> Government cannot make men prosperous any more than it can make men good. Government cannot produce anything. It can merely seize and divide up what individuals produce. Government can give the people nothing which the government has not first taken away from them. And the amount which government doles back to the people or spends to promote their welfare is always less than what it takes because of the excessive cost of governmental administration.[22]

Looking unto the Hill

The preamble to the Constitution of the United States declares that one of the six reasons for establishing a constitution was to "promote the general Welfare." Mention the word *welfare* today, and most people would think of government-funded social programs. But that's not what the founders had in mind. By "welfare" they meant simply the well-being of the people. I doubt they could have imagined our present system, which taxes the citizenry to the point of bondage and strips people in need of their personal dignity and incentives.

In the Psalms, the Bible asks the rhetorical question: "I lift up my eyes to the hills—where does my help come from?"[23] Too many people today are lifting up their eyes to the Hill—as in Capitol Hill—instead of looking to God to supply their needs. The psalmist doesn't make the same mistake. Instead, he says, "My help comes from the Lord, the Maker of heaven and earth."[24] When we look to divine providence as our source, we will be moved with active compassion toward all who suffer, and every need will be addressed.

But isn't it the government's responsibility to provide for its citizens? Certainly the government should create an atmosphere of opportunity so that every individual has a shot at success. But success is never guaranteed. Government must do everything possible to give citizens an equal chance to achieve, but it cannot and should not guarantee the same outcome for everyone. The effectiveness of our political system is not proved by how many people are *on* welfare, but rather on how many have been moved *off* welfare and into productive employment. Extending our helping hands to those in need, rather than giving handouts, will bring about the kind of interaction and support required for people to rise above poverty and hardship.

I grew up in a dysfunctional family in a poor neighborhood.

But I was encouraged to believe it was possible to improve my lot in life. I was inspired to succeed and move beyond my miserable circumstances by others I saw who had done it. When I was given small opportunities, I worked hard to take advantage of them. I was never taught to sit back and wait for a government agency to take care of me. When I was twelve years old, I started working in a grocery store six days a week for a mere forty cents an hour—but I was not complaining. I was grateful for the opportunity, and I gave it all I had. After I had been there a year, the manager said to me, "Some day you can manage this store." A year later, I thought, *I can* own *this store*. I set my sights on the possibilities, and this attitude developed as I grew up. By the way, I lived in an area where only 10 to 20 percent of the population was white, but I never considered race an issue in our neighborhood or anywhere.

The Limits of Government

191

We must move beyond the mind-set that causes so many people to believe that somebody owes them something because of wrongs that were done in the past. If we focus on the failure of our predecessors, not only will we never advance, but the strength of our country will be dissipated. When we insist on reparations for the evils done by society, we cheat ourselves out of the potential for true restoration and repair.

I thought that President Bush made a classic statement in April 2002 when he addressed the Palestinian-Israeli conflict. He said the two sides cannot continue to feed their grievances and focus on all the reasons they are fighting. If they did, he said, they would miss the opportunity to resolve those grievances. Not that the grievances are not real—they are *very* real. But the focus must be on the opportunity to move beyond them.

When we consider the very real grievances held by certain

groups in our society, we don't in any way want to disregard or diminish those issues. Nevertheless, we must find ways to move past our differences to unite around principles and practices that will "promote the general welfare" of all our citizens and others around the world. Instead of forever looking back, can we instead look *forward* to a better and brighter future—together?

People ask me, "How do we do that?" I'll tell you: Draw a circle around where you're standing and get everything inside that circle right with God. Begin to pray. Begin to love your enemies. Begin to focus your energy on giving people—including yourself—the opportunity to achieve. Great things happen when we help remove the limitations on people and encourage them, as the apostle Paul said, to "[forget] what lies behind and [reach] forward to what lies ahead, . . . [to] press on toward the goal for the prize of the upward call of God in Christ Jesus."[25]

The Power of Government Can Be Dangerous

The reason for such caution is simply that government is, by its very nature, dangerously powerful. As George Washington warned, "Government is not reason, it is not eloquence—it is force." Likewise, journalist Joseph Sobran has written:

> The essence of government is force: whatever its end, its means is compulsion. Government forces people to do what they would not otherwise choose to do, or it forces them to refrain from doing what they would otherwise do. So, when we say, "Government should do *x*," we are really saying, "People should be forced to do *x*." It should be obvious that force should be used only for the most serious reasons, such as preventing and punishing violence. The frivolous, improper, or excessive use of force is wrong. We used to call it tyranny. Unfortunately, too many people

think that calling for the government to do x is merely a way of saying that x is desirable. And so we are increasingly forced to do things that are not genuine social duties but merely good ideas. The result is that the role of state coercion in our lives grows greater and greater.[26]

When government serves its proper role, it is a welcome hedge against chaos. But when it ceases to *serve*, it inevitably enslaves. That is precisely why our efforts at social reform should be designed to avoid the "interference of the state beyond its competence."[27] As C. S. Lewis said, "Of all the tyrannies, a tyranny sincerely expressed for the good of its victims may be the most oppressive. It may be better to live under robber barons than under omnipotent ideological busybodies."[28]

Love and Faith-Based Solutions

Everyone should recognize that there is a significant need for change in our nation and around the world. By now it should also be clear that although government is important, it is not all-important. We know that the only truly effective force for change is people, but how do we apply this knowledge to get results? Two words: *faith* and *love*.

Our oldest daughter, Rhonda, went to Bolivia in 2001 with Life Outreach International. Part of the team's mission was to provide basic necessities to people who otherwise wouldn't have them. While she was there, Rhonda met a little nine-year-old boy who had lived on the streets his whole life. After receiving a bath, a shirt, and a bed, the boy had decided to lie down for a nap. Rhonda was sitting next to his bed watching him when he woke up. Do you know what he said to her? He said, "This is the greatest day of my life." It brought tears to my daughter's eyes to hear such pure gratitude expressed in response to receiving a few things that you and I would take completely for granted. That's the power of love! Without love, the attempts of government to meet pople's needs through programs amount to little more than throwing money at the problem.

People Power

In order for positive change to occur, people must get involved. Government can't do it alone. I think the spirit of President Bush's Faith-Based Initiatives program is an important step toward resolving the tough issues facing Americans and people around the world today. The bottom line is that love and faith *can* work together with the incredible power of government to deal with many of the human dilemmas we face in our society. I'm talking about food for the hungry and shelter, bedding, and clothing for those who need them. The government and the faith community *can* work together toward solving many of the world's problems. We desperately need to build a system of accountability in which government and faith-based organizations can work together in a nonintrusive way so that each can hear and appreciate what the other has to share. But we need to realize that the government *cannot* do it alone; it urgently needs the involvement of the faith community to make any real progress toward solving real problems. Our faith has to enter the equation.

Sadly, President Bush's idea has been denounced as a horrible mistake by hundreds of people involved in faith-based organizations—not to mention secularists in government and the media. These representatives of faith-based groups claim that the government will interfere with the Church. What nonsense! Can you imagine the revolution that would occur in this country if the government tried to tell the Church what it could and could not preach? If you ever want to see people of faith stand up with overpowering effect, just try to tell them that they *can't* preach and share the gospel. Watch and see what would happen! It isn't as if we're asking the government to fund the sharing of the gospel. Believers don't need that and don't want it. The government will never control the Church. What I *am* saying is this: *Why don't we find a way for faith-based organizations that change people's lives to effectively use some of the nearly 9 trillion dollars we have thrown at the poor over the past few decades?*[29] We could have bought every poor person in America a house and a Lexus with that kind of money. And yet we still have needy people everywhere we look. There's got to be a better solution. I *know* that faith and love work. So why can't we find a way for faith and love to work *together* with the government?

If an organization is doing a good work in love and faith and needs more beds or some food or some room, can we not provide it with resources out of the government's vast supply? Consider the serious problem of inner-city drug addiction. It has been confirmed that Teen Challenge, the ministry founded by David Wilkerson (author of *The Cross and the Switchblade*), has one of the highest success rates of recovery. Why shouldn't the government find a way to cooperate with Teen Challenge? Is that asking too much? Consider this: Many Americans pay income tax to the tune of 15 to 30 percent a year. Add in additional taxes like sales tax and property tax, and it quickly adds up to roughly 50 percent of the gross income of millions of our citizens. That means if you are a working American, you work half the year to pay some form of taxes, an enormous portion of which goes to the federal government. *If you're going to take money out of my pocket, why not give it to someone who's helping somebody?* Why can't you give it to someone who loves a fatherless child? or to somebody who feeds those who are hungry? or to somebody who will give a bed to a person sleeping under a bridge?

Cooperation Is Possible

During my days as a traveling evangelist, I spoke in more than two thousand public schools, and I never talked about God. I talked about godly principles—principles that work—but I didn't deliver an evangelistic message. The school administrators were gracious enough to allow me to tell the students that if they wanted to hear more of what I had to say, I would be speaking that night at the local stadium or coliseum. There was a spirit of cooperation between the school officials and me because they knew I wasn't going to impose my beliefs or intrude on the rights of the students. Instead, they knew that I would impart truth to the students and help them understand how to strengthen their relationships at home and at school, how to assume responsibility for their actions, and how to deal effectively with addictive practices and sexual promiscuity. I spoke about the absolutes, and faith naturally followed.

My experience with these many schools is one example that there are ways to forge a good working relationship between the government and faith-based organizations that are directly serving the needs of people in the community. Too often Christians become so focused on defending their faith that they fail to share the power of love—which is the transforming power of Jesus Christ at work in their lives. The Bible says there is no way to limit the power of love when it is freely released. Certainly we ought to be able to implement a system of accountability that will satisfy the government's requirements without tying the hands of faith-based groups to serve people.

I am constantly encouraged by how much good I see coming out of our minority communities. Do you know that we have minority groups in this country that work nonstop to help people, to clothe people, to feed people? Yet much of the time these important groups lack the resources to continue to work their effective ministries. I've seen these groups in action. I've talked with people in the African-American community and the Hispanic community who want nothing more than to be able to help others. But they just don't have the capital. These are good, gifted, dedicated people just waiting for the means to reach out to others. I would love programs put in place, perhaps by corporations and the business community, that could benefit groups in minority communities. Also, many minorities have established successful businesses but lack access to capital for growth or expansion. It's a shame. I can think of no reason why Republicans and Democrats shouldn't be able to work together to reach such a worthy goal. This is not a political idea, it's a *people* idea. The government could possibly set aside some resources for qualified people, establish an achievable means of repayment, and then let those people do their work helping others or growing their businesses. I'm convinced there would be incredible results. I'm positive that such an approach would be a big step toward resolving the hurt in minority communities. I also firmly believe that any charity receiving government assistance must accept total accountability for their use of those funds. We must be willing to refrain from imposing religious requirements or insisting that those who come for help must listen to our message. Let's just love people from a pure heart. When they experience the unconditional love of God poured out in service to them, believe me, they will want to know what makes us different. And then we can tell them. But let's not make religion a prerequisite for love.

197

Stop Worrying . . .
Some in Christian circles here have said, "If the government starts funding faith-based organizations, the Scientologists, New Agers, Hindus, Muslims, and others will get government

money, too. And what about the Satanists?" I love how Mike Huckabee, governor of Arkansas, responded to that. He said, "If the Satanists can get government money because they're doing good, I'll put the love of God up against a Satanist's efforts any day of the year."[30] He's right—we should stop worrying about what other people might do and just concentrate on what *we* can do with God's help. If we would simply share God's love freely, we would have nothing to fear, because "perfect love casts out fear."[31] It seems many people would rather fight than find a legitimate way to help those who are suffering.

Where Are the Christians?

When our mission team visited Somalia's refugee camps, I saw thousands upon thousands of hungry, hurting people. And who was there offering assistance? Muslim aid groups with their hospital tents and their soup lines. Do you know where the food came from? USAID. The Muslims were feeding the Somalian refugees American food. What was my response? After I had walked through their hospitals and observed their feeding lines, I went to the Muslim leaders and said, "Thank you for saving the lives of these little children."

As I walked back outside and looked at the multitudes of needy people, I prayed, "God, why are there no Christian workers in this refugee camp?" Perhaps they were too busy discussing theology and debating church policy to come make a difference where it really counts. Woe to us if we allow "fruitless discussion" to cause us to miss opportunities for serving the needs of people.

I certainly don't mean to imply that Christians seldom help in these dire circumstances, because there are countless examples of wonderful Christian organizations that do help, sacrificially and continuously. But imagine the impact if *all* Christians were as committed to helping as the Muslims I met in Somalia. Before the children in those refugee camps could eat, they quoted Muslim verses. What if they were in a camp run by Christians? What if we fed them without making them quote any verses? What if we just loved them? All over the world there are millions of people just waiting to be loved. That's where Christians belong. Not arguing among ourselves! And when people ask us why we care, why we showed up and loved them, then we can tell them about Jesus. Do you see the progression? We must *show* them Jesus before we *tell* them about Jesus. And how do we show them Jesus? Simple—we show them love by offering help and hope in times of distress. Through Life Outreach, we've been doing this for years—and it works!

Where is the Church, by and large? Rather than seeking to solve the dire problems we find in the world, far too many Christians are busy defending their theological positions. Either that or they're living life as if they're oblivious to what's going on. We've got people lying in the street starving while we're discussing insignificant issues. How many people do you think that's helping?

In Washington D.C., it seems that Congress is more interested in fighting to protect Republican positions and Democratic positions than in working together to meet our country's needs. Meanwhile, the problems continue to grow without being solved.

I look at all these groups and it's like watching a bunch of billy goats butting heads—and it breaks my heart. How long are we going to fight while people are in pain, many without shelter, many suffering from addiction, malnutrition, fatherlessness? There is no real substitute for compassionate action. We need people who are willing to act. And I believe that God is looking for those people, too.

199

Three Keys to a Better World

We can move forward into a better future for our world, not by imposing our ideals on others, but by demonstrating the love of God through our lifestyles, our commitment, and our concern for other people. In his Gettysburg Address, Abraham Lincoln referred to a government *of* the people, *by* the people, and *for* the people. In order to preserve this vision, *we the people* must step up to our responsibility in three key areas: inspiration, information, and involvement.

Citizens Must Be Inspired

In his diary account of his voyage to the New World, Christopher Columbus said the purpose of his mission was to spread the gospel of Jesus Christ to a heathen land. If the greed of others had not corrupted that noble purpose, the proclamation of God's truth and the demonstration of His love would have been the spiritual basis even for the discovery of America. Christians should be inspired by the realization that spiritual people, seeking freedom of worship for themselves and future generations, established this country on a spiritual foundation.

We should also be inspired by the dedication of those who secured and preserved our freedom from our country's inception right up to the present. Through the pages of history, we can trace a trail of blood spilled by the thousands—on foreign battlefields and here at home—who laid down their lives defending rock-solid absolutes and Bible-based principles, along with the freedom we enjoy.

As we consider the sacrifices made by these heroes and patriots, we can be assured of one thing: These people didn't lay their lives on the line to defend the perverse expressions of "freedom" we see in America today. The founders acknowledged and exalted a benevolent and righteous God and affirmed the worth and dignity of humanity—unlike the brand of liberty exalted by some today, which disregards or rejects the values on which this nation was built. Although our Constitution provides for and protects the right to protest and disagree—and I would defend those rights with my life—we mustn't overlook the absolute truth that ideas have consequences, and we must recognize that the consequences of a blatant disregard of moral absolutes is a steady decline in our moral character. If the ideas set forth by the purveyors of profanity, pornography, and exploitation become the prevalent mind-set in America, the foundations of our freedom will have cracked. Ultimately, our nation will deteriorate and true freedom will be lost.

As a result of political freedom proceeding hand-in-hand with economic freedom, America blossomed into the richest and most powerful nation the world has ever known. Along the way, however, aspects of socialism crept in, threatening our great free enterprise system. Secular humanism—the man-centered religion that rejects the idea of God and elevates humanity to the center of all life—has become the dominant school of thought for many Americans. Humanism invariably generates momentum toward rule by an elite class of supposedly superior individuals and groups, and this in turn leads to concentration of power in the central government. We've seen this trend in the United States over the past half century, as the federal bureaucracy has mushroomed and government regulations have crept into every area of our lives. This drift of power into the hands of the elite will ultimately lead to bondage and the destruction of true liberty.

The only way to turn America from this treacherous path is to rally those who believe in eternal values—the sanctity of life, the importance of the home and family, godly authority, freedom of religion, of speech, and of the press—and unite in opposing the forces that threaten our precious heritage.

If decent citizens are no longer inspired by the magnificent ideals and principles that have made America the greatest nation in history, I can guarantee you that small, focused special-interest groups will be inspired to fill the gap with their own self-serving ideas.

Whenever I see groups of children or families together—whether playing in the park, out in the front yard, or taking walks in the neighborhood—I'm inspired to make a difference, to preserve the privilege of freedom for the next generation. The Bible says that we're to pray for those in authority, "that we may live peaceful and quiet lives."[32] I pray that God will protect our nation and restore its solid foundation.

The challenges that face our nation should inspire us to heed the words of President John Quincy Adams, who said, "Posterity, you will never know how much it has cost my generation to preserve your freedom. I hope you will make good use of it."

202

Citizens Must Be Informed

To be effective in the political arena, we must study the candidates, the officeholders, and the issues. Every American who cares about liberty must read, study, and seek counsel from knowledgeable people. True knowledge does not come easily. It demands time and energy. We must all begin seeking to be informed about government at every level, from the local school board, to the state legislature, to the halls of Congress. We cannot afford to be ignorant or tongue-tied when it comes to political developments that will encroach on our freedom, our beliefs, and our society. Otherwise, the persistent voices of radical activists will dominate every forum as they articulate their carefully crafted positions on every issue that concerns them.

If decent, principled, moral people do not stay abreast of what is happening in our nation and around the world, in effect they are relinquishing control of the future to people who *have* taken the time and trouble to be informed; people who *have* learned how the system works—and work at it; people who *have* taken the time and trouble to run for office and now control portions of the government; people who *will* introduce and pass self-serving legislation and policies.

The government today is influenced in too many ways by tax-supported lobbyists; highly organized, self-seeking special interest groups; and greedy, corrupt political opportunists. This situation persists because too many Christians have fallen for the notion that Christianity and politics do not mix. This perspective may be based partly on a misinterpretation of the biblical command to "be separate" from the world.[33] Whatever its source, I believe the withdrawal syndrome that prevails among Christians and other decent citizens is mistaken and dangerous. If we don't stand up for absolute principles, who will?

We must insist that our leaders be guided by absolute, time-tested principles and not by mere preferences. We must not be deceived by candidates whose winsome personalities disguise a lack of moral integrity and courage. We must take the time to study the issues and vote for those candidates who have the character and commitment to govern wisely.

Citizens Must Be Involved

I have had the privilege over the years of speaking directly to many of America's leading political figures, including several presidents. I have taken those opportunities to share my heart and my convictions about the importance of seeking spiritual guidance for dealing with the affairs of government. I would encourage you to share your spiritual wisdom with those in authority and those seeking positions of authority at every level. Talking with leaders and potential leaders is not a privilege or

203

responsibility reserved for evangelists, pastors, or other religious leaders.

If you cannot directly contact a leader or candidate, I encourage you to write letters about issues that are important to you. Letters can have a tremendous effect, especially when unsolicited by political interest groups.

What can we do, as concerned citizens, to help ensure enduring freedom in America? Here are several suggestions:

1. *Pray* for government figures at every level, for potential leaders, for America, and for the world. This may be the most important thing you can do, and it is a necessary foundation for the other steps.

2. *Study* public issues. We have a responsibility to speak out, but first we must know what we're talking about. The Scriptures say, "My people are destroyed for lack of knowledge."[34] Believers in Christ and all caring citizens should be informed about the issues. We should resist the negative effects of those who are committed to defending their partisan political positions and who sacrifice the well-being of the American people in their self-serving pursuit of political power.

3. *Select and campaign for politically and morally qualified candidates.* It has been proven time and again that fifty to one hundred dedicated volunteers actively campaigning can elect a candidate to local or state office. Activist organizations have proven how much influence a committed group can have on public policy. Some people refuse to participate in party politics at the "grassroots" ward and precinct level, because they believe that politics is a "dirty business" that is beneath their dignity. But in a free country like ours, politics is nothing more or less than the process of

deciding who is going to run the government and how. If it's a "dirty" business, it's only because the "clean" people have abandoned the process and let the "dirty" people take over. By getting actively involved, we can be instrumental in placing principled representatives in our local communities, state houses, Congress, and the White House.

4. *Register and vote.* As a general rule, only 50 percent of the American people vote in presidential elections, the lowest percentage of any free country in the world. We must not be guilty of such pathetic indifference. It is unfathomable that any American, knowing the sacrifices that have been made to secure the privilege of public participation in the election process, would be too lazy or careless to exercise this privilege by going to the polls to vote. I will admit that too often I have allowed my schedule to interfere with my own participation, and I deeply regret this. On occasion, the candidates have seemed too similar or the issues of little importance to me, but I know it's a mistake not to vote. If we feel we can do nothing else to influence the course of political events in this country, we can at least vote. God help us if we neglect the privileges and responsibilities of freedom.

205

Edmund Burke said, "All that is necessary for evil to triumph is for good men to do nothing." The future depends on our willingness to focus on more than our own private concerns. As long as mainstream Americans find more compelling things to do than vote on election day, the doorway is open for organized special-interest groups to elect men and women who will advance their particular agendas for America.

Some people pride themselves on being members of the "silent majority." How naive! A silent majority is a servile majority, blindly catering to the interests of the militant minorities to whom it has abdicated the responsibilities of government. The silent majority needs to wake up and speak up.

If the challenge seems overwhelming, I ask you to consider the words of Edward Everett Hale, the great poet and one-time chaplain of the U.S. Senate, who said: "I am only one—but still I am one. I cannot do everything, but still I can do something. And because I cannot do everything, I will not refuse to do the something that I can do."[35]

I challenge you to *be inspired, be informed,* and *be involved.* You are only one, but you are one. You can't do everything, but you can do something.

THE ABSOLUTES IN ACTION

PART THREE

CHAPTER THIRTEEN

Our practice of religion is powerful enough to make us hate one another but not powerful enough to make us love one another. **ALFRED JOHNSON (1791–1877)**

Tolerance is a virtue practiced by no religion anywhere in the world at any time—except perhaps in those few rare cases where Christianity is actually Christian. **JOSEPH ADDISON (1672–1719)**

Anyone who studies the religions of the world will quickly come to the conclusion that there is nothing more powerful, more dynamic, or more dangerous than faith apprehended wrongly. **ANTHONY TROLLOPE (1815–1882)**

Religion Can
Be Dangerous,
but Repentance
Is Redemptive

Mere religion is a poor substitute for a relationship with the
living God, made possible through true repentence.

More than any other place on earth, Jerusalem has been the focal point of wars, invasions, rebellions, terrorist attacks, crusades, persecutions, and occupations—paradoxically because it is a holy city for three of the world's major religions. A close friend who has visited Jerusalem on several occasions shared with me this image of the historic city:

> From a balcony in the King David Hotel, at the very heart
> of the city, the austere enchantment of the Old City comes
> to life with its scarred exteriors and trampled paths. Clus-
> ters of tourists—still a fairly common sight even in these
> days of terrorist attacks and suicide bombings—walk
> slowly toward the Jaffa Gate, savoring every precious
> morsel of time and space, hushed by awe. A few blocks
> away, quiet processions of monks make their way toward

the Church of the Holy Sepulcher. The sweet fragrance of their incense and the haunting refrain of their chants waft through the air. Beyond the ancient battlements of Suleiman, still deeper into the city, the Hasidim gather at the Western Wall in their long, black coats and wide, perched hats, prayer shawls unfurled, to cry out to Jehovah separately and together. Above them, on the site where Herod's Temple once stood, a ragged line of Muslim faithful walk silently into the shrine of Muhammad's mysterious transport. They kneel down, touching their foreheads to the ground in prayer.

How is it that such pious men and women, intent on living lives pleasing to God, can live in such deep enmity with one another? In an atmosphere of piety and prayer, how is it that suicide attacks on innocent bystanders meet with approval and inspire more violence in return? How can such a place of peace tolerate and even encourage such hatred?

Since September 11, 2001, millions of Americans have asked the question, "How is it possible that someone could commit such horror in the name of religion, in the name of faith, in the name of Allah—or in the name of God?" Scenes of spontaneous celebrations erupting on the streets of Arab cities as news of the terrorist attacks spread across the globe shocked us. How is it that human beings could take glee in such an awful calamity? And how could they justify their feelings in the name of faith in God?

We expect more of the religious, and well we should. Yet we see that the face of religion is often ugly and sometimes deadly. Throughout history, there have been many religious traditions and prejudices that sought to force others into submission and bondage. And though it is natural for us as Christians to point to the radical Muslim Taliban and the terrorist al Qaeda network as examples of religious extremism, we must remember that our Christian history is not without blemish, from the Crusades of the Middle Ages, to the Spanish Inquisition, to the justification of slavery and oppression of blacks here on American soil.

It does not take an atheist, skeptic, agnostic, or liberal to stand up and point out the radical fringes of some religions. The appalling effect of some people's religious devotion on those around them is inexcusable.

The Religion of No Religion

Equally dangerous are those who profess no religion, who instead have cobbled together a set of beliefs around the creed of relativism and humanism, which they promote with nothing less than religious zeal. Indeed, some ardent atheists make a religion out of hating religion.

Thomas L. Friedman, for instance, writing in the *New York Times,* asserts that "the real war" we face today is against religion that believes it must be applied in life. "We have to understand what this war is about. We're not fighting to eradicate terrorism. Terrorism is just a tool. We're fighting to defeat an ideology: religious totalitarianism."[1]

And what is this "religious totalitarianism" that Friedman is so concerned about? It is "a view of the world that my faith must reign supreme and can be affirmed and held passionately only if all others are negated."[2] In other words, religious totalitarians are those who believe that their religion is true! According to Friedman, such notions are inherently dangerous. True religious freedom, then, as Friedman apparently would have it, is being able to worship the God of our choice so long as we don't really believe that our faith actually means anything in an absolute and objective sense.

Comparing any belief in revealed truth to Nazism, Friedman goes on to argue that every social institution must be enlisted to eradicate the belief that anyone's religion is actually true: "Unlike Nazism," he says, "religious totalitarianism can't be fought by armies alone. It has to be fought in schools, mosques, churches, and synagogues, and can be defeated only with the help of imams, rabbis, and priests."[3]

Thus, according to this renowned commentator, writing in the world's most influential newspaper, religion must be relegated to the level of preference. It must never be allowed to rise to the level of principle. If religion behaves itself by being essentially irrelevant, then it will not have to be banned. But in order to tame and train religious passion, all religious people must join the state, the schools, and the courts in seeking to destroy the notion that their religion is actually true. Although I disagree with Friedman in the above statement, as well as on other occasions, I also acknowledge and appreciate the often brilliant observations shared by this gifted writer.

Secular fundamentalism is becoming more and more prominent. According to sociologist James Blanchard

> The fervor of atheism is no less religious than the piety of evangelical Christianity. The real danger of religion is not the belief in ultimate things, it is the impulse to power. It is the determination to exert force. It is the imposition of values against the will of others. Any religion can be guilty of such dangerous behavior—but no religion is as frequently guilty as that religion which pretends not to be religious.[4]

Religion vs. Relationship

As John Koster demonstrates in *The Atheist Syndrome* and Paul Johnson shows in *The Intellectuals,* religion is at its most dangerous when it either fails to live up to its high ideals or it attempts to force those ideals on the unwilling masses through coercion. At such times, that which is best about us quickly becomes that which is worst about us.

It is obvious to Christians and non-Christians alike that the Church's behavior is often incongruous with the heart and character of God as revealed in the Bible and in the blameless, exemplary life of Jesus Christ. One can quote Scriptures, axioms, and creeds, but if one's life is not a demonstration of the transforming power of the God who inspired them and Christ, who demonstrated their true meaning, the results can be dangerous. The ultimate test of the effectiveness and validity of any belief system is its overall benefit to humanity. The God in whom Christians believe is a God who cares so deeply about humanity that He sacrificed His Son to purchase our redemption. The great difference between the world's religions and genuine faith in God is our response to this undeniable expression of God's love for us.

As Dr. Richard Halverson, the late pastor of Fourth Presbyterian Church in Washington D.C., once wrote:

> Jesus Christ transcends all religions! Judaism—Islam—
> Buddhism—Hinduism. . . . He is greater than all these—
> including Christianity. Religions are the inventions of
> men. They may begin with a great leader in mind—Moses,
> Jesus, Mohammed, Buddha . . . but human tradition soon
> reduces the original to a mere set of ethical standards and
> a dead letter of the law which no one can follow. The origi-
> nal sin was not murder, adultery, or any other action we
> call sin. The original sin was, and still is, the human choice
> to be one's own god—to control one's own life—to be in
> charge—to be religious. Rising out of this choice evolved
> religion: mankind's attempt to please God. Jesus tran-

scends religion because he is the incarnation of all that is true, good, loving, gentle, tender, thoughtful, caring, courteous, and selfless. Jesus does not want you to become a Christian. He wants you to become a new creation! There is a great difference between the two.[5]

What Christianity offers is the opportunity of knowing God personally and letting His divine nature become part of our daily lives. We can experience a new life born of the Holy Spirit. As a matter of fact, according to Jesus, we *must* be born from above not only to have eternal life, but also in order to experience "abundant life" right now, here on earth.[6]

Trouble in the Pulpit
Joining a church or a religious organization will not suffice. Many people do that. Some of the meanest people on the planet are not only members of church organizations, they are often leaders within their churches and denominations! Some people assassinate one another with their words, misrepresentations, accusations—even using the Bible as a weapon of unholy warfare.

I have and always will boldly defend the "reliable, inerrant Scriptures," but I also recognize that they can be manipulated, misquoted, and twisted. Far too often in the history of the Church, Christian leaders and "defenders of the faith" have used the Bible to destroy the reputation of others.

Instead of demonstrating unity in the Spirit for the entire family of God to emulate, some leaders refuse to interact with one another. It seems as if they are more interested in building their own little empires than in building up the entire body of Christ. As a result, the Christian community suffers and fails to grow into full maturity.[7]

Some individuals will not even allow themselves to be seen with a person who is perceived to be part of another group—even with those whose basic beliefs are the same. Instead, they separate themselves based on petty disagreements over the interpretation of certain passages of Scripture, or they dismiss one another on the basis of whatever label will most effectively discredit the other party: conservative, liberal, charismatic, fundamentalist, modernist, or whatever. God help us! What a miserable way to live. Christ's own disciples manifested these same tendencies, arguing over which of them was the greatest; hindering others who were not a part of their group but who were casting out demons in Jesus' name; and wanting to call down fire on some who didn't relate to Jesus the way the disciples thought they should. Jesus rebuked the disciples for allowing themselves to be influenced by an evil spirit.[8]

We're so quick in the Church to identify each other according to label, doctrine, or position. But Jesus said, "Let your good deeds shine out for all to see, . . ." not so you can look good and win others to your side of the argument; not so you can win friends and influence people, but "so that everyone will praise your heavenly Father."[9] As Christian leaders, we must *demonstrate* the importance of servanthood. After all, Jesus said that He Himself did not come to be served, but to serve others. That's how we who profess to be His followers must live. We must work with one another, not duplicating each other's efforts, but working together with others in the body, all the joints fitted together. There is one head—and it's not some highly visible preacher, but Jesus Christ. He expresses Himself through His body, true disciples working in harmony together.

216

Trouble in the Pews
Many people go through the motions of worshiping God, but they do not have a life-giving, energizing relationship with Him. Jesus said, "These people honor me with their lips, but their

hearts are far away. Their worship is a farce, for they replace God's commands with their own man-made teachings."[10] As a result, some churchgoers express characteristics that are totally contrary to a life surrendered to Jesus.

In the book of James it says, "If you have bitter jealousy and selfish ambition in your heart, do not be arrogant and so lie against the truth. This wisdom is not that which comes down from above, but is earthly, natural, demonic. For where jealousy and selfish ambition exist, there is disorder and every evil thing."[11] Unfortunately, jealousy and ambition corrupt far too many lives, even among some evangelical Christian groups. I have experienced these evil tendencies in my own life and ministry, and I know how quickly they can inflict damage. These things are not from God—they are exactly what the Scriptures say they are: earthly, natural, demonic. James goes on to say: "But the wisdom from above is first pure, then peaceable, gentle, reasonable, full of mercy and good fruits, unwavering, without hypocrisy."[12]

217

In Galatians 5, where Paul talks about the fruit of the Spirit, he also talks about the fruit of the flesh, which religious people too often manifest. He describes fleshly expressions as "enmities, strife, jealousy, outbursts of anger, disputes, dissensions, and factions." Sadly, all of these characteristics are typical within some churches and other religious groups. Yet Paul said those who practice these things will not inherit the kingdom of God. If the spirit of fleshly appetites and attitudes control us, we will not be able to live according to God's transforming power. If a person has no desire to overcome unwholesome practices, it clearly illustrates a lack of spiritual transformation in his or her life.

What the Church Should Look Like

The New Testament Church was born in the spirit of Pentecost, when the Holy Spirit came just as Jesus had promised. The apostles, who were the early leaders of the Church, had been with the crucified and resurrected Messiah. They and others had sat in His presence, had walked in the aura of His miraculous power, and had seen Him ascend to heaven. Then they waited until they were suddenly consumed by the onrushing power of the Spirit, which not only transformed them with the character of Jesus Christ but also enabled them to express His character in the most undeniable fashion, so that even their detractors—and the whole world, the Scriptures say—stood in awe.

To this day, many people spend time discussing and defending the elements of Pentecost—whether the manifestations were spiritual manifestations or just the boldness of the apostles' witness; whether the gift of tongues was an impartation of spiritual languages or simply common dialects given only for that day and age; and countless other discussions of the characteristics of God's work. But the ultimate characteristic of the early Church that seems to have been forgotten—and which we must now reclaim or risk losing our hope and our freedom—is that everyone in the Church had nothing that possessed them. Unlike our contemporary society—and, sadly, much of the contemporary Church—which has succumbed to the siren song of materialism and individualism, the early Christians would willingly and gladly part with anything and everything in order that no one would be without. This spirit of generosity, compassion, and care was not something imposed by the government—far from it! It was not a religious demand or some sort of tradition. It was not an appeal by a persuasive preacher or a burden placed upon the people to become somehow more charitable. Instead, it was the result of a genuine encounter with the Spirit of God that brought about an overflow of love and selflessness, so the interests of others became more important than one's own interests. In other words, the real needs of others became the primary focus of the Church—and nobody suffered a lack of anything.

No government program—or Church program, for that matter—can manifest the concern and care for others that we in the body of Christ will naturally demonstrate when we are fully given over to the will and ways of God. Only then will we see that no one is left without. Whatever it takes, we will give it to others out of the abundance of our hearts to meet their needs. If the Church of Jesus Christ—the Christian community—is to move beyond its present place to fulfill its highest calling, all of us must surrender ourselves to the transforming power of God and Christ. Through the Holy Spirit and without restraint we must begin to deliver food to the hungry, water to the thirsty, clothing to the naked, and freedom to the captives. When the Church unites in godly cooperation, it will no longer be just a few people doing a lot, but all Christians seeking to do their part, however large or small—not motivated by guilt but moved by the over- 219 whelming spirit of love and compassion.

Jesus said that one day "all the nations will be gathered in his presence, and he will separate them as a shepherd separates the sheep from the goats. He will place the sheep at his right hand and the goats at his left. Then the King will say to those on the right, 'Come, you who are blessed by my Father, inherit the Kingdom prepared for you from the foundation of the world. For I was hungry, and you fed me. I was thirsty, and you gave me a drink. I was a stranger, and you invited me into your home. I was naked, and you gave me clothing. I was sick, and you cared for me. I was in prison, and you visited me. . . . I assure you, when you did it to one of the least of these my brothers and sisters, you were doing it to me!' "[13]

The mission of Life Outreach International is to help inspire people to feed the hungry around the world and help provide clean water to thousands of people who don't have it. Some critics have told me I've become like a beggar on behalf of the poor. In fact, one lady even said she'd found the perfect epitaph for my tombstone in Luke 16:22. I asked her what it said, and she replied, "And the beggar died." Well, the Jewish leaders in the Old Testament were scolded for not pleading the cause of the widow and the orphan.[14] I will at least be pleading the cause of the needy as long as I have breath.

Others have said, "James, you continually ask us to feed more children, to provide water for more people. You can't feed every hungry child, and you can't give clean water to every thirsty person." I know I can't do everything, but I can do something. I have determined that I will live my life to help inspire the desire in others to help feed every hungry child in the world, and if possible, provide access to clean water to every person on earth. I can't do it alone, but with the help of others, and by the grace of God, it is possible to reach everyone.

God has invited us to come freely into His presence by faith, to understand and experience His compassion for us and for others, and to accomplish His will as expressed in the Bible. He has invited us to pour out blessings and love, food, water, and shelter out of our abundance and out of our hearts of love. As Jesus said, "Give as freely as you have received!"[15] He now invites us to a unity of spirit, a harmony of heart, a oneness of mind—not that we will agree in all areas necessarily, but that we will understand how to relate to other people in love and with positive effect all over the world. He has given us an invitation to come into His presence, to be a part of His family, and to reveal His heart of compassion to others. How will we respond?

God Invites Us and Allows Consequences
Somehow, while discussing our theology and defending our

positions on various doctrines, we have dulled the process of spiritual renewal, which quenches and grieves the Holy Spirit. Too many of us, as Paul says, have been bewitched, and we no longer walk in freedom and liberty but we have returned to bondage.[16] What God intended when He sent the Holy Spirit to indwell us is that we would be filled to the point of overflowing with His presence—which means the Spirit is not something to be contained but Someone who overwhelms and overflows us so that the spilling over of beauty touches everything around us.

But if the invitation to come freely into relationship with God, to experience freedom in Christ, and to walk in the power of the Holy Spirit is not sufficient to draw us, then the pressures that come naturally from tragic circumstances and catastrophic events—be they natural disasters or premeditated assaults by the forces of evil—will pressure us until we are pushed to the breaking point. If that's what it takes to wake us up, then that's what will happen. Even if that happens, we may not necessarily respond properly. Throughout history, many have continued to ignore God despite the most disastrous events.

I'm concerned that if we don't respond now—with the memory of September 11 still fresh in our minds and the news of the world set before us daily, with the obvious needs of so many who are suffering and the pain of oppressed people so evident— if we really don't care, if we refuse to respond with compassion while there's still time, then you can rest assured the pressure will intensify. It won't necessarily be as a direct judgment from the hand of God, but as a natural consequence of suffering by people who will lash out in destructive ways.

There has never been a more critically important moment for the Christian church. All professing believers must begin expressing love, compassion, and their convictions through consistent life practices. By the power of God we must increase our compassionate care and missions outreach to all nations, especially to developing countries. We need the transforming power of God to change the attitudes of potential terrorists. Without a righteous influence worldwide, false religious leaders will continue to convince young men that if they kill American "infidels" they will wake up in paradise with a harem of virgins. It's not hard to understand how that prospect would sound more inviting than life in a dusty cave, a squalid refugee camp, or a sand-blown desert. We must demonstrate love and truth in order to offset the deadly impact of false religious teaching.

Repentance Is the Tipping Point

How can this positive moral influence actually spread and bring about positive change on a national or global level? We need to discover the tipping point.

The "tipping point" is a term used by scientists who study the spread of diseases to refer to events or circumstances that cause a virus or other disease to "tip" out of equilibrium and begin spreading in epidemic proportions. Journalist Malcolm Gladwell, in his fascinating book titled *The Tipping Point*, explores how this same phenomenon also can account for a wide variety of social changes, including the sudden emergence of fads and crazes, the rapid increase or decrease in rates of crime, the meteoric ascent of a new book on a best-seller list, and word-of-mouth promotion of a hot new restaurant. Gladwell writes, "The best way to understand the emergence of fashion trends, the ebb and flow of crime waves . . . or any number of the other mysterious changes that mark everyday life is to think of them as epidemics. Ideas and products and messages and behaviors spread just like viruses do."[17]

Much could be said about how the "tipping point" principle might be applied to promoting a resurgence of the absolutes in our society, but I want to focus on three key factors that Gladwell identifies:

– Small changes can produce big results.
– Changes at the margins can have a big effect.
– The efforts of a few key individuals can tip widespread changes.

Small changes can produce big results.
An intriguing and important component of the tipping point equation is that relatively small changes can produce disproportionately big results. It's also possible, and often true, that big changes produce meager results. What makes the difference is how close the situation is to the tipping point, and how well focused the changes are. So, for example, a company might pour millions of dollars into a marketing campaign for its product and achieve only a small increase in sales, but if a few "connected" individuals start using the product, or if a few key "mavens" promote the product to their friends and acquaintances, sales could explode virtually overnight.[18] Often it takes a series of small changes or the culmination of several factors to tip a situation into an epidemic.

223

Changes at the margins can have a big effect.
Sometimes we are tempted to confront problems head-on in an effort to turn the tide. But a full-frontal assault—in physical warfare as well as spiritual warfare—is not always the best strategy. Gladwell talks about how the New York City Transit Police successfully reduced the crime rate by turning their primary attention away from confronting major crime in the subways and focusing instead on cleaning up graffiti and prosecuting fare jumpers. By addressing these two seemingly marginal issues,

they changed the *atmosphere* on the subway, which helped to tip the situation, leading to a dramatic decline in crime. The key is to focus on contextual factors to counteract the idea that "nobody cares." By changing the perception in parts of the world that we don't care—through focused applications of genuine, heartfelt, godly love—there's no telling what a positive impact we could have on our society and the world.

By calling graffiti and fare jumping "marginal" issues, I don't mean to imply that they were minor problems or easy to address. As Gladwell explains, it took a purposeful commitment of resources and a dogged persistence to outpace the graffiti artists and stem the epidemic of fare jumping, but they proved to be achievable objectives with an exponential payoff. The key to the tipping point is to make the changes that will have the biggest effect.

The efforts of a few key individuals can tip widespread changes. It isn't always visible and established leaders who bring about major changes. More often, the words and actions of a few key individuals will trigger the tipping point. Jesus said to His disciples, "You are the light of the world. A city that is set on a hill cannot be hidden. Nor do they light a lamp and put it under a basket, but on a lampstand, and it gives light to all who are in the house. Let your light so shine before men, that they may see your good works and glorify your Father in heaven."[19] Christians have a unique opportunity—in fact, it is a mandate from Jesus Himself—to be a light in the darkness. Regardless of how much our postmodern society may seek to marginalize Christians and their influence, we have the potential to tip widespread positive changes by releasing the power of God to work in our world. But first we must stop trying to make spiritual clones of ourselves and just start loving people. We must stop just preaching to the choir and start reaching into our communities with care and compassion. We must stop infighting over doctrinal differences and start outfighting our common enemy—the forces of evil—through unity in the Spirit; through focused, deliberate, persistent prayer and focused, deliberate, persistent action. To accomplish our purpose here on earth, it's going to take a change of heart.

In that sense, the ultimate tipping point is *repentance*. It is the mechanism that puts genuine change into action in our lives and in our culture. It is what will enable us to move beyond the past—and all of the mistakes of the past—and into the future with bright hopes and new dreams. Repentance is the fulcrum upon which cultural transformation hinges. Without repentance, we will never secure enduring freedom.

Defining Repentance

Pride, stubbornness, and self-centeredness are like a dam that keeps the river of life from flowing through us. Repentance is a decision of the will to open the floodgates and release the transforming power of God. It is a change of mind and heart that produces undeniable changes in our habits and actions and in how we respond to people around us. Repentance moves us in a whole new direction that imparts life. Wherever the river of life flows, life springs up. Like trees planted along a river, the outgrowth of repentance is life and fruitfulness.

I live for the day when I open my mouth and the heart of God flows out. After all, isn't that what Jesus said—that if we believed in Him out of our "innermost being shall flow rivers of living water"?[20] But if what we say and what we do are corrupted by our own selfish ambition, our own sin, or any motive that doesn't reflect the pure heart of God, then the water that flows out of our lives is just as unclean, just as sickening, just as use-

225

less for life as any polluted stream. It's time we tested the water of our lives—and if it isn't pure and holy, then we need to repent. But what is repentance?

We might best approach a definition of *repentance* by looking first at what it is not. Repentance is not *reform*. It is not simply straightening up our act and resolving to do better. Repentance is not *regret*. It's not merely saying we're sorry and that we wish something hadn't happened. Nor is repentance *religion*—the decision to conform our behavior to an external standard. No, repentance is deeper. It involves a change of heart and a change of mind such that *redemption* and *love* become our primary motivations.

Redemption literally means to buy something back, often from a harmful or detrimental situation.[21] Implicit in the idea of buying something back is the necessity of investing something of value. When we have a genuine change of heart and decide to adopt a redemptive mind-set, we must be willing to invest ourselves in caring for other people, in setting people free from that which binds them, and in making something good from otherwise bad situations. A redemptive mind-set asks the question, "What one thing can I do right now to make a positive difference?"

The answers to our nation's and the world's needs and our continuing hope for the future will be found first and foremost in the hearts and minds of people, not in more laws or the promises and plans of governments. Conservatives and liberals alike must repent of the idea that we can solve our problems by skillfully combining incentives and disincentives, or by artfully devising political solutions. The pathway to a better future will not be established by enacting the right bills, electing the right politicians, reclaiming the right legacies, initiating the right reforms, or restoring the right priorities. Genuine cultural solutions can only emerge when people are willing to commit them-

226

selves to upholding the absolutes and are willing to turn away from everything that stands in the way. In other words, it will only be accomplished by a work of repentance and redemption in individual hearts and minds.

There's something about human nature, however, that makes us hate to admit when we're wrong. We're quick to rationalize or justify our actions and our attitudes, and we immediately put up our guard whenever someone even hints at our mistakes and our failures—not to mention our sins. Unfortunately, we all make mistakes, we all fail, and we all sin. And as long as we try to cover up our faults and deficiencies, there's no chance for improvement. In fact, if we remain steadfast in our denial of wrongdoing, we only make matters worse. The only way for us to learn from our mistakes is first to admit that we've made them. Second, we must be willing to correct what's wrong. And, third, we must have a fundamental change of heart to keep us from falling back into our old ways. This three-step process is called repentance.

British psychologist James Ulrich says, "Since sin is the source of virtually all human ills, it is only when we directly deal with sin that we can hope to solve those ills in our hearts, in our homes, and in our communities." Indeed, suggests Ulrich, we will achieve the greatest advances in mental, social, and national health "when we . . . finally . . . come to the threshold of genuine repentance. . . . It is only then we can actually begin to hope for authentic change. It is only then that we can lay the groundwork for a new beginning. It is only then that the pieces are in place for us to have a fresh start."[22]

The Return of the Prodigal

The clearest example of true repentance is revealed in Jesus' parable of the prodigal son.[23] In this story I see some connections to the current state of our nation. The parable opens with a picture of a young man who was blessed with an inheritance (much as we have been blessed with our inheritance of freedom). But instead of appreciating his inheritance and seeking to preserve its value, he became focused on his own rights, needs, and personal freedom to do as he pleased. Eventually he left home and squandered the very gift he'd been given. In demanding his rights, he stepped outside the provision that had been made for his welfare and safety at home.

It wasn't that his father's resources were not available to him when he was living at home—they were, but with constraints. With freedom came certain responsibilities. When the son chose instead to pursue freedom without responsibility, the results were disastrous. Not only did he lose everything he had, but he also became a slave to his appetites and his circumstances. That's what happens when we don't consider the consequences of our ideas and our actions, when we put our "rights" before our responsibilities. In our nation, we must never forget the absolute principles and the sacrifices that have been our solid foundation for more than two centuries.

When the young prodigal finally hit bottom—feeding pigs as a servant to a foreigner in a far-off land—he had a decision to make. If he stayed where he was, he would likely starve. But if he returned home, he couldn't expect to be more than a slave in his father's house. Ultimately, his hunger drove him home.

When the son took the first step out of the pigpen, that wasn't repentance—because repentance isn't reform. And he didn't just say, "I'm sorry I ended up in a pigpen and I'm sorry I ever left home"—because repentance isn't merely regret. But when he returned to his father with a broken and contrite heart and said, "I'm willing to be a slave," that was an act of repentance. And his father, welcoming him and forgiving him, said,

"I'm not interested in having a slave. I want a son who will serve others gladly." True repentance occurs when we return to God with our whole heart, and it results in a relationship that produces in our lives action that reveals the character of our loving Father.

The Prodigal Nation

As a nation, I believe we are somewhere on the road between the father's estate and the pigpen—with the very real possibility of experiencing serious pain and deprivation. We still have our freedom, but we have placed it in jeopardy through our choices as a society. The privileges afforded us in a free society can easily be abused. Such is the nature of freedom. But when we base our attitudes and our actions on our right to do what we please rather than on the character to do what is right and what is best, we are in trouble. When we improperly define freedom as "my right to do whatever I choose" and then defend the most despicable practices, we make ourselves vulnerable to all manner of evil.

The battle between good and evil is as old as time itself. When we allow the nature of evil to shape our thinking and control our actions, we place ourselves on that wide, well-trodden path to destruction. To reverse course, we must repent. We must begin to demonstrate with our lives the truth of our national motto: "In God we trust."

Repent of What?

If America is to remain a genuinely free, prosperous, and civil society, we must adopt an attitude of genuine repentance. Freedom's only hope for the future lies in our ability to recognize the dangerous drift of our culture toward relativism and selfishness, and then our willingness to turn from the error of our ways and acknowledge and adhere to the absolutes. Unless we re-engage with these timeless, rock-solid principles, our future is dim.

We will always have those who defend their actions and attitudes by saying, "I was born this way" or "I just can't help it." Truly, they have set their minds at war against their hearts to justify their rebellion. Our society will always have the downcast, the addicts, the rebels, the defiant, the weak, and the poor. But if our nation repents—a true change of heart—we will care about every one of these individuals.

I cannot emphasize the following point enough:

IF THE ABSOLUTES THAT ARE ESSENTIAL FOR FREEDOM'S SURVIVAL DO NOT BECOME THE BASIC INFLUENCE THAT SHAPES OUR DECISIONS AND OUR ACTIONS, THEN FREEDOM AS WE HAVE KNOWN IT WILL VANISH—NOT ONLY IN THE UNITED STATES, BUT ULTIMATELY FROM THE EARTH.

Jesus said that there would be "wars and rumors of wars" until the end, but we do not have to be overwhelmed by the devilish intentions of evil people and greedy warmongers who impose their wickedness on the rest of the world.[24] We can live free and be a "light set on a hill." We cannot solve every nation's problems, nor end their civil wars and national turmoil, but we can be an example of hope and offer help where it will be received. We can stand for human rights, including the rights of the innocent unborn. We do not have to subsidize or in any way condone the plundering, self-serving, and wicked actions of rogue leaders.

We must recognize the reality of evil and conquer it with love. We must dispel the fog of relativism and pursue truth. We must examine the consequences of our ideas, and we must pursue understanding and wisdom.

We must admit that God exists, and that people matter. We must graciously uphold the family and protect human life. We must abandon the destructiveness of greed. Our country may have "In God We Trust" printed on our coins, but far too many tend to place more trust in the money itself and in the systems of productivity and enterprise built around it. Although lately there has been a resurgence of the song "God Bless America," many people have been deceived into believing that our blessings as a nation come from other sources. We must repent of this foolishness.

We must recognize that character counts, and we must learn from our mistakes. We must not be swayed by the attitudes and opinions of the often-wrong majority. We must make government our servant or we will become its slave.

We must restore sex to its proper place, so that it can bloom into something beautiful. We can agree to disagree, but we must pursue righteousness. We must uphold the strengths of others, while building up their weaknesses. We must address our spiritual nature, ensuring that a genuine relationship with God, through Jesus Christ, is not replaced by a dangerous religion of intolerance.

The absolutes speak for themselves. Their truth is self-evident and irrefutable. We can choose to throw ourselves against them, but they will stand firm as they always have.

The Power of Individual Repentance

Repentance, which is the essence of true religion and leads to a restored relationship with God, will not result in our imposing or forcing our belief system or standards on others. Instead, it means that we will live our lives in such a way that the results will be magnetically attractive to all who see us. We will live with such freedom that only the foolish will fail to recognize the posi-

231

tive effect of our beliefs. They will observe the joyful interaction we have with others, our readiness to accept responsibility, and our willingness to share the benefits of what we are privileged to enjoy. They will see us bear up under suffering and calamity with fortitude and a spirit of peace—and they will want to know what makes the difference in our lives.

One great example of an individual who reached the tipping point of repentance and had his life transformed as a result is President George W. Bush. For many years before his political star began to rise in our home state of Texas, I had known Mr. Bush as a typical yuppie—professionally successful, politically connected, self-absorbed, self-confident, and not interested in a political future. Still, he and I shared some common interests in sports and the outdoors, and in my capacity as a Christian leader I had opportunity to offer him some spiritual insight. I'll never forget the occasion in August 1998 when Betty and I visited with then-Governor Bush and his advisor Karl Rove in the governor's office. As we were talking, Governor Bush began to share how an encounter with God had transformed his life. He talked about spending time in Kennebunkport, Maine, with Dr. Billy Graham, whom he greatly respected. He said, "I can't totally describe what happened. It was something about the humility and yet the strength and character of this man that moved me deeply."[25]

About a year after his conversation with Dr. Graham, Governor Bush gave up drinking. "Although I would not have considered myself an alcoholic by any stretch of the imagination," he said, "I do believe that drinking alcohol had become a problem in my personal life, with my wife and family, and I believe it could have become a very serious problem. I just had a heart change, and I knew that I would never drink again. My life was changed. I can't explain it perhaps in the terms you would as a minister, but it happened."

Later in the conversation, Governor Bush shared how he now had a new sense of destiny, focus, and purpose. He said, "I don't understand all this, but I would appreciate your prayers. I know my life has changed, and I know I want to do God's will. There isn't anything more important."

Had George W. Bush not reached this tipping point of repentance in his life, I for one would not have been excited to see him become the leader of the free world. In fact, I'm convinced that if he had not committed his life to Christ and experienced an undeniable change, George W. Bush would not have become president of the United States. But over the years since he first told me about the changes in his life, I have observed the difference firsthand and have gained a deep admiration and appreciation for him. Something profound and life-changing had occurred, and it was evident to all who knew him that he was walking in a new direction, pursuing a divine destiny. As the president has stood strong during the challenging days of his presidency, others have begun to see the compassion and character that has caused people like his adviser Karl Rove to say on more than one occasion: "We are standing in awe and amazement of what we have observed in his everyday life. We are impressed with how this man develops daily in his leadership strengths. We admire him beyond words, and we watch him all the time." That's an obvious effect of true repentance.

233

Another example of life-changing individual repentance can be found in the story of the Philippian jailer told in the book of Acts.[26] When all things were shaken in his life, he experienced a tipping point that was absolutely undeniable, irrefutable, and unstoppable. Placed in charge of Paul and Silas after their arrest on trumped-up charges, the jailer no doubt witnessed their joyful and peaceful response in their dire circumstances—which itself was the fruit of their earlier repentance. Indeed, they were praying and singing hymns despite being placed in stocks in the inner prison after having been beaten with rods.

When God sent an earthquake to open the doors of the jail, the jailer feared for his life to the point of contemplating suicide by his own sword because he thought the prisoners had escaped. But when he went in and saw that everyone was still there, he fell down at the feet of Paul and Silas and said, in essence, "What must I do to be like you?" When they told the jailer about Jesus and His transforming power, it changed his life. Not only that, but this same jailer who had once been frightened to the point that he almost took his own life, now boldly took Paul and Silas to his own home so that his entire household might also experience the power of his encounter with God. This man was so radically changed that there was no longer any fear.

The Bible says that when all things are shaken that can be shaken, that which cannot be shaken will remain.[27] I'm convinced that what cannot be shaken are the absolute principles on which every stable society can securely stand. In repentance, we will acknowledge that God is the unshakable center of the universe, the Creator of all life, and the source of our well-being. In repentance, we will discover an abundance of life that will help us secure our enduring freedom.

14

CHAPTER FOURTEEN

Train your tongue to offer solace, your heart sympathy, and your hand mercy. **PETER LORIMER (1812–1879)**

Mercy has converted more souls than zeal, or eloquence, or learning, or all of them together.
SOREN KIERKEGAARD (1813–1855)

Nothing costs so little, goes so far, or accomplishes so much as a single act of mercy.
PIERRE-AUGUSTE RENOIR (1841–1919)

We who are named of the truth have a mandate to not merely love in word and tongue but in action and truth. Thus, our unanimity on the matter must not merely be rhetorical. It must be translated into action.
VINCENT DE PAUL (1581–1660)

14

Servanthood:
The Key to Success
and Significance

*At no other time than when we serve others do
our meaning and purpose in life become so clear.*

I have a friend named Otis Winters, a successful businessman who has served on the boards of several of the largest, most highly respected and prosperous companies in the United States. He is a member of Augusta National Country Club, Cypress Point, Pine Valley, Southern Hills, and the prestigious Royal and Ancient Golf Club of St. Andrews in Great Britain. If you know anything about prestigious golf courses, you would no doubt say that Otis Winters has "arrived."

I shall never forget the day during the summer of 2001 when we were bass fishing together. Otis turned to me and said, "James, I've had it with success. I want to live the rest of my life for significance—real significance. I want to make a difference in light of eternal issues. I want to make a difference in God's kingdom. I want to use all I have and all that I am for the rest of my life, all to the glory of God. I want to bless others. I want to bless you and your ministry. I want to be a help." After a long career of achievement and opportunity, he had come to understand that there is far more to success than the accumulation of recognition, awards, and material gain. He discovered that servanthood is the key to genuine success and significance, and he encouraged me to help others, especially businessmen, discover this truth. As he put it, "I want to use all God has blessed me with to accomplish God's will and fulfill His kingdom purpose."

The headlong pursuit of success has captured the hearts and minds of so many in Western societies, especially in America. Our culture measures significance in materialistic terms: how big, how much, how many. In this age of accumulation, money talks, so people grab all they can. Many Americans seldom see success in terms of sharing and caring, but we should. It is sad to hear ministers on TV and in churches attempting to justify materialism as a measure of God's blessing while failing to proclaim the necessity of sacrifice for the sake of others in order to truly experience God's greatest blessings.

In times of national catastrophe, we seem to wake up momentarily and pay attention to the noble deeds that constitute true success. But servanthood should be a lifelong attitude, not just a temporary response to crises when they arise.

Eliza Doolittle, the heroine of *My Fair Lady,* captured the sentiment of most of us when she complained: "Words, words, words—I am so sick of words. I get words all day through, first from him, now from you. Is that all you blighters can do?"[1] She was tired of hearing and practicing empty rhetoric—as high-sounding as it was. Instead, she wanted to see something real.

Talk is cheap. Promises are a dime a dozen. Most of us have had just about all the spin-controlled sound bites we can stomach. The truth is, actions speak far louder than words. And that is universally true, whether in love or politics, religion, friendship, business, or technology. Mere good intentions are not sufficient in any area of life. There has to be follow-through on what we say. There must be substance behind our words.

Love is not just something we feel; it's something we express through our actions. Mercy is not just something we intend; it's something we extend by showing compassion and forgiveness and working toward reconciliation in our relationships with others. Hope is not just something we harbor; it's something we act on by finding a goal and working toward it or helping others work toward a goal they have. That is why a posture of servanthood is one of the most powerful inducements to both success and significance in life. After all, it really is "more blessed to give than to receive."[2] The sooner we realize that, the better off we—and those around us—will be.

It is not surprising then to discover that the idea of servanthood is showing up just about everywhere, even in places you might least expect it. Many business and management consultants, for instance, are beginning to see a life of selfless service as the key to prosperity and progress. Servanthood is a widely celebrated concept in the expanding literature of business success and personal management. The advent of the information age has almost completely transformed our predominantly industrial economy into a service-oriented economy. "Service Factor" is the new maxim for success in the crowded global marketplace. Good service promotes customer loyalty, management efficiency, and employee morale. It provides a competitive edge for companies in an increasingly cutthroat business environment. It is a means of gaining empowerment, flexibility, and innovation at a time when those qualities are essential for business survival. It prepares ordinary men and women to outsell, outmanage, outmotivate, and outnegotiate their competition. It enables them to "swim with the sharks without being eaten alive."[3]

According to businessman Jack Eckerd and Chuck Colson

238

of the Wilberforce Forum, service on the job and in the workplace can mean many things: "Valuing workers. Managing from the trenches. Communicating. Inspiring excellence. Training. Using profits to motivate."[4]

Corporate prognosticators, motivational speakers, and management consultants, from Tom Peters, John Naisbitt, and Stephen Covey to Richard Foster, Michael Gerber, and Zig Ziglar, agree that servanthood is an indispensable key to success in business or in life.[5]

These analysts have long promoted the idea that selfless service is essentially a complex combination of common courtesy, customer satisfaction, and the spirit of enterprise. It is realizing that "the customer is always right" and then going the extra mile to satisfy the customer. It is a principle-centered approach to human relationships and community responsibilities. It is putting first things first. It is the recovery of the medieval concept of chivalry, which is behavior characterized by "honor, generosity, courtesy, and gracious consideration."[6]

239

The genuine spirit of service inherent in servanthood isn't simply a tactic designed to boost profit margins, protect market shares, keep customers happy, or improve employee relations. It isn't just a strategy designed to instill patriotism, strengthen community relations, or attract more investments. It is not merely a technique to pad résumés, garner votes, or patronize constituents. It isn't just a style of leadership, a personality bent, or a habit of highly effective people. Instead, servanthood is a function of mercy. It stems from a genuine desire to seek the best for others, to put their interests before our own, and to exercise authentic love. Thus, the difference between the *ministry* of service and the *business* of service is like the difference between faith in God and faith in faith. Faith in God is personal and objective. Faith in faith is impersonal and subjective; that is, when our feelings change, our faith is likely to change too. Faith in God transcends self-interest and self-fulfillment. Faith in faith descends into self-reliance and self-assurance. Faith in God is a belief in someone who has revealed Himself to man "at many times and in various ways."[7] Faith in faith is simply "a belief" in something or anything.[8] It is difficult to think of a better example of true servanthood than Mother Teresa. Few people in modern history have stimulated compassionate acts as significantly as this humble woman who lived a life of servant leadership.

Public Success, Private Failure

When I was a young man, some of the most respected and admired people in America told me that I could be a success because of a special gift that enabled me to communicate effectively to the masses. Many called me "the next Billy Graham." Others were pushing me in a more political direction. In 1967, when I was twenty-three years old, one of the wealthiest men in the world, H. L. Hunt, approached me. He had followed my speaking ministry for two years and said he thought I was the most powerfully effective communicator he had ever heard. Further, he said he believed that I could one day be elected president of the United States if I followed the plan he had masterminded for me. He placed before me a long-term, carefully crafted strategy designed to gain enough visibility and credibility to build the foundation for a lifelong political career, one he hoped would put me in the White House in 1980. He thought by then that America would have moved toward more conservative leadership—quite amazing foresight in light of Ronald Reagan's election that year!

Mr. Hunt was disappointed when I declined his offer to utilize his influence and wealth to move me toward the lofty goal of becoming the nation's leader, but I believed that my ministry as an evangelist would fulfill the role that God intended for my life.

Nearly everyone assumed that I would make my mark through public speaking opportunities across the nation and throughout the world. In fact, for many years I spoke in stadiums and coliseums often filled to overflowing. At one point, Dr. Frank Harber, now a pastor in Texas, wrote a doctoral thesis in which he stated that by the time I was thirty, I had preached to more people in person than anyone else in history. I say this only to document the fact that by every external standard, I was considered a "success." But the sad truth is that great success brought the greatest temptations and battles I could imagine. I often found myself unable to control my appetites, attitudes, and—in many instances—my actions, because I had foolishly moved away from the necessary intimacy with God.

Such is the case with many people who have succeeded according to our society's standards. Look at how many have failed after gaining so much: athletes who are in and out of prison, entertainers who are hooked on drugs, businessmen who are under investigation by Congress, politicians who are caught in scandalous situations, and even ministers who have found themselves in the midst of moral, ethical, and legal controversies. Few things can destroy a person as quickly as the pressures and temptations that often accompany great success.

I am convinced that had it not been for my wonderful, patient wife, my loving family, and truly caring friends who became the stabilizing force in my life, I could have been destroyed. I was successful in my public life, but I was failing in my private and personal life. It was at that time that I discovered that servanthood is the source of true success and significance. As Jesus said, "The servant is greatest of all" when it comes to the impact we have in the world. Through the love of God, I also

241

found restoration, renewal, and the resolve to move away from what the world had defined as success and to begin working toward true significance.

A remarkable thing happened in my life, and it would be wonderful if it happened in the life of every person: I became a servant and discovered the real key to success. I found significance when I began serving others. After my release from the pull of "success" that had seemed to hold me captive, I no longer felt the need to compete with others in order to be recognized. From that time on, I adopted a new lifetime motto: "I have nothing to prove. I have Someone to please." I began living with the goal of always trying to give more to others than I ever received from them.

The Cult of Self

Selfishness is epidemic in our day. Our culture teaches us from our earliest days to look out for number one, to pamper ourselves, and to encourage self-actualization, self-awareness, and self-esteem. As a result, we have become self-absorbed, self-concerned, and self-consumed. We also have become supremely unhappy and unfulfilled. The reason, says psychologist Paul Kellerman, is that "the only path to genuine happiness and fulfillment is through service to others. It is only as we give ourselves away that we can truly discover ourselves."[9]

The whole of history contradicts our society's emphasis on self-service and self-satisfaction. We can learn some great lessons about servanthood and significance by observing the lives and work of men and women who put the interests of others before their own, who put the safety of others before their own, and who put the happiness of others before their own. Compare the lives of men like George Washington, Patrick Henry, John Quincy Adams, Abraham Lincoln, and Teddy Roosevelt with our modern-day obsession with self. The enormous contrast quickly becomes clear. Our contemporary culture beckons us to "find ourselves" by turning inward. It entices us to "satisfy ourselves" by "being true to ourselves." But these heroes resisted the siren song of self-aggrandizement. They fought for justice, cared for the needy, worked for mercy, fed the hungry, and rescued the perishing. Their greatest accomplishments were the result of their servanthood—the key to significance, success, and even authority.

Sociologists have identified a link between social service and social authority. Whoever meets the needs of the people will gain the allegiance of the people. The administrators of many of our social service institutions understand this concept of social development very well. As a result of the entitlements they have bestowed on others, they have gained increasing authority. But as Jesus taught his disciples, real authority comes when we humbly serve others:

243

> The kings of the Gentiles lord it over them; and those who exercise authority over them call themselves Benefactors. But you are not to be like that. Instead, the greatest among you should be like the youngest, and the one who rules like the one who serves. For who is greater, the one who is at the table or the one who serves? Is it not the one who is at the table? But I am among you as one who serves.[10]

Sadly, all too many of us have not fully grasped the link between charity, mercy, kindness, and authority. We have not fully understood that authority comes through service. When people are needy, fearful, or desperate, they seek out protection. They seek out benefactors. They seek out authorities with whom they can trade allegiance for security.

Early in our nation's history, the Church was largely responsible for operating the hospitals, orphanages, almshouses, rescue missions, hostels, soup kitchens, welfare agencies, schools, and universities. The Church was a home to the homeless and a refuge for the rejected. The Church willingly took up the mantle of servanthood. As a result, it was able to demonstrate its cultural significance. It tasted genuine success. The Church had cultural authority, which it had earned by serving.

Somewhere along the line, much of the Church at large seemed to lose its focus when it comes to loving and serving people. That's not to say we ever abandoned those ministries, but many began to look for political solutions to our nation's needs. It is sad to note that political activists did more to secure civil rights for minorities than did the Church. Although many in the Church did diligently seek to help tear down the walls of discrimination, there were also those who were committed to continuing a spirit of separation and racism. The truth is, the critical issues we face today are far more than political issues. The roots of these issues are spiritual. And it is the consistent proclamation of spiritual truth, received and lived out daily in the lives of believers, that will lead to effective solutions to the problems people face.

Please don't misunderstand me. Canvassing neighborhoods is effective. Registering voters is essential. Evaluating candidates is very important. Mobilizing phone banks, direct-mail centers, and media campaigns are all necessary. But if we really want to make a difference in our nation and in our culture, we must not only organize ourselves politically, we must also reinvest ourselves in authentically caring for those in need. We must reinvigorate our central mission of love and service. We must help offer sanctuary to the poor, the aged, the handicapped, the unborn, the abused, and the downtrodden—and we must keep at it until every need is met, much of it through the private sector, which will prevent government waste and the misuse of our tax dollars. I personally thank God from the bottom of my heart for every person and organization that holds to the importance of moral absolutes and family values while promoting active participation in the political process.

Discovering a Servant's Heart

Several years ago, God clearly pointed out to me that I would find the essence of life—true significance—if I would begin serving others. So I started looking for people to help, not only the poor and suffering but also other ministers and leaders. If a couple's marriage was floundering, I wanted to help them get back on solid ground. If a child was in trouble, I wanted to reach out. If a staff member was in need, I wanted to be there. In serving others, I learned how to develop relationships that became dynamically effective in turning multitudes in a new direction.

245

Adopting a servant's heart means that we will seek every way possible to give love and support to others. When I saw starving children in Africa, I knew that I needed to do something. I didn't know whether the viewers of *Life Today* would respond to a "missions emphasis," but we did what we had to do. In order to raise money to immediately feed a few thousand children, we sold our ministry airplane. Many people might associate private aircraft with excess, but in our case it was a necessity, not a luxury, because of all the traveling our team did. (There were always ten to twelve staff members accompanying me for ministry purposes, and I often spoke in several states each week and was away from home 265 to 300 days a year.) Even though the airplane was an important asset for our ministry, we sold it and used the funds to launch our mission feeding efforts. I became a servant to Peter Pretorius—a servant himself—who was already working to feed the hungry in Africa. Within a matter of months our ministry was seeing more people come to faith in Christ in a single year than we had in a decade of public speaking.

We were suddenly making an even greater difference than before and found real significance. We had come to see first-hand what Jesus meant when He said, "The greatest among you shall be your servant."[11] He did not mean great in recognition, appreciation, or admiration. He meant great in impact and effectiveness for eternity. Truly, those who serve others are the greatest in bringing about positive change and results.

The Old Testament prophet Isaiah said it well:

Feed the hungry and help those in trouble. Then your light will shine out from the darkness, and the darkness around you will be as bright as day. The Lord will guide you continually, watering your life when you are dry and keeping you healthy, too. You will be like a well-watered garden, like an ever-flowing spring. Your children will rebuild the deserted ruins of your cities. Then you will be known as the people who rebuild their walls and cities.[12]

The Power of One Person of Principle

Can one person dedicated to servanthood make a difference? The answer, unequivocally, is yes. Consider the example of the great English statesman William Wilberforce. With the perspective of 20/20 hindsight, we can now see the extraordinary effects of his leadership on the course of history. Though he was a remarkable orator; though he successfully assembled powerful political, social, religious, and cultural coalitions; though he was able to serve his nation ably and faithfully from the time he was a young man to the time he was an elder statesman; and though he was privileged to receive the acclaim of friend and foe alike during his long career, the real effects of his leadership were not readily evident in his lifetime. It is only by the legacy he left that we are able to gauge the true impact of his life.

Shortly after he was elected to Parliament as a very young man, Wilberforce underwent a dramatic conversion to Christianity. From that day forward he determined to use his office as a force for selfless service to the poorest of the poor and the neediest of the needy. He devoted himself to a host of social reforms, including child-labor laws, equitable weights and measures, and fair immigration statutes. He worked for farm-labor reform, colonial-administration reform, progressive tax reform, factory-labor reform, and franchise-rights reform. His greatest cause, however, was the fight to abolish the African slave trade, which by the late 1700s had become a massively lucrative global enterprise. Wilberforce quickly became the emerging abolitionist movement's chief spokesman in the House of Commons—indeed, he became its chief spokesman anywhere and everywhere throughout the world.

247

In 1807, Wilberforce finally secured enactment of legislation prohibiting the slave trade and thus banning the import of newly captured Africans into any of the far-flung British colonies. But he did not rest on his laurels. He immediately went to work writing legislation that called for the complete abolition of slavery, banning not only commerce in human flesh but transferred-ownership rights as well. He devoted the rest of his life to the cause. Though old age and ill health ultimately forced his retirement from Parliament in 1825, the legislation he had worked so hard to secure, the Emancipation Bill abolishing slavery altogether, became law as he lay dying.

Like a latter day Athanasius, Wilberforce was forced to stand "all alone against the world," most of his life. He was a nonconformist in a day of enforced conformity. He was a genuine reformer and a man of unswerving principle in a day of blatant compromise. At times he was considered a single-minded fanatic. But it was precisely because he was willing to risk such stigmatization for the sake of justice and truth that he was able to prevail.

Thomas Chalmers, the great Scottish pastor, professor, and reformer, likened Wilberforce to George Washington, "who had the knack of losing every battle on his way to winning the war."[13] His tenacious and steadfast commitment to the cause of ending the African slave trade knew no moderation, accepted no defeat, and gave no credence to setbacks, mishaps, or obstacles. Chalmers continued: "William Wilberforce is that rarest of all breeds, a man of great influence and station willing to sacrifice all for the sake of truth. When we pray that the Lord might be pleased to deliver us from the hands of politicians and to entrust our future to statesmen, we are unwittingly praying that He would raise Wilberforce—and those few like him—to ever higher positions."[14]

If our elected officials—from the president, through both houses of Congress, to the Cabinet and all the appointed posts—could understand clearly that their roles are those of servants, then our country will continue to flourish.

Although most servants will never have the widespread historical impact of a man like William Wilberforce, I am moved by individuals who have a profound effect on the communities where they live. For example, Jackie Holland, a Texas native, has been feeding the poor in the Dallas/Fort Worth area for many years. Her ministry began when she discovered good, untouched food in a grocery store's dumpster near her home. The store was discarding the products because they were close to the code dates for freshness, but the food was still safe to eat. At first she took the boxes out of dumpsters and gave the food to those in low-income apartments. Eventually, she got up the nerve to ask the grocery-store manager if he could save those boxes for her. She was paid nothing for her service—she was simply being obedient to God. Today, Jackie is on staff as care pastor at Restoration Church in Euless, Texas, and oversees a food line on Tuesdays and Thursdays. "I tell my volunteers to treat the next person in line as if it could be Jesus," she said. Before the locals walk through the line, filling their bags with a variety of groceries, they are invited to attend a service that Jackie leads. Jackie Holland's care and compassion have changed numerous lives.

Another powerful example of servant leadership is Dr. Howard Hendricks, who has taught at Dallas Theological Seminary for more than fifty years. Early in the seminary's history, there were months when Dr. Hendricks didn't get paid—but that didn't seem to deter him. Fortunately, some local grocers and clothing stores helped out the dedicated professor. When Dr. Hendricks received an invitation to teach at prestigious Yale University, he turned down the offer. His calling was to help prepare future ministry leaders instead of Ivy League scholars. Truly, Dr. Hendricks helped put Dallas Theological Seminary on the map. He has mentored thousands of students who, in turn, have influenced many more people with the gospel. Some are very well-known leaders like Dr. Bruce Wilkinson, author of the widely read book *The Prayer of Jabez*; Dr. Chuck Swindoll, noted author, speaker, and chancellor of Dallaas Theological Seminary; and Dr. Joseph Stowell, president of Moody Bible Institute. Dr. Hendricks still teaches, speaks across the country, and serves as chairman of the Center for Christian Leadership at the seminary.

There are many "unsung heroes" who are making a difference in America, and we need to follow their lead. Does the idea of accomplishing something significant seem overwhelming or

249

so big that you don't know where to start? Keep in mind that in the two examples above, neither Jackie Holland nor Dr. Hendricks went out of their way to look for needs to meet or opportunities to have an impact. Rather, the opportunities presented themselves in the course of their daily lives, and they responded to those opportunities in ways that were in line with their own gifts and abilities. In the same way, we must learn to serve our families, neighbors, friends, and even our enemies. All of us must learn to do things that will last beyond this lifetime. Then and only then will we be able to find success as a nation and significance as citizens.

15

CHAPTER FIFTEEN

To be capable of steady friendship or lasting love are the two greatest proofs, not only of goodness of heart, but of strength of mind. **WILLIAM HAZLITT (1778–1830)**

Love doubles our joy and halves our grief.
DOLLEY MADISON (1768–1849)

Love, for therein lies true strength, and whosoever loves much performs much, and can accomplish much, and what is done in love is oft done well.
VINCENT VAN GOGH (1853–1890)

Love Conquers All

*Love never fails. Ultimately, it can overcome
every obstacle and solve every dilemma.*

One of the more enduring images from the World Trade Center disaster was the sight of rescue workers rushing *into* the building while frightened office workers were streaming out. Many of those valiant firefighters, police officers, and emergency-response workers paid with their lives. Nevertheless, later, after the towers had collapsed, another wave of rescuers combed the wreckage—ignoring their own exhaustion, hunger, and safety—in a desperate search for survivors.

What caused these heroes to endanger their lives for the sake of their fellow citizens? Was it duty? responsibility? courage? . . . Or was it love?

What motivated the passengers of United Airlines Flight 93 to attempt to overcome their attackers and thwart their plans for mass destruction, though it cost them their lives? Was it desperation? anger? an instinct for self-preservation? . . . Or was it love?

Jesus said there is no greater expression of love than to lay down one's life for another person. Genuine love is innately sacrificial, putting the interests of others before our own. It sees the opportunities, not the obstacles. It is tenaciously persistent and boldly active. We can *say* that we love other people, but do we also show that we love them by our actions? Are we willing to roll up our sleeves and get involved in their lives? True love cannot be faked. It has a certain air of authenticity about it. It doesn't give in when the going gets tough. It doesn't give up when the loved one doesn't respond.

The absolute principle is pretty simple: If we truly love other people, we won't stand by watching while they suffer. When we see people in need—and depending on our circumstances, we may not have to look far—we find ways to meet those needs. If we can't do it on our own, we can team up with others or find an organization that is already working to meet those needs and get involved. If for some reason we cannot get involved directly, we can contribute financially to help worthy organizations get the job done. Good people out of the good treasure of their hearts bring forth good things.[1]

We've seen the power of sacrificial love at work countless times in modern history:

- Families in the Dutch and French Resistance hiding Jews from the Nazis during World War II.
- Poets and writers in the Russian samizdat, a clandestine organization for publishing and distributing government-suppressed literature, forming an underground system to care for the families of Siberian exiles.
- Missionaries in India standing against the barbarities of suttee, the voluntary cremation of a widow on her husband's funeral pyre.
- Emancipationists liberating captive slaves in West Africa.

– Freedom fighters throwing off the shackles of tyranny in Nicaragua, Malaysia, Sudan, Croatia, Belarus, and Tibet.

Betty and I have worked for years alongside missionaries and their children who have left behind the comforts of home to give hope and life to suffering people throughout the Third World. In the end, the worst that evil can do is no match for the best that love in action can accomplish. If we want to overcome evil in our nation and around the world and make a positive difference in the lives of people everywhere, we must demonstrate deep, sacrificial love and commitment.

Fighting Evil on Two Fronts

Following the September 11, 2001, terrorist attacks, a reporter from the *New York Times* called me to ask what spiritual advice or counsel I might offer the nation. I told her we must fight the terrorist threat on two fronts: militarily and with love. We fight militarily to defend freedom, protect the innocent, and punish the perpetrators of evil. That's justice in action, and it fulfills the rightful responsibility of government: providing security for its citizens and punishing wrongdoers.

At the same time, we must recognize that military action is not the final answer. To achieve the ultimate victory, we must fight our enemies with love. How do we do that? First, we must be very clear about the identity of the enemy. It's not the people; it is the force of evil that holds people in bondage. We all have tendencies toward evil—it's part of our fallen nature—and people are, in various degrees, controlled by the power of evil. But love can break that power, and people can be redeemed—set free from evil's grasp. If love is our motivation, our hearts will feel compassion and a deep desire to see people released from their bondage and captivity.

We must love the Afghan people, who have been suffering under the harsh hand of a corrupt system, and not think of their country only as a place where we must uproot the terrorist training system. It will take genuine love to give us the endurance to secure the opportunities for freedom in Afghanistan and to meet the needs of the people there.

To extend the argument even further, we must have love for the Taliban even though we detest their ways. Perhaps you've heard it said that we should hate the sin but love the sinner. I believe that's exactly what we must do. I hate what Osama bin Laden and his associates have done. There's no excuse for the evil they brought to bear on the victims in New York City, Washington, D.C., and rural Pennsylvania. But if I rightly perceive Osama bin Laden as a mortal man caught up by the forces of hatred and evil and living out the inevitable consequences of his worldview, then I must love him as I would love any other person whom God created and for whom Christ died.

255

If you think about it, there isn't a lot of difference between Osama bin Laden and Saul of Tarsus (in the New Testament) before his conversion on the road to Damascus. For all intents and purposes, Saul was a Middle Eastern terrorist who thought he was doing God a service by trying to destroy everything connected with the Church of Jesus Christ. In the name of religion, he was filled with hatred. He watched approvingly as an innocent man was stoned to death.

What turned Saul around? It wasn't persuasive preaching; it wasn't reason or rhetoric or military action. Instead, it was the love of God expressed through the words of a dying man—a man named Stephen—who offered forgiveness with his final breath.[2] If we want to break the power of evil in this world, it's going to take a Stephen-like commitment to love other people.

I've met some people who have that kind of love for Afghanistan. People like Dayna Curry and Heather Mercer, whose lives were spared by the Taliban but who were willing to risk it all to bring the love of God to the suffering Afghan people.

Loving the Unlovely

Of course, having compassion for other people and loving our enemies does not mean we stand idly by while those who are bent on destruction perpetrate their evil in the world. You can be certain that if someone breaks into my home to harm my family or me, I am not going to say, "I love you, brother," and offer him a sandwich. I am going to defend my family.

We have an obligation to resist evil in all its forms, and the government has the express responsibility to protect the lives and safety of its citizens by bringing criminals and evildoers to justice. Just because we love other people doesn't mean that criminals shouldn't pay for their crimes, but we must be certain that our motive is justice and not vengeance. Nevertheless, as we rightfully seek to bring wrongdoers to justice, as Christians we also ought to be praying that God will transform their hearts and fill them with his love.

How is it possible to love someone like Osama bin Laden? My personal opinion is that sacrificial love is the result of a supernatural work of God in the life of those who have received the love of God themselves. God's love moves beyond human compassion and care, which is as natural as a mother lion's care for her cubs. All created beings have a basic instinct to protect certain aspects of life around them. But for us to love our enemies and yet not condone what they do takes a supernatural change in our hearts. And if sacrificial love is not expressed in the life of every person in a given community or society, then those who have the love of God in their hearts must, by their example, influence those who don't.

We won't win everybody over. Some people will not accept our love for them. Many people rejected the perfect love of Jesus when He walked on the earth, and instead, they nailed Him to a cross. It's possible to reject love, and many have done so down through the ages. Nevertheless, love has had its effect, and it has caused some dramatic, positive changes in society.

The Transforming Power of Love

Let me tell you how I've seen the power of love transform some otherwise hopeless situations through the work of Life Outreach International.

Angola

In Angola, the most dangerous place on earth to be a child, we discovered that even the most hard-nosed Marxists would relent when they saw that our only concern was to care for the children of their country. As a result, even though the situation there is far from safe, we have been able to feed, care for, and save the lives of thousands of children.

Perhaps you've seen the photo of the late Diana, princess of Wales, holding a chubby little African child in her arms at a hospital in Luanda, Angola. Life Outreach International was the supplier of food, medicine, and supplies to that hospital, and the beautiful, healthy child with Diana in the picture was among the children for whom we had been caring for years. I'm telling you, the power of love *works*.

Mozambique

On my first visit to Mozambique more than twelve years ago, in the region of Tete where thousands of people were dying, Peter

257

Pretorius had established a feeding program that after a matter of months was producing positive results. Already, some of the hungry children were being strengthened and given new hope.

I'll never forget a young boy there we nicknamed "Little Buddy." He became like a poster child for the mission. When I met him, he had on a tattered red shirt and was carrying a cup of hot soup. We were filming that day and I turned toward the television camera as this beautiful child walked up and stood beside me with a smile. I pointed at the cup of soup in his hand, looked at the camera and said, "See, he's been given a cup of soup. Look how happy he is. He's grateful."

That little boy, unsolicited and for all the world to hear, immediately said, "Yaw."

That "yaw" was like an injection of pure inspiration that stirred compassion in the hearts of everyone who witnessed it. It became a tipping point for a lot of people to become involved in feeding the hungry. That's the power of love.

258

When Life Outreach first went into Mozambique, the iron grip of the Marxist government was clearly evident: Helicopters, machine guns, and tanks were everywhere. We just went into the country to love people. We loved the members of the Renamo opposition party, we loved the people in the government, and we loved the children. Both sides arrested us, and both sides turned us loose. By God's grace, neither side killed us. For ten years, evangelist Peter Pretorius was the only Christian who could speak publicly in the country, and he told the people about Jesus.

Today, Mozambique, once the poorest nation in the world, is the greatest example of democracy in any developing nation. Mozambique still has its struggles, but it's a miracle how rapidly the country has come out of the doldrums. We're continuing to help them with education and feeding programs, and school attendance has skyrocketed.

We're seeing Mozambique change, and I was thrilled when the president of Mozambique, Joaquim Alberto Chissano, visited the White House early in 2002 to talk about how a nation can change.

I've seen what the power of God has done in Rwanda. I've watched the beginning of an incredible turnaround. I'm watching it happen slowly in the Congo. And I've seen the first glimmers of hope in, of all places, Sudan. It hasn't happened yet, but it might. And if it does, will it be because of American ingenuity and strong-arm diplomacy? No. It will be because of the transforming power of love. Nigeria, a strong Muslim country, has now elected a committed Christian as its president. God's love is also at work in the former Communist bloc of Eastern Europe.

Sudan

The difference between mere religion and a genuine faith in God is an undeniable expression of love. Love is the one thing we've seen that does work. It is the very force that stopped the advance of radical religious forces that threatened to sweep throughout Africa, from the north down into the sub-Saharan area. In Sudan you can draw a line that marks the border where Christian missionaries, fifty to one hundred years ago, left such a mark on the lives of the people that Franklin Graham said to me, "You must go here. I promise you, you will see people more like Jesus than any people on earth since the New Testament."

When Franklin and I visited areas of the Sudan that had been devastated by repeated bombing (even the medical clinics were targets), the pilot of our plane had to take off again almost immediately after dropping us off, for fear of being attacked. As we watched the aircraft disappear into the distant sky, I wondered if it would be able to return to pick us up. In the midst of this uncertain and horrible situation, we walked into the presence of some of the most beautiful and radiant people I have ever met. Despite their dire circumstances, they were singing and praising God and offering prayers of thanksgiving. The love and the glory of God shone in their faces. They spoke of the missionaries who had taught them about Jesus as if they had been there yesterday, even though many of these spiritual leaders have been dead for more than thirty years. The people still recall their names and refer to them as grandparents. What makes this story particularly remarkable is that it demonstrates how the influence of Christian missionaries from years ago stopped the aggressive spread of Islam as it sought to sweep southward throughout Africa. Much like the Israelites who would not bow before King Nebuchadnezzar, the Sudanese Christians refused to succumb to intense persecution from their government. They stood firm and insisted that God would deliver them. Even as many of them died, they persevered in glorifyng God.

We need a similar caliber of faith to sweep through the entire Church if we ever hope to stop the aggressive spread of evil throughout the world. We need a similar level of commitment to the absolutes if we want to experience a new day in America; if we genuinely desire to feed every hungry child and see to it that no person is forced to drink unsanitary water. It can be done. We can touch the heart of the world. God has never given us an assignment without the resources to fulfill it.

China

In China, our mission was to help the people who struggled the most, such as the thousands of orphans. When we met with the leaders in Nanchung and other places south of Beijing, our focus was always on how to alleviate the suffering, how to help the workers in the orphanages, and how we could supply medical personnel. All of our workers were Christian, and it never became an issue with the Chinese. In fact, the leaders gave us permission to pass out Christian literature in their language as long as they printed it. It was all accomplished through discussion and the love of God.

How did it work? We just kept talking, not about making deals but about what we could do to help them with a very serious problem: how best to care for the children. The more we talked, the more they listened to us. And they were intrigued because we didn't conform to their preconceptions about what Americans or Westerners would be like. We weren't the deal makers they expected. They talked to us about how their media portray the United States. They really see our weaknesses, and they're accurate in some of their observations. When they pointed out something negative, we acknowledged that, yes, there are some areas in which we need to improve. We'd say, we're not necessarily the model, but here are some things that are the model. Here are things we've tried that *do* work, and this is *why* they work.

261

We continued to just love the Chinese as people—and it disarmed them. We learned from our interpreters that behind our backs the leaders were saying, "These people are strange. They're not like typical capitalists from the West. These people love us. They love our people. They love our children. They want to help."

They were also intrigued and captivated by my life story. I told them everything, including how I was conceived as the result of rape and raised in poverty and how I came to love Jesus. They were very interested and asked if I would like to speak in their city squares. I had the opportunity to speak publicly and on television, as long as I didn't proselytize. We were allowed to share some printed materials about the West and explain what we believe.

We watched firsthand as the power of love moved the Chinese people deeply. And because we had built such incredible trust, they allowed our cameras to go anywhere, in all facilities, to see the worst of sites. Our camera crews went all the way to Beijing and filmed in hospitals, orphanages, and other facilities. The Chinese leaders trusted us because they said, "You want only to improve us. You're not trying to hurt us. You care about us." That is the transforming power of love.

We didn't accomplish all of this overnight. It was a slow process, with interaction and dialogue. Because our motive was love, we took time to build relationships and trust. The mission of Life Outreach International to feed hungry children has been successful because we genuinely love the people we serve. If they never gave us a chance to talk about the love of God, we would still love them and do everything we could to help them. We would still do our best to show them God's love in action, and that opens the door to relationship. Sadly, our efforts in China were largely undermined by a news crew from another country that came to do an exposé of Chinese atrocities. The government saw this as a betrayal of trust and clamped down on foreign involvement, including many of our projects.

Before President Bush made his first trip to China, I shared privately with him that I thought he would accomplish far more than he might ever imagine if he simply treated the Chinese leaders with honor and respect. We know we don't agree with them in numerous areas, but we can show them love. I can tell you this: We'll never get anywhere with the leaders of China or any other nation by pointing out everything that's wrong with their country. They look at us in America and listen to what we say. Then they observe some of our lifestyles and the evident disregard some Americans have for the law, and they think we're nuts. "Why do you have laws if you don't enforce them?"

Chinese leaders asked me. They then went on to say, "We are not afraid to sit out on our porches at night. If you drop your wallet on the street, it will be there for you when you come back. We don't have a drug problem." We can talk all we want about how the Chinese achieve their results through oppression, but unless and until we demonstrate to them the transforming power of love, the impact of our diplomacy will be diminished. I know that President Bush believes in the power of love, and I believe he was successful in establishing a good rapport with the Chinese precisely because he showed them love and respect. On his way to China for his second visit, President Bush told a group of armed forces personnel, who greeted him at a stop-over, that he had shared with Chinese president Jiang Zemin how his faith in Christ has changed his life. He encouraged Jiang not to write off religion and to discontinue intolerance.

How Can a Nation Show Love?

263

It may not be particularly difficult to understand how an individual can show love or how a private enterprise can be organized around the principles of love, but what about applying these principles at the national level? I won't for a moment suggest that it's easy, but it *is* possible. As long as the United States remains a picture of hope to the world, we Americans will have our place at the table, but if we want to continue to be effective in our diplomacy and in our foreign aid, we need to change our mind-set and our motives. We must set aside our partisan differences and show the world what one nation under God can do to reveal this love to all people. I'm not talking about exporting the Christian religion, but I *am* talking about using all the power God has given us to have a positive impact on world leaders.

If we approached our domestic and foreign policy on the

basis of love and what is best for the people involved rather than focus on what would advance our national interests or on what we could gain in terms of resources, influence, or the balance of power, we could begin to transform the world.

Again, I'm not suggesting that this process will be easy—principled decisions never are—but if we don't put the interests of people first, we risk making situations worse instead of better. In the 1980s, when the United States supported the extreme fundamentalist Afghan leaders in their fight with the Soviets, we had been warned that they were ruthless and that once they had control of the country, they were likely to do exactly what they did: establish a repressive regime. In many respects, when we left the Afghan people under the control of the extreme fundamentlists, they might just as well have been under Soviet dominion. Of course, there were other reasons we didn't want that to happen—we didn't want the Soviets to control the Persian Gulf, for example, and we were resisting the spread of Communism. But the point is, we were resisting something to protect our own security and defend our own interests without adequately providing for the security and stability of the people who were directly affected.

It's true that we can't police the world. But love will cause us to stretch the boundaries of our efforts beyond anything we've ever done before. We need to look at situations around the globe with new eyes and with a view to protecting and providing for the people. President Jimmy Carter was instrumental in making the issue of human rights violations a central part of our foreign policy, and we need to build on the foundation of those suggestions. Persecution, oppression, and corruption are serious issues. It should matter to us how other countries use the foreign aid they receive from us. We're not going to solve the problem of corrupt and repressive regimes overnight, and only love will compel us to persist in finding ways to do it, but love should motivate us to try to find a solution when people are suffering abuse anywhere in the world. We should apply all of our resources, our business acumen, and our technological and industrial abilities to serve the best interests of *all* people, not just the interests of America or the corporate bottom line. If we don't start thinking that way, our freedom is in serious trouble.

British prime minister Tony Blair addressed this in one of his speeches following September 11, when he said that it will be a black mark on the conscience of all humanity if we ignore Africa and don't do better at addressing the needs there. I agree. I pray continually that the United States government and we as a people will see all of Africa as a glorious opportunity to share love. The African continent is rich in natural resources, yes, but there is no greater resource than the beautiful African people, and their well-being must be a top priority.

There are opportunities around the world for God's love to transform entire populations and enable nations to reach their full potential sociologically, economically, and spiritually: the war-torn enclaves of the former Yugoslavia, the oppressive slums of Bolivia, the remote villages of India, the wastelands of sub-Saharan Africa. There are so many places for love to give birth to life.

We can be certain that extremist Islamic groups and others with a terrorist mind-set will seek to convert and exploit the poor, underdeveloped nations. It has been the influence of Christian missionaries that has slowed the advance of radical Islam into the southern part of Africa. Love is the greatest force on earth to resist, limit, and ultimately halt evil's deadly progression. This is the greatest hour in human history for us to take hold of the power of God's love, "not in word only, but in deed."[3]

Corporate Love

It is not only our government that must act on the basis of love; corporations must take responsibility as well. The business community could change the continent of Africa, the nation of India and south Asia, and Central and South America—for the better. But that won't happen as long as American businesses move into countries only for what they can take out, without considering what they can put back, what they can establish, and what they can build for the future. Take Enron, for example: Enron could have helped to restructure some of the Third World. When they went into India to develop the power industry there, they could have done something good and established longstanding relationships. But the way they manipulated the situation and hurt others by taking water to drive their power plants, with no consideration of needs for irrigation, revealed their true motivations: greed and power. They did not have the best interests of the Indian people in mind. Their bottom line was controlled by greed, and it was wrong. President Bush, speaking at Notre Dame in 2001, emphasized that the business community must become more committed to charity in behalf of the poor. He's right. We can't simply leave caring for the poor up to the government. Businesses must do more to help others. If we're to be successful, everybody must decide to make a difference, and we must act with integrity.

An Appeal to the Church

I'm convinced that before this attitude of love will sweep our nation and the world, it must first take root in the Church of Jesus Christ. After all, isn't love the signature gift of the Spirit? We need to show people that Jesus sends us out first to *demonstrate* what He taught in His life—and *then* to teach them the life of love. All too often we have misinterpreted "making disciples" to mean making members of our own group. By seeking to spiritually clone ourselves, we have succeeded in making "like kind," but we have not necessarily made "Christlike kind." If we show people that we love them—period—the way a parent loves a child, their lives can be transformed by the power of the Holy Spirit.

If you had asked me years ago if I loved other people, I would have said yes, but I think I had developed a spirit of intolerance that was not healthy. The fact is, we can hold our religious positions even more strongly than we do our political positions. Denominationalism has as much potential to damage people as racism or any other "ism" does. God got my attention and showed me I had developed a very intolerant attitude through my association with other like-minded individuals and groups.

I remember calling Billy Graham and criticizing him quite forcefully for his association with people I deemed too liberal or non-Evangelical, because of his friendship with Catholics in other countries and his association with charismatics and Pentecostals. Dr. Graham was unfailingly gracious to me in that conversation, and he said, "I really want to be careful that I'm not compromising. I don't want to do that. But tell me this: Do you know these people? Have you been around these people that you're talking about? Have you spent much time with them?"

I said, "No, I haven't."

And he replied, "Well, I have, and I've found them to be very Christlike. As a matter of fact, I couldn't have a crusade outside the United States without their help. If it were not for the Pentecostals and charismatics, I couldn't have an effective crusade overseas."

As I look back on that conversation, I realize that the same small-mindedness and hard-heartedness I exhibited is a tendency of many in the church. And we need to stop it. It's not

267

healthy, and it makes us insensitive to the heart of God. It deafens us to what the Lord is saying to His people.

Showing love does not mean we'll never have disagreements, but let's learn how to resolve those disagreements without being hateful. What have we accomplished if we "win" a debate but lose a brother?

I still have deep convictions about things—and I still have my hot-button issues—but my convictions now are aimed more toward tearing down the walls that separate people and building a dialogue that leads to healing and reconciliation. I'm tired of the division in the Church and in our nation. I want to help bring people together, "speaking the truth in love."

That's why I am heartbroken when people refuse to dialogue, when they refuse to interact honestly or try to hear one another. And it disturbs me when I see the media misrepresent the truth, or when I see Hollywood filmmakers misrepresent the truth, or when religious people misrepresent the truth. Let's stop hiding behind our party lines, our denominational differences, our stereotypes, and our rhetoric. Let's speak the truth lovingly to each other and continue to build on the absolute principles that have made our nation great.

Love As Forgiveness

I am personally convinced that love has no greater expression than forgiveness—sincere, wholehearted forgiveness that seeks to reconcile relationships and restore the fallen. We should never accept or tolerate evil, but love can be released without condoning sin. Steven Mosley's book *A Tale of Three Virtues* gives a powerful example of this truth put into practice:

Tommy Pigage was a convicted killer. He had grown up in a troubled family, and by age sixteen he was addicted to alcohol. One night in 1982, after drinking himself into a fog, he climbed into his car, went careering down the highway, and collided head-on with a car driven by eighteen-year-old Ted Morris. Ted, the only son of Frank and Elizabeth Morris, was killed in the crash.

The Morrises were devastated. Frank lived for the day when Tommy would be cinvicted and sentenced, and Elizabeth found herself imagining Tommy's execution—where she would be the one to throw the switch on the electric chair.

When Elizabeth finally confronted the intensity of her hatred, she was alarmed. Convicted by Christ's words on the cross, "Father, forgive them," she began praying for a change of heart. One day, after hearing Tommy speak at Ted's high school as part of his rehabilitation, Elizabeth gathered the strength to speak to him. When she discovered that no one ever visited Tommy in jail, she decided to visit him herself.

At one point during the visit, Tommy blurted out, "Mrs. Morris, I'm so sorry. Please forgive me."

For a moment time stood still. Then, as it dawned on Elizabeth that God had also lost His only Son—yet had forgiven the killers—she forgave Tommy and asked him to forgive her for the bitter hatred she had harbored against him.

The Morrises subsequently became involved in Tommy's rehabilitation, picking him up at jail and driving him to his speaking engagements. On one of these nights, as they were driving Tommy back to jail, he began talking about a Bible study course the Morrises had told him about and how he felt it had strengthened him. It became evident that Tommy had committed his life to Christ.

"Have you been baptized?" Frank asked him.

"No, but I'd like to be," Tommy answered.

Frank pulled into the parking lot of the Little River Church of Christ, where he and Elizabeth were members. Once inside,

Frank led Tommy to the baptsimal pool at the front of the sanctuary, and the two waded into the chilly water.

As Elizabeth watched her husband baptize the young man who had killed their only son, she recalled the day several years before when Frank had baptized Ted.

Although Frank Morris had joined his wife in their involvement with Tommy, he had continued to wrestle with forgiving him. Now he was baptizing him. When Frank lifted Tommy out of the water, the young man embraced him tightly and begged, "Please, I want you to forgive me, too."

In that moment, something changed and the grieving father replied tearfully, "Yes, I forgive you."

When Tommy was released from jail, the initial prospects for his rehabilitation weren't good. He still carried emotional scars from his childhood experiences and the physical consequences of his addiction to alcohol. But Elizabeth and Frank continued to involve themselves in Tommy's life. Elizabeth called him every day, and Frank occasionally asked him to help with outdoor work. Largely because of the Morrises' active concern and involvement, Tommy was able to achieve sobriety, find a steady job, and develop a strong sense of purpose. In the process, the Morrises also found the pathway of true forgiveness, regarding the killer as their son.[4]

It is vital to our freedom that evildoers are brought to justice. The thief on the cross who sought salvation received it freely from Jesus Christ, but he still had to pay for his earthly crimes. Tommy Pigage spent time in jail to pay for his crime, but the story of his life took a significant turn because of the Morrises' forgiveness and their involvement in his life as they worked for reconciliation and restoration.

We must overcome evil wherever it rears its head, but once the battle is over, we must also reach out to the people who have suffered retribution. In the same way that America forgave Great Britain, Germany, Japan, the Soviet Union, and other former enemies, we must help to rebuild ravaged nations like Afghanistan, to bring reconciliation and hope to the people. If we are truly able to forgive our enemies and demonstrate God's love in practical ways, we will overcome much of the world's hostility and hatred.

We must also apply the power of forgiveness within the borders of our own country. We must work to change unjust practices and resolve the issues that divide us. As the Morrises did, we must refuse to allow the past to hold us captive. We must forgive the wrongs we have done to one another and move forward in a spirit of reconciliation. Forgiveness releases the full power of love to transform people's lives.

There is little doubt that we will face great challenges in the days ahead. These are perilous times, and difficulties lie in wait at every turn. But if we will commit ourselves to the principle that love conquers all, we will find that love is sufficient for the task.

CHAPTER SIXTEEN

The prevailing spirit of the present age seems to be the spirit of skepticism and captiousness, of suspicion and distrust in private judgment; a dislike of all established forms, merely because they are established, and of old truths, because they are old. **SAMUEL JOHNSON (1709–1784)**

If men will not be governed by the Ten Commandments they shall be governed by the ten thousand commandments.
G. K. CHESTERTON (1874–1936)

There are those who believe that a new modernity demands a new morality. What they fail to consider is the harsh reality that there is no such thing as a new morality. There is only one morality. All else is immorality. There is only true Christian ethics over against which stands the whole of paganism. If we are to fulfill our great destiny as a people, then we must return to the old morality, the sole morality.
THEODORE ROOSEVELT (1858–1919)

The Absolutes
Have a Source

There are many other absolutes—and they have been
forthrightly revealed to us throughout the ages.

In the preceding pages, we have touched on just a few of the many absolutes that undergird our civil society. They are truths that dissenters can try to deny but can never escape. Recorded history confirms the negative consequences of rejecting the principles necessary to establish moral standards. Although the absolutes may be discovered in the course of life through observation and experience, and although they are visible in the character and nature of the created world in which we live, there is also a catalog of absolutes readily available to us. Within the pages of that remarkable text, we can find absolute principles that apply to every age and every situation.

The Book of the Ages containing the inescapable fixed principles of life is also the world's number one best-seller: the Bible. It comes from a source beyond our human capacity, and its sixty-six books contain a consistent and beautiful thread of grace, wise principles, and absolute truths. It was written over a span of hundreds of years, by writers who never met one another, yet the consistency of the themes is so remarkable that only a supernatural explanation will suffice.

Because the Author of this book is living and active and has sent His Spirit to help teach us everything we need to know and to remind us of everything He has said, it is imperative that when seeking the truth we do not strain the truth through a screen of preconceived notions, ideas, or prejudices—including religious positions.[1] The Bible often interprets itself, which means that when we read it, we can—and must—consider each passage in light of other passages of Scripture. The bottom line for proper interpretation and application is to consider the results. Are they consistent with the revealed character and works of God? Is Christlikeness the end result?

Everyone comes to the Bible with some existing presuppositions. No one is totally objective. Some approach the Scriptures demanding that any concept pass the logic test. If it is not "reasonable," then it is rejected. Others come with tradition as their interpretive key. They rely on the definitions and explanations of church historians or admired theologians, often excluding the guidance of the Holy Spirit. And others are unwilling to accept anything they cannot relate to their own experience.

Extremists in every age have used the Bible to support some of the worst heresies ever conceived. They have quoted it to justify domination, exploitation, murder, slavery, greed, and other life-destroying behaviors, including the recent bombings of abortion clinics. But here is an absolutely essential principle for evaluating the truth and reliability of Scripture: The Bible judges us; we don't judge the Bible. And if our behavior and our attitudes do not match the revealed truth of the Scriptures, then our behavior and our attitudes are wrong and must be changed. When rightly apprehended, the Bible is a book that conveys life, love, and peace. Just as the Genesis account of creation records God speaking the world into being, when the Word of God comes through the Scriptures, new worlds of light and purpose appear. The key question is: How do we get life rather than death from our reading of the Scriptures? The Bible itself reveals the truth: "The letter kills, but the Spirit gives life."[2]

If we treat the Bible as a book of religious rules and regulations—instead of recognizing that it is a living and active revelation of the truth about God, Jesus Christ, and the Holy Spirit—we will be doomed to a life of never quite measuring up to the high standard of Scripture. But if by faith we understand that on our own we never will measure up, and that our only hope is to accept the pathway to reconciliation with God that comes through the death and resurrection of Jesus Christ, then we can experience an abundance of life.

Taking a Step of Faith

Some people attempt to discredit a belief in God and the Bible by calling it a "leap of faith," but that's nothing out of the ordinary. After all, *every* belief system is based on faith at some level. Humanists, for example, who believe we exist by chance and that the source of truth—if it even exists—must come from within us, cannot prove their case, so at some point they take a step of faith. As Christians we unashamedly confess that we believe in the veracity of the Bible and the faithfulness of God. We, too, have taken a step of faith in choosing who will be our ultimate interpreter of truth. It is not ourselves, our experience, or our traditions, but Jesus Christ, God's Son. Jesus is the only one who can faithfully explain God and the Scriptures to us.[3]

Some would argue that Christians are too exclusive and narrow-minded for believing that Jesus is the only way to God. Actually, this is not our choice. Jesus is the One who said, "I am the way and the truth and the life. No one comes to the Father except through me."[4] By embracing Jesus, we surrender the right to add to or subtract from His claims. To deny His assertions would be to deny Jesus Himself.

Our step of faith requires total commitment, but it is not a blind step into the dark, because the Bible shines the light of truth into every corner of our lives. All of humanity is looking for the answers to some basic but vital questions: How did we get here? What is our purpose? Why is evil present and what can we do about it? How do we find answers to solve the human dilemma?

The Bible gives the best answer: A personal, all-powerful and loving God created everything that exists with the purpose of sharing His joy with the highest of His creatures: human beings. Because God gave humans the dignity of making choices that have real consequences, we each have the opportunity to accept or reject the Creator's plan. Without exception, in our carnal hearts, we have all turned our backs on God, and the consequences have affected all of creation. These consequences can only be reversed by God, who chose to redeem His creation by sending His own perfect Son into the world to die as a sacrifice for our sins. In effect, He transferred the consequences of our rebellion onto Jesus, while transferring the consequences of Jesus' perfect faithfulness onto us. The heart prepared to receive truth accepts Jesus as the final authority.

The Book of Books

God has authored an extraordinary book—its very name means "book of books"—and in its pages can be found all the absolutes. Its beauty and truth have inspired untold generations with its extraordinary vision of faith, hope, love, and redemption. In addition, it has provoked the most glorious cultural flowering the world has ever known. As Yale University professor William Lyons Phelps observed, "Our civilization is founded on the Bible. More of our ideas, our wisdom, our philosophy, our literature, our art, our ideals come from the Bible than from all other books combined."[5]

According to D. James Kennedy in his remarkable work titled *What If the Bible Had Never Been Written?* there is not a single aspect of Western civilization—from the prosperity we enjoy to the freedoms we cherish; from the comforts we have to the security we rely on—that is not directly attributable to the teaching and influence of biblical absolutes.[6] Our worldview, our music, our economics, our technology, our stories, our education, our health care, our law, our industry, our science, and our art are all rooted in basic scriptural truths.

The wise men and women who have gone before us looked to the Bible as their blueprint for living. They took it seriously—studying it, applying it, and obeying it—because they understood and accepted that the Bible is the Word of God. As theologian Cornelius Van Til says, "The Bible is authoritative on everything of which it speaks, and it speaks of everything."[7]

John Locke was the political and philosophical theorist whom the Founding Fathers most relied upon as they were laying the foundations of the great American experiment in liberty. Because the basis of Locke's reasoning was the Bible, the basis of the distinctive American approach to freedom is also the Bible. He said, "The Bible is one of the greatest blessings bestowed by God on the children of men. It has God for its author, salvation for its end, and truth without any mixture of error. It is all pure, all sincere; nothing too much; nothing wanting."[8]

Likewise, the pioneering psychologist Henry James writes, "The Bible contains more true sublimity, more exquisite beauty, more morality, more important history, and finer strains of poetry and eloquence than can be collected from all other books, in whatever age or language they may have been written."[9]

John Quincy Adams said, "The Bible is the book of all others to read at all ages and in all conditions of human life; not to be read once, or twice, or thrice through, and then laid aside; but to be read in small portions of one or two chapters every day."[10]

As Abraham Lincoln later asserted, "Without the Bible we would not ever be able to tell right from wrong. It is not just the source of man's conscience, it is our only hope that our conscience may ultimately be satisfied."[11]

Napoleon Bonaparte argued that "the Bible is no mere book, but a living power that conquers all those who oppose it."[12]

Even Immanuel Kant, a philosopher not known for his orthodoxy or faith, writes, "The existence of the Bible as a book for the people is the greatest benefit which the human race has ever experienced."[13]

279

President Theodore Roosevelt quoted Scripture often, manifesting his intimate familiarity with the Bible. He believed that biblical principles were woven into the very fabric of Western civilization, and were essential for maintaining order, civility, and prosperity. Indeed, without the truth of Scripture, the great American experiment in liberty would be thrown into very real jeopardy. He believed that the absolutes expounded in the Bible were altogether indispensable:

> Every thinking man, when he thinks, realizes that the teachings of the Bible are so interwoven and entwined with our whole civic and social life that it would be literally impossible for us to figure ourselves what that life would be if these standards were removed. We would lose almost all the standards by which we now judge both public and

private morals; all the standards which we, with more or less resolution, strive to raise ourselves.[14]

Writing in his blockbuster book, *The Closing of the American Mind,* Allan Bloom reflected on the remarkable experience of his immigrant grandparents who were "ignorant by our standards" and yet were very well educated in the absolutes of the Bible. He concluded:

I do not believe that my generation, my cousins, who have been educated in the American way, all of whom are MDs or PhDs, have any comparable learning. When they talk about heaven and earth, the relationships between men and women, parents and children, the human condition, I hear nothing but clichés and superficialities, the material of satire. A life based on the Book is closer to the truth. The Bible is not the only means to furnish a mind, but without it . . . a mind will remain unfurnished.[15]

Clearly, the Bible is not just a marvelous and inspiring collection of quaint sayings and moralistic stories. It is God's own revelation of Himself and of His actions in this fallen world. It is a proclamation of God's ultimate wisdom, knowledge, and understanding. It is His message to humanity. It is His guideline, His plumb line, and His bottom line. It is a comprehensive catalog of His absolutes.

Returning to the Absolutes

Every time a problem or a crisis arises in our society, we can expect to hear the same litany of responses: "The government needs to do more"; "There ought to be a law"; "The president, or Congress, or the state legislature, or the governor, or the courts, or the CIA, or the FBI must act—and it must act immediately." We are prone to look for the quick fix, and far too many Americans are prepared to turn anywhere and everywhere except back to the absolutes.

The fact is, it took us quite some time to get into the culture-wide mess we currently find ourselves in, and it may take us a long time to get out of it. We don't need more restrictive laws, more intrusive regulations, or more bloated government agencies. What we need is a grassroots renewal of the things that made America great in the first place. The root of our current crisis is not economic, educational, institutional, scientific, or political. It is spiritual. Because as a nation we have ignored or suppressed the absolutes, we have ventured onto the battlefield of life bereft of our most essential weaponry, including truth, justice, and love. As a result, our culture is in dire straits in many areas. But we can turn things around; we can renew our commitment to the absolutes—and indeed we must.

281

The strength of our national character that was revealed in the aftermath of the September 11 terrorist attacks is a solid foundation on which to base a return to the absolutes. What the terrorists thought would destroy America actually helped to awaken and revive us. Instead of weakness and fear, the whole world saw our conviction, resolve, and determination. At the same time, they witnessed our compassion, our respect for the rule of law, and our commitment to the principles of freedom. As President Bush said in his State of the Union address in January 2002, "America has never been stronger." But if we hope to remain strong, if we hope to preserve our freedom and continue to be a light set on a hill that draws others to freedom, we must remain strong on the foundation established by the absolutes.

Already, in the months following the September 11 attacks, we've seen a tendency among the citizens of the United States to return to business as usual. In a sense, we've hit the "snooze" button on the alarm clock of world events. My concern for our nation is that we will doze off and miss the greatest opportunity we'll ever have to secure enduring freedom and make a positive difference in the world. In the words of Jesus to the church at Sardis:

> I know your deeds; you have a reputation of being alive, but you are dead. Wake up! Strengthen what remains and is about to die, for I have not found your deeds complete in the sight of my God. Remember, therefore, what you have received and heard; obey it, and repent. But if you do not wake up, I will come like a thief, and you will not know at what time I will come to you.[16]

The truth of this proclamation will be proved over time if America fails to re-engage with the absolutes. But if we apply them, we will begin to see revealed in our midst the characteristics of the man most admired in human history: Jesus Christ. We will adopt an attitude that puts others first, just as Jesus did. We will openly acknowledge our dependence on God—the very principle that made our nation great, that makes our families great, and that could make our corporations truly great. We will move away from corruption and greed, the tendencies that sacrifice everything of value on the altar of self-centered, idolatrous pursuits.

Americans will become more like the Good Samaritan as described in the parable told by Jesus.[17] When we see others in the ditch of despair, defeat, and pain, we will not merely cross to the other side of the road and continue on our own way of comfort and convenience as the priest and the Levite did. We will invest ourselves and our resources to meet the needs of others;

we will become our brother's keeper. When necessary, we will lay down our lives for the cause of freedom and for the benefit and blessing of others—as our servicemen and women have done throughout our history. We will not back down in the face of adversity or challenge, but we will be overcomers, demonstrating the spiritual truth that "greater is he that is in [us], than he that is in the world."[18] The influence of the world will not pull us away from our guiding principles.

If we will follow Jesus and adhere to the absolutes revealed in Scripture, our lives will display the values of Jesus. Like Jesus, we will love unconditionally. We will give generously. We will forgive repeatedly. We will honor God with our words and our deeds. We will love the Scriptures. And ultimately, through the power of the Holy Spirit, we will win every battle decisively. Far from being a boring religious figure, Jesus is the exciting Lord of everything, and He desires to share with us the unspeakable privilege of working with Him to bless the world.

The future is indescribably bright for all who accept the unshakable, reliable, time-tested principles of the absolutes. For those who refuse, the future is dim, and they will contribute to the efforts of the enemy, who wishes to deceive, divide, conquer, and destroy. Those who walk in the truth and hold fast to freedom-giving truth will help secure freedom's hope. For the sake of freedom, may we be bold enough to return to the absolutes. For the sake of all that is dear to us, may we be wise enough to hear and to heed the call of Scripture:

My child, listen to me and treasure my instructions. Tune your ears to wisdom, and concentrate on understanding. Cry out for insight and understanding. Search for them as you would for lost money or hidden treasure. Then you will understand what it means to fear the Lord, and you will gain knowledge of God. For the Lord grants wisdom! From his mouth come knowledge and understanding. He grants a treasure of good sense to the godly. He is their shield, protecting those who walk with integrity. He guards the paths of justice and protects those who are faithful to him.

Then you will understand what is right, just, and fair, and you will know how to find the right course of action every time. For wisdom will enter your heart, and knowledge will fill you with joy. Wise planning will watch over you. Understanding will keep you safe.

Wisdom will save you from evil people, from those whose speech is corrupt. These people turn from right ways to walk down dark and evil paths. They rejoice in doing wrong, and they enjoy evil as it turns things upside down. What they do is crooked, and their ways are wrong.

Wisdom will save you.[19]

A Final Word

Will freedom as we have known it survive here
in the United States and the rest of the free world?

We are moving rapidly into an age of extremes. We see it undeniably in acts of hatred, violence, intolerance, and destruction. Almost daily we hear the news of escalating conflicts throughout the world—in Jerusalem and the West Bank, Pakistan and India, many African nations, and parts of South America. In all likelihood, it's only a matter of time before a direct attack comes once again to North America. My prayer is that before then we will begin to witness extreme expressions of love, compassion, self-sacrifice, courage, strength of character, and unshakable resolve in our nation, which can only result from a genuine commitment to moral absolutes and the truth of Scripture.

Our nation must express more courage, conviction, and compassion than at any previous time in our history. The Church must begin to move in demonstrations of godly love— even going beyond the sacrificial love exhibited by the early Church in the book of Acts—to fulfill the challenge Jesus set forth in Matthew 25 to meet the needs of "the least of these" through genuine concern and care.

We must not be deterred. Any attacks against us must deepen our resolve and strengthen our character. We must live according to the absolutes and if necessary be willing to give our lives before we would allow freedom to perish. If our nation does not begin to move back toward absolute truth, I predict we will repeatedly experience firsthand the pain of unrestrained evil with its many horrors. Our decisions regarding the absolutes and our attitude toward God, the Source of life and true liberty, will determine the extent to which the horrors of evil will be felt within our borders. The forces of evil will certainly affect us, but whether or not they will destroy our way of life has yet to be determined. Apart from a miraculous move of God producing expressions of mercy and grace, however, I predict we will witness the most extreme attempts ever in human history—by terrorists and others—to destroy our freedom and our lives.

The Middle East is a time bomb with a rapidly burning fuse. Eventually the conflict there will result in Armageddon, as foretold in the book of Revelation. However, as Christians we must not be lulled by a sense of inevitability about world events, but we must increase our efforts to demonstrate love to our enemies and pray for those who curse us. Jesus said there would be wars and rumors of wars in the last days. But how long it will be before the ultimate explosion occurs will be determined in part by the moral resolve of the free world, our willingness to respond with force—and forcefulness—to terrorist and military threats, and the positive effects of love and compassion to soften the hearts of people throughout the Middle East, in developing countries, and around the globe.

I think all would agree that the events of September 11 woke us up as a nation to the possibility—and even the likelihood—

that we could suffer catastrophic destruction within our own borders. Don't think for a moment that al Qaeda and other terrorist organizations are not trying to find a way right now to detonate weapons of mass destruction within the United States, and don't think for a moment they won't attempt it if they have the chance. Even short of a major attack, however, we could soon find ourselves in a situation similar to Israel's, with smaller bombs being detonated randomly. The amount of pain and destruction that will occur within the United States as a result of the intense stream of hatred presently erupting throughout the world will largely be determined by America's response to the rock-solid truth of the absolutes. The psalmist has said that the "shields of the earth belong to God,"[1] and we must look to the Lord for our protection. That's why in an address to the nation early in 2002, President Bush encouraged people to pray for a shield of protection for our country, and that's why I believe so strongly that we must return to the absolutes in order to receive divine guidance.

Because of its relevance to current events, Betty and I decided to see the movie *The Sum of All Fears,* based on the Tom Clancy novel. Near the conclusion, while we watched a graphic portrayal of the aftershock of a nuclear explosion within our own nation, I silently prayed, *God grant us mercy and guidance.* In my heart I felt that I heard God reply, "I'm offering it—if only people will receive it."

The world has already begun to see radical expressions of hatred, vengeance, retaliation, and intolerance with all the ugly and devastating consequences. It's time for all free nations to call the Islamic leaders of the world to account for their beliefs concerning those they consider infidels. Do they believe, as Mohammed declared shortly before his death, that the Jews and Christians must perish? Muslims in the United

States expect protection, acceptance, and tolerance while enjoying the freedom and privilege they are afforded in this country; yet most Muslim countries offer no such benefits within their borders. In fact, their policies and practices demonstrate just the opposite. This intolerant practice must change, and change soon! Or has the line already been drawn in the sand? Has much of the Arab and Islamic world indeed already declared war on the rest of the free world, with a primary focus on Israel and the United States?

If moderate Arab and Muslim leaders will courageously renounce extreme acts of terror and suicide bombings and begin to advocate good relationships with Israel and the West, then I believe there will be a period of peace. But if they refuse to renounce their commitment to acts of terror as a means of furthering their cause, then they should feel the full brunt of our military strength. It is the terrorists and those committed to evil who should live in fear—not Americans and other lovers of freedom.

288

If an easing of tensions does occur, then American and global businesses, the Church, and the government of every free nation must move quickly to demonstrate a greater interest in the well-being of others. The strength of our alliances will depend on how deeply other nations value absolute principles such as loyalty, commitment, and sacrifice. Some countries will slowly distance themselves from the United States lest they also become a primary target for terrorists. They will talk about freedom and democracy, but they will not be counted with us. It will require courage, resolve, and a steadfast commitment to positive expressions of love to offset the influence of evil in the world. Our peace and security—and peace throughout the world—will be directly affected by our legitimate care and compassion for those who are less fortunate.

Stand Up and Be Counted

One Sunday, more than a year before the September 11 attacks, I was having lunch with a couple after speaking at their church. The wife asked me, "What do you believe will happen of significant importance in the United States and the world?"

I said that I think this is a day of great polarization in America. I believe we will tend to divide—liberal and conservative, good and evil, light and dark, Democrat and Republican—as many competing forces vie for our loyalty. However, Christians must refuse to *polarize*—they must *penetrate* all areas of life. Believers must not be drawn into divisive movements; instead, they must *demonstrate* unity as a model for others. There has never been a better time for the Church of Jesus Christ to have a positive impact on the world.

This is the hour for all freedom-loving people to stand up and be counted. This is the time for people of compassion to begin to reach out all over the world. To all of my fellow Christian believers, to all who claim to have a personal relationship with Jesus Christ, if you have experienced the transforming power of what He referred to as "the spiritual new birth," you are going to hear God's call to commitment—not just commitment to national and world freedom and privilege as we have known it, but commitment to His eternal purposes.

The most powerful force available to stop the spread of deadly extremist ideologies is the love of God freely expressed through His people and through citizens who are compelled by compassion to reach out to the less privileged. Islamic extremists and other radical groups tend to flourish in areas of poverty and deep-seated human need, just as the Communists did in Eastern Europe, Russia, and Asia during the twentieth century.

Now more than ever, Christians must take the Good News

of Jesus Christ to the ends of the earth, proclaiming it in word and demonstrating it in deed. All Americans must seek ways to serve and to share with the less privileged in our own country and especially in developing nations. As we bless others, so shall we be blessed. As I previously mentioned, the path to abundance of life is to give as freely as we have received.

Further, we must all assume responsibility for preserving the great privileges of freedom we enjoy in the United States by participating intelligently in the political process. We must make decisions based on principle, not preference or the personality of candidates. We must stand courageously and lovingly against the trends and beliefs that seek to undermine our freedoms. We must live in such a manner that people will be inspired by the undeniable characteristics and the positive results that are produced through our commitment to Jesus Christ and His commission.

We need the kind of commitment expressed by our president to Betty and me when we visited him in the Oval Office in late spring 2001. During our conversation, I shared how it disturbed me to see him sometimes stereotyped as a conservative politician lacking in compassion. I said, "You get the typical bad rap placed on many conservatives that they don't love people, and I know you do."

In response, the president leaned forward on the front edge of his chair and said firmly, "I *do* love people, and I want you to know I love the Lord, and I'm serious about my faith."

When I heard the president and leader of the free world affirm everything I had observed about him during the numerous times he and I had prayed together over the past few years, I knew he had just voiced the key to the future hope of America: We *must* love people. We *must* love the Lord, and we *must* be serious about demonstrating our faith through acts of righteousness and compassion. These are attitudes and actions birthed in the hearts of those who properly respond to the absolutes.

The Power of Compassion

All over the world, we have seen the effectiveness of Christian ministry and relief efforts motivated by compassion. History confirms one reason for America's greatness is the characteristic of love and compassion and our sincere desire to share with others not only our freedom but also the blessings of our prosperity. Third World countries and every other nation can be influenced, redirected, and even transformed by the love we share.

It is time for all Christians and all freedom-loving Americans to rise up without fear and stand for truth. As King David says in the twenty-third Psalm, "Even when I walk through the dark valley of death, I will not be afraid, for [God is] close beside me."[2] Believe me, the only way we will ever come to fear no evil is if we know beyond a doubt that the Lord God Himself is with us, and we are with Him.

Whether people believe the Bible or not, and whether or not they accept my personal testimony of God's grace that can be experienced in Jesus Christ, the absolutes I've shared in this book are irrefutable, steadfast, and proven throughout all of history. Some may not like them; they might resist them with all their might or simply try to ignore them. But if they do, this grave mistake will ultimately lead to decay, division, and destruction—for individuals, for our nation, and for our priceless liberty.

The powerful truths of the absolutes cannot be imposed. They must be received and embraced freely. To refuse to walk in the security afforded by the absolutes is to take a step toward ruin. To embrace them wholeheartedly is the most positive step possible toward securing enduring freedom.

NOTES

INTRODUCTION: OUR MOMENT OF TRUTH

1. Cotton Mather, *Magnalia Christi Americana* (Boston: Long and Daye, 1881), xii.
2. Ravi Zacharias, *Light in the Shadow of Jihad* (Sisters, Ore.: Multnomah, 2002), 20.
3. "President Outlines War Effort," Remarks by the president at the California Business Association Breakfast, October 17, 2002, www.whitehouse.gov/news/releases/2001/10/print/20011017-15.html.
4. www.worldnetdaily.com, November 20, 2001.
5. Harold Goverenan, ed., *Great American Speeches* (Dallas: Presidio Books, 1978), 227.

CHAPTER 1: EVIL IS A HORRIBLE AND PRESENT REALITY

1. Proverbs 14:12, *Holy Bible*, New International Version.
2. Robert Goguet, *The Origin of Laws* (New York: John Taylor, 1821), 302.
3. Nathan Villard, *The Founding Era* (New York: Baker, Harbridge, and Wilson, 1958), 47.
4. Philippians 3:19, *Holy Bible*, New Living Translation.
5. Richard Weaver, *Ideas Have Consequences* (Chicago: University of Chicago, 1948), 23.
6. Ravi Zacharias, *Light in the Shadow of Jihad* (Sisters, Ore.: Multnomah, 2002), 19.
7. Ibid., 22.
8. Os Guinness, *The American Hour* (New York: Free Press, 1993), 148.
9. Thomas Paine, *The American Crisis*, no. 1, December 23, 1776, quoted in *Bartlett's Familiar Quotations*, fifteenth edition (Boston: Little, Brown and Company, 1980), 384.
10. Aleksandr Solzhenitsyn, *A Warning to the West* (New York: Harper and Row, 1978), 64.
11. James Q. Wilson, *Forbes*, ix.
12. Luke 23:34, *Holy Bible*, King James Version.

13. Psalm 139:23-24, *Holy Bible,* New Living Translation.
14. 1 Peter 5:8, *Holy Bible,* New Living Translation.
15. 2 Thessalonians 3:2-3, *Holy Bible,* New Living Translation.

CHAPTER 2: IDEAS HAVE CONSEQUENCES

1. Alvin Toffler, *Future Shock* (New York: Bantam, 1971), 158.
2. E. F. Schumacher, *Small Is Beautiful* (New York: Harper and Row, 1975), 52.
3. James Sire, *How to Read Slowly* (Wheaton, Ill.: Harold Shaw, 1978), 14–15.
4. Francis Schaeffer, *A Christian Manifesto* (Wheaton, Ill.: Crossway, 1981), 17.
5. Ibid.
6. Romans 1:18-19, 21-22, 25-31, *Holy Bible,* New Living Translation.
7. See James 1:22.
8. Quoted in Os Guinness, *The Journey* (Colorado Springs, Colo.: NavPress, 2001), 43.
9. C. S. Lewis, *The Weight of Glory and Other Addresses,* revised and expanded edition (New York: Macmillan, 1980), 92.

CHAPTER 3: WE ARE SPIRITUAL BEINGS

1. "What changed on September 11, 2001. And what didn't," www.spirituality.com, October 17, 2001.
2. B. Pascal, quoted in W. Bright, *Jesus and the Intellectual* (San Bernardino, Calif.: Campus Crusade for Christ, 1968).
3. Janine Robertson, *The Theological Implications of Weber's Sociology* (Los Angeles: University Society Press, 1987), 88.
4. See 2 Peter 1:9; Titus 3:3; Isaiah 56:10; and Proverbs 24:2.
5. See 2 Thessalonians 1:6; 1 John 2:29; and John 8:32.
6. Robertson, 89.
7. 2 Corinthians 5:17, *Holy Bible,* New Living Translation.
8. Robertson, 92.
9. See Matthew 25:13-30; Matthew 7:24-27; James 5:7; and Ephesians 4:25-32.
10. See Galatians 5:22-23; James 3:13-17; and Genesis 1:28.
11. Robertson, 94.
12. See 2 Peter 2:2-3.
13. See Philippians 2:3-4.
14. See Ephesians 5:16.
15. See Colossians 4:5.

16. See 1 Peter 4:10; Deuteronomy 8:18; 1 Timothy 5:8; Luke 22:25-30; and 1 Peter 3:1-17.
17. Robertson, 95.
18. George Gilder, *Wealth and Poverty* (New York: Basic Books, 1981), 74.
19. See Deuteronomy 28:1-14.
20. See Romans 8:28.
21. Hebrews 11:6, *Holy Bible,* New International Version.
22. Romans 1:19, adapted from the *Holy Bible,* New Living Translation.
23. See Colossians 1:15, 18.
24. Jeremiah 29:13, *Holy Bible,* New International Version.
25. Samuel Fallows, *The American Manual and Patriot's Handbook* (Chicago: Century, 1889), 26, 28, 30, 99, 38, 60, 111.
26. See Proverbs 3:6.
27. Galatians 5:1, *Holy Bible,* New International Version.

CHAPTER 4: THE MAJORITY IS NOT ALWAYS RIGHT

1. Matthew 7:13-14, *Holy Bible,* New Living Translation.
2. See Numbers 13:1–14:12, 24; 32:12; Joshua 14:6-14.
3. See 1 Kings 18.
4. See John 1:29; 18:38–19:18.
5. Quoted in *Stirling Bridge Newsletter,* December 2000.
6. George Grant, *The Patriot's Handbook* (Nashville, Tenn.: Cumberland House, 1996), 252.
7. Ibid.
8. Quoted in *Stirling Bridge Newsletter,* December 2000.
9. Theodore Roosevelt, *Realizable Ideals* (New York: Scribners, 1924), 650.
10. Ibid.
11. Quoted in *Stirling Bridge Newsletter,* December 2000.
12. Ibid.
13. Ibid.
14. Grant, 183.
15. Herman Young, *American Education in the Era of the Founders* (New York: James Benning and Sons, 1964), 144.
16. For an excellent overview of the classical model of education, see "The Lost Tools of Learning," from a 1947 lecture at Oxford by writer Dorothy Sayers. The text of Sayers's speech is available on several Web sites, including www.biola.edu/academics/torrey/docs/sayers-tools.cfm.

17. Proverbs 2:6, *Holy Bible,* New Living Translation.
18. Proverbs 4:7, *Holy Bible,* New Living Translation.

CHAPTER 5: TRUTH WITHSTANDS DEBATE

1. Alexis de Tocqueville, *Democracy in America* (Boston: Tupperville and Sons, 1899), xxi.
2. George Grant, ed., *The Patriot's Handbook* (Nashville, Tenn.: Cumberland House, 1996), 233.
3. Nat Hentoff, *The First Freedom: The Tumultuous History of Free Speech in America* (New York: Delacorte, 1980), 58.
4. Cal Thomas, "ABC's Rosie scenario," Tribune Media Services, March 19, 2002.
5. See Proverbs 27:17.
6. See Romans 1:18-32.
7. Ibid.
8. Os Guinness, *The Journey* (Colorado Springs, Colo.: NavPress, 2001), 45.
9. Lionel Ceveada, *Spanish Literature of the Sixteenth Century* (New York: Longmans Press, 1967), 248.
10. See Isaiah 1:18; Proverbs 1:5; and 2 Timothy 4:2-5.

CHAPTER 6: PEOPLE MATTER MOST

1. Jon Yates, "Fire Guts Church in Wheaton," *Chicago Tribune,* 19 March 2002, sec. 2, p. 1.
2. Ibid.
3. The author first heard this story from Ravi Zacharias, who also recounts it in his book *Light in the Shadow of Jihad* (Sisters, Ore.: Multnomah, 2002), 112–13.
4. Psalm 103:12, *Holy Bible,* New International Version.
5. Thomas Paine, *Common Sense and Other Essays* (New York: Signet Classics, 1977), 19.
6. Harold K. Lane, *Liberty! Cry Liberty!* (Boston: Lamb & Lamb Tractarian Society, 1939), 31.
7. Abraham Lincoln, *Speeches, Letters, and Papers: 1860–1864* (Washington, D.C.: Capitol Library, 1951), 341–42.
8. Dave Grossman, *On Killing: The Psychological Cost of Learning to Kill in War and Society* (Boston: Little Brown, 1995), 3, xxix.
9. Robert Bork, *Slouching Towards Gomorrah* (New York: ReganBooks, 1996), 182.
10. Ibid., 185.

11. Alan Keyes, *Our Character, Our Future* (Grand Rapids, Mich.: Zondervan, 1996), 6.
12. See Luke 10:30-37.
13. Galatians 5:14, *Holy Bible,* New Living Translation.

CHAPTER 7: GREED DESTROYS

1. Proverbs 16:18, New King James Version.
2. *Parade,* December 2, 2001.
3. Thomas Chalmers, *The Economics of Large Towns* (Glasgow: William Collins, 1838), 45.
4. Ibid.
5. Leviticus 23:22, *Holy Bible,* New Living Translation.
6. Acts 2:45, *New American Standard Bible.*
7. Acts 20:35.

CHAPTER 8: CHARACTER COUNTS

1. John C. Maxwell, *The 21 Indispensable Qualities of a Leader* (Nashville, Tenn.: Thomas Nelson, 1999), 3–4.
2. Peggy Stanton, *The Daniel Dilemma: A Moral Man in the Public Arena* (Waco, Tex.: Word Books, 1978).
3. WorldNetDaily, December 4, 2001.
4. Ibid.
5. Ibid.
6. Ibid.
7. Robert A. Wilson, ed., *Character Above All: Ten Presidents from FDR to George Bush* (New York: Simon & Schuster, 1995).
8. Herman Dockery, *The Era of Juvenile Fiction* (New York: Laramie and Sons, 1956), 23.
9. Ibid.
10. Luke 6:43-45, *New Revised Standard Version of the Bible.*
11. Maxwell, 4.
12. Hilaire Belloc, *The Biographer's Art: Excerpts from Belloc's Florid Pen* (London: Catholic Union, 1956), 33.
13. E. Michael Jones, *Degenerate Moderns: Modernity as Rationalized Sexual Misbehavior* (San Francisco, Calif.: Ignatius Press, 1993), 9.
14. Job 4:8, *Holy Bible,* New Living Translation.
15. Steven Berglas, *The Success Syndrome: Hitting Bottom When You Reach the Top* (New York: Plenum Press, 1986), 77.
16. 1 Corinthians 10:12, *New American Standard Bible.*
17. 1 Timothy 4:2; Philippians 3:19, New King James Version.
18. See John 5:24; 1 John 3:14.

19. George Grant, *Carry a Big Stick* (Nashville, Tenn.: Cumberland House, 1996).
20. Maxwell, 6.
21. Philippians 3:13-14, *Holy Bible,* New Living Translation.

CHAPTER 9: SEX IS A GREAT GIFT THAT MUST BE PROTECTED

1. Sol Gordon, *Ten Heavy Facts about Sex* (Syracuse, N.Y.: Ed-U Press, 1975).
2. *Sexuality Alphabet,* Planned Parenthood Federation of America, 1982.
3. Ibid.
4. *Planned Parenthood News,* 1963.
5. Sheri Tepper, *The Perils of Puberty* (Denver, Colo.: Rocky Mountain Planned Parenthood, 1974).
6. Sheri Tepper, *You've Changed the Combination* (Denver, Colo.: Rocky Mountain Planned Parenthood, 1974).
7. Sheri Tepper, *The Great Orgasm Robbery* (Denver, Colo.: Rocky Mountain Planned Parenthood, 1977).
8. Thomas Sowell, *Inside American Education: The Decline the Deception, the Dogmas* (New York: Free Press, 1993), 53.
9. Ibid., 54.
10. Ibid.
11. Mary Calderone and Eric Johnson, *The Family Book About Sexuality* (New York: Bantam, 1981), 226.
12. Randy Alcorn, *ProLife Answers to ProChoice Arguments* (Sisters, Ore.: Multnomah, 1992, 1994, 2000), 267.
13. Ibid., 266.
14. Louis Harris and Associates, *American Teens Speak: Sex, Myths, TV, and Birth Control* (New York: Planned Parenthood Federation of America, 1986), 19.
15. Ibid., 4.
16. *Family Planning Perspectives*, August 1986.
17. Roberta Wiener, ed., *Teen Pregnancy: Impact on the Schools* (Alexandria, Va.: Capitol Publications, 1987), 17.
18. Ibid., 17, 24.
19. Wendy Baldwin, *Adolescent Pregnancy and Childbearing Rates* (Bethesda, Md.: NICHD, 1985, 1989), 5.
20. Weiner, 10.
21. Harris, 8, 18, 60.
22. 1 Corinthians 6:18, *Holy Bible,* New Living Translation.

CHAPTER 10: STRONG FAMILIES ARE THE CORNERSTONE OF SOCIETY

1. Deuteronomy 6:5-7, *Holy Bible*, New Living Translation.
2. The list of six ways children suffer from divorce is based on Karen S. Peterson, "Unhappily Ever After: Children of Divorce Grow into Bleak Legacy," *USA Today*, 5 September 2000, which summarizes the findings in Judith Wallerstein, Julia Lewis, and Sandra Blakeslee, *The Unexpected Legacy of Divorce* (New York: Hyperion, 2000).
3. Child development specialist E. Mavis Hetherington indicates that 43 percent of all marriages in America will end in divorce and nearly 60 of all remarriages will suffer the same fate. E. Mavis Hetherington, *For Better or For Worse: Divorce Reconsidered* (New York: W. W. Norton, 2002), 272, 262.
4. Judith Stacey, "Good Riddance to the Family," *Journal of Marriage and the Family* 55, no.3 (August 1993):545–47.
5. William D. Watkins, *The New Absolutes* (Minneapolis: Bethany House, 1996), 112.
6. See Ephesians 5:21-33.
7. George Grant, *Bringing in the Sheaves* (Atlanta: American Vision Press, 1996), 67.

CHAPTER 11: EQUALITY IS NOT SAMENESS

1. Gregory Wilbur and George Grant, *The Christian Almanac* (Nashville, Tenn.: Cumberland House, 2000), 550.
2. George Grant, ed., *The Patriot's Handbook* (Nashville, Tenn.: Cumberland House, 1996), 435.
3. 1 Corinthians 12:14-26, *Holy Bible*, New Living Translation.
4. See 1 Peter 2:4-5.
5. Luke 12:48, *Holy Bible*, New Living Translation.
6. See Matthew 23:11-12; Mark 9:35; and Luke 22:25-27.
7. See Matthew 25:31-46.
8. Isaiah 58:6-12, *Holy Bible*, New Living Translation.

CHAPTER 12: IF GOVERNMENT DOESN'T SERVE, IT WILL ENSLAVE

1. Quoted in James Robison with Jim Cox, *Save America to Save the World* (Wheaton, Ill.: Tyndale House, 1978), 8–9.
2. Proverbs 25:28, New King James Version.
3. From the preamble to the Constitution of the United States of America.

4. *Nashville Banner* 25 January 1993.

5. Ibid.

6. *Washington Post,* 5 July 1990.

7. E. J. Dionne, *Why Americans Hate Politics* (New York: Simon and Schuster, 1991), 9, 18.

8. Conservative Action PAC Survey, December 2001.

9. Ibid.

10. Gallup Poll, January 1999.

11. Wirthlin Poll, January 1999.

12. *Human Events,* November 21, 1992.

13. American Demographic Report, February 1993.

14. Remnant Review, November 6, 1992.

15. A. James Reichley, *The Life of the Parties: A History of American Political Parties* (New York: Free Press, 1992).

16. Michael Drummond, *Participatory Democracy: A New Federalism in the Making* (New York: L.T. Carnell and Sons, 1923), 19.

17. Ibid, 22.

18. Ralph Ketcham, *The Anti-Federalist Papers* (New York: Mentor, 1986).

19. Ibid., 46.

20. Ross Lence, *Union and Liberty: The Political Philosophy of John C. Calhoun* (Indianapolis, Ind.: Liberty Press, 1992).

21. G. K. Chesterton, *Omnibus* (London: Stratford Lewes, 1966), 142–43.

22. Robert Minor, ed., *The Rebirth of a Nation* (Third Century Fund, a division of the National Heritage Foundation, 1978), 176.

23. Psalm 121:1, *Holy Bible,* New International Version.

24. Psalm 121:2, *Holy Bible,* New International Version.

25. Philippians 3:13-14, *New American Standard Bible.*

26. www.sobran.com.

27. James Hollis, ed., *American Conservative Writing* (Los Angeles: Spirit of 76 Press), 48.

28. C. S. Lewis, "The Humanitarian Theory of Punishment," from *God in the Dock: Essays on Theology and Ethics* (Grand Rapids, Mich.: Eerdmans, 1970).

29. According to the Heritage Foundation, since the "War on Poverty" began, the United States has spent nearly 9 trillion dollars on welfare programs (8.3 trillion dollars from 1965 to 2000, and an estimated total of 8.9 trillion through the first half of 2002). The figures are in 2002 dollars.

30. This quote from Governor Mike Huckabee came from a conversation he and the author had while fishing together in 2001.
31. 1 John 4:18.
32. 1 Timothy 2:2, *Holy Bible,* New International Version.
33. 2 Corinthians 6:17.
34. Hosea 4:6, *New American Standard Bible.*
35. John Bartlett, *Bartlett's Familiar Quotations,* 15th ed. (Boston: Little, Brown and Company, 1980), 590.

CHAPTER 13: RELIGION CAN BE DANGEROUS, BUT REPENTANCE IS REDEMPTIVE

1. *New York Times,* 27 November 2001.
2. Ibid.
3. Ibid.
4. James Blanchard, *The Atheist Threat* (Dallas, Tex.: Theos Press, 2001), 9.
5. Richard C. Halverson, *Perspective.*
6. See John 3:3; 10:10.
7. See Ephesians 4.
8. See Luke 9:46-56.
9. Matthew 5:16, *Holy Bible,* New Living Translation.
10. Mathew 15: 8-9, *Holy Bible,* New Living Translation.
11. James 3:14-16, *New American Standard Bible.*
12. James 3:17, *New American Standard Bible.*
13. Matthew 25:32-36, 40, *Holy Bible,* New Living Translation.
14. See Isaiah 1:23.
15. Matthew 10:8, *Holy Bible,* New Living Translation.
16. See Galatians 3:1; 4:8.
17. Malcolm Gladwell, *The Tipping Point* (Boston: Little, Brown and Company, 2000), 7.
18. According to Linda Price, marketing professor at the University of Nebraska, as quoted by Malcolm Gladwell in *The Tipping Point* (p. 62), "A Maven is a person who has information on a lot of different products or prices or places. . . . This is the person who connects people to the marketplace and has the inside scoop on the marketplace." Gladwell later adds his own comment (p. 67): "What sets Mavens apart, though, is not so much what they know but how they pass it along. The fact that Mavens want to help, for no other reason than because they like to help, turns out to be an awfully effective way of getting someone's attention."
19. Matthew 5:14-16, New King James Version.

20. John 7:38, *New American Standard Bible.*

21. *Merriam Webster's Collegiate Dictionary,* 10th ed., s.v. "redeem." 1a: to buy back : REPURCHASE; b: to get or win back; 2: to free from what distresses or harms: as a: to free from captivity by payment of ransom, b: to extricate from or help to overcome something detrimental, c: to release from blame or debt : CLEAR, d: to free from the consequences of sin; 3: to change for the better : REFORM; 4: REPAIR, RESTORE; 5a : to free from a lien by payment of an amount secured thereby; 5b (1): to remove the obligation of by payment, (2): to exchange for something of value, c: to make good : FULFILL; 6a: to atone for : EXPIATE, 6b (1) : to offset the bad effect of; (2): to make worthwhile : RETRIEVE; synonymy see RESCUE.

22. James Ulrich, *The Stages of Mental Health* (London: Galloway and Sons, 1978), 34–35.

23. See Luke 15:11-32.

24. See Matthew 24:6; Mark 13:7.

25. President Bush has spoken openly on a number of occasions about his faith experience, including several times during the 2000 presidential campaign and after his election. The details recounted here are based on conversations he and the author had in 1998 and in subsequent visits. Quotes attributed to the president are to the best of the author's recollection and may not be verbatim.

26. See Acts 16:22-34.

27. See Hebrews 12:27.

CHAPTER 14: SERVANTHOOD: THE KEY TO SUCCESS AND SIGNIFICANCE

1. James Jerome, *Great Hollywood Moments* (New York: Broadway Books, 1976), 89.

2. See Acts 20:35.

3. *Houston Chronicle,* 18 May 1986; *Forbes,* 14 September 1992; *Forbes,* 9 September 1993; *Wall Street Journal,* 16 April 1992; Harvey Mackay, *Swim with the Sharks* (William Morrow, 1988), 1.

4. Chuck Colson and Jack Eckerd, *Why America Doesn't Work* (Dallas, Tex.: Word, 1991), 168.

5. George Gilder, *The Spirit of Enterprise* (New York: Simon and Schuster, 1984); Michael Gerber, *Power Point* (New York: HarperCollins, 1991); Tom Peters, *Thriving on Chaos* (New York:

Knopf, 1987); Stephen Covey, Roger Merrill, and Rebecca Merrill, *First Things First* (New York: Simon & Schuster, 1994).

6. *Webster's Collegiate Dictionary*, 10th ed., s.v. "chivalrous."
7. Hebrews 1:1.
8. See James 2:19.
9. Paul Kellerman, *The Cult of Self* (New York: Holtzman Publishers, 1988), viii.
10. Luke 22:25-27, *Holy Bible*, New International Version.
11. Matthew 23:11, *New American Standard Bible*.
12. Isaiah 58:10-12 *Holy Bible*, New Living Translation.
13. Thomas Chalmers, *Essays and Speeches* (Edinburgh: William Collins, 1846), 174.
14. Ibid., 171.

CHAPTER 15: LOVE CONQUERS ALL

1. Paraphrased from Matthew 12:35, New King James Version.
2. The Bible tells the story of Stephen's martyrdom (Acts 7) and Saul's eventual conversion when he is confronted by a vision of Jesus on the road to Damascus (Acts 9). Although Saul continued to persecute the Christian Church after the death of Stephen, and in fact became even more militant for a time, the author is convinced that the power of love expressed by Stephen and other Christian martyrs broke the power of evil and made possible the conversion of a rabid persecutor like Saul.
3. See 1 John 3:18.
4. This story was adapted from Steven R. Mosley, *A Tale of Three Virtues* (Sisters, Ore.: Questar, 1989), 129–30.

CHAPTER 16: THE ABSOLUTES HAVE A SOURCE

1. See John 14:26.
2. 2 Corinthians 3:6, *New American Standard Bible*.
3. See John 1:18 and Luke 24:27.
4. John 14:6, *Holy Bible*, New International Version.
5. William Lyons Phelps as quoted in Lee Williams, *No Room for Doubt* (Nashville, Tenn.: Broadman, 1977), 36.
6. D. James Kennedy, *What If the Bible Had Never Been Written?* (Nashville, Tenn.: Thomas Nelson, 1998), 4.
7. Cornelius Van Til, *Complete Works* (Philipsburg, N.J.: P&R, 1999).
8. Kennedy, 5
9. Ibid.
10. Ibid.

11. Byron Tallmadge, *Lincoln and the Faith* (Oklahoma City, Okla.: Western Historical Society, 1988), 99.
12. Kennedy, 5.
13. Ibid.
14. James Austin Wills, *The Letters and Speeches of Theodore Roosevelt* (New York: Billington and Sons, 1937), 86.
15. Allan Bloom, *The Closing of the American Mind* (New York: Simon & Schuster, 1987), 60.
16. Revelation 3:1-3, *Holy Bible,* New International Version.
17. See Luke 10:30-37.
18. 1 John 4:4, *Holy Bible,* King James Version.
19. Proverbs 2:1-16, *Holy Bible,* New Living Translation.

A FINAL WORD
1. Psalm 47:9, *New American Standard Bible.*
2. Psalm 23:4, *Holy Bible,* New Living Translation.

ABOUT THE AUTHOR

Since 1962, James Robison has presented the gospel to millions of people—first through crusade evangelism, and today through television. When James was eighteen years old, God called him into the ministry and he began speaking in churches. The doors soon opened for him to expand his preaching into a nationwide crusade ministry in stadiums and indoor arenas. Over the years, more than twenty million people attended his crusade meetings and more than two million people made commitments to Christ.

In 1968, at the suggestion of Dr. Billy Graham, the James Robison Evangelistic Association launched a TV ministry, taking James's crusade-preaching format to the airwaves. As Dr. Graham had predicted, thousands of viewers accepted Christ.

By the late 1970s, James was spiritually burned out, largely due to his intense schedule. Through the faith-filled prayers of a humble Christian brother, James experienced newfound freedom and spiritual fullness, along with a renewed vision for reaching the lost. He believes that God very clearly moved him into a servant's role of trying to help others.

In 1992, the James Robison Evangelistic Association changed its name to Life Outreach International, as part of an effort to make the ministry purpose-centered rather than personality driven. They also changed the format of the television program, *Life Today,* into an interactive thirty-minute talk show. James and his wife, Betty, co-host the daily broadcast, which airs on major Christian networks nationwide, hundreds of independent stations, as well as on the PAX TV and ABC Family networks. *Life Today* can be seen by more than one hundred million households in the United States, and throughout Canada, Europe, and Australia. Each month, an average of sixty thousand viewers call the ministry's twenty-four hour Prayer Center seeking counsel.

Although James believes that media outreach is the most effective way to evangelize, he also feels strongly about helping those in need. Much of the ministry's focus is in parts of the world where the physical needs are staggering. Life Outreach helps feed more than 300,000 children every month in parts of Africa. Schools, medical clinics, orphanages, fruit and vegetable farms, and a food processing plant are also part of the ministry's outreach in Africa. Life Outreach has helped support ministry outreaches in nearly 40 countries, including Bolivia, Romania, China, and India.

James is the author of more than a dozen books, including *My Father's Face, Thank God I'm Free, The Search for a Right Mate,* and *Knowing God as Father.* James and Betty Robison have been married since 1963 and make their home in Fort Worth, Texas. They have three children—Rhonda, Randy, and Robin—and eleven grandchildren.